MODERN GERMAN DRAMA

By the same author

GERHART HAUPTMANN
(*Yale University Press, 1954*)

Modern
German Drama

H. F. Garten

GROVE PRESS, INC.   NEW YORK

Preface to This Edition

Since this book was first published in 1959, the general picture of contemporary German drama has scarcely changed. The leading position of the two German-Swiss playwrights, Max Frisch and Friedrich Dürrenmatt, and the Austrian Fritz Hochwälder, is still unchallenged. Hochwälder wrote a modern mystery play, *Donnerstag* (Thursday, 1959), which shows a new departure from his earlier, mainly historical, plays. Max Frisch had his greatest success so far with *Andorra* (1961), a striking parable on the problem of anti-Semitism, while Dürrenmatt continued his line of tragical farces with a musical, *Frank der Fünfte* (Frank the Fifth, 1960), and *Die Physiker* (The Physicists, 1962), dealing with the predicament of nuclear scientists in our time.

In Germany proper, Carl Zuckmayer published a new play, *Die Uhr schlägt eins* (The Clock Strikes One, 1961) which proved rather a failure. A few new names are beginning to emerge: Karl Wittlinger, whose play for two characters, *Kennen Sie die Milchstrasse?* (Do You Know the Milky Way?, 1959) had a marked success; Leopold Ahlsen, with a forceful play about Greek resistance fighters, *Philemon und Baukis*; Wolfgang Hildesheimer, with a sophisticated version of the Turandot story, *Der Drachenthron* (The Dragon Throne); and Mattias Braun, who has recast Greek tragedies in a modern idiom *(The Trojan Women, Medea,* and *The Persians).* Lastly, Siegfried Lenz has scored a major success with a play, *Zeit der Schuldlosen* (Time of the Guiltless), one of the first valid attempts to deal, in terms of drama, with the problem of collective guilt. However, none of these authors has as yet developed a clear profile. The stagnation of the German theatre persists.

London, April 1962   H.F.G.

PREFACE

This book is not intended to be a comprehensive history of modern German drama; nor is it a portrait gallery of individual playwrights. Its aim lies somewhere between the two: while tracing the main trends of German drama since the rise of Naturalism in the 1890s, it concentrates on those dramatists who made a vital impact in their time. This impact cannot be measured in terms of popular success. A great number of theatrical 'hits' have not found a place in this survey: they belong to the routine business of the theatre, and have vanished with the moment for which they were written. On the other hand, it has been my aim to include all authors and plays that have contributed, in one way or another, to the main stream of modern German drama.

The book is designed for the English reader interested in drama generally, or in German literature in particular. It should also be useful to the historian, who will find many trends, political, social, and intellectual, of this turbulent period in German history reflected in the contemporary theatre. It deals with a branch of modern European drama of which comparatively little is known in this country – due, partly, to the two great wars which have divided the nations, but also to deeper causes implicit in the differences of national character and taste. Yet there can be little doubt that the German drama of this period has had its full share in the evolution of the modern theatre, and that it has exercised a strong influence, directly or indirectly, on the drama of other countries, including England and America.

I have tried to restrict critical analysis in order to preclude personal prejudice, as far as this is possible. It has been my ambition to meet the works discussed on their own ground, that is, to take them as seriously as they wanted to be taken. Nothing would be easier than to ridicule many of the products, say, of the expressionist movement. But it seemed pointless to introduce plays only to dismiss them with a sneer. Their aspirations, if nothing else, were sincere enough to warrant serious consideration.

I may add that the subject-matter of this study is drawn largely from personal experience. I had the good fortune to witness at close quarters an important part of the period under review, the twenties and early thirties. I have seen many of the plays performed on the living stage, and I was lucky enough to have close personal contact with two of the leading dramatists of the time, Gerhart Hauptmann and Georg Kaiser. It is to the memory of these two masters of the stage, whose work, more than any other, has kindled my love for the theatre, that this book is dedicated.

One more word about details. Since the book is intended for English readers, all quotations are given in translation, with the emphasis on accuracy rather than on style. Only in verse quotations, or whenever the English did not seem adequate to convey the meaning, the original also is given. If not otherwise stated, the translations are my own. In the bibliography, unpublished dissertations or articles published in periodicals are not included. I have added a list of English translations of the plays mentioned in the text, as far as they are available in print; this list does not claim to be complete.

I wish to express my thanks to Professor J. Boyd and Professor E. L. Stahl of Oxford University for the interest they have shown in my work in its earlier stages; to Dr. K. Mitchells, London, to the late Dr. Peter Suhrkamp and Herr Hans-Geert Falkenberg, Frankfurt am Main, for furnishing me with valuable material; to Professor B. Q. Morgan, University of Stanford, Calif., and Mr. Eric Bentley, New York, for their help in compiling the list of translations. I also wish to thank Mrs. Gerty von Hofmannsthal, Miss Doris Hutton of *Drama*, Dr. Richard Southern, Messrs. Heffers & Sons, Cambridge, the Schauspielhaus, Zürich, the Theatermuseum, Munich, and the Ullstein Bildarchiv, Berlin, for providing the illustrations. Most of all, I am indebted to my wife for the invaluable help she has given me throughout.

H. F. G.

London, May 1959.

CONTENTS

ILLUSTRATIONS

SOURCES: *Ullstein Bildarchiv*, Berlin (1, 8, 9); *Theatermuseum*, Munich (2, 3, 6, 11, 13); Mrs. Gerty von Hofmannsthal (4); R. Samuel and R. H. Thomas, *Expressionism in German Life, Literature and the Theatre* (5); *Das Theater* (7); J. Bab, *Das Theater der Gegenwart* (10); Dr. Richard Southern (12); Gerda Goedhardt (14); *Schauspielhaus*, Zürich (15); *Kunst und Bühne*, Baden-Baden (16)

INTRODUCTION

In Germany drama may be said to take first place among literary forms. The proportion of serious plays, both old and new, presented on the German stage is considerably larger than in almost any other country. Moreover, the number of theatres showing a first-rate repertory is far greater than in the Western countries where theatrical life is almost exclusively confined to the capitals. This keen and widespread interest in drama can be attributed to various causes. A predilection for tragedy, for the sharp conflict of passions and ideas, seems deeply ingrained in the German character. The novel, on the other hand, has never attained the place it holds in French, English, or Russian literature. Instead, drama has served as the main vehicle for all currents of thought, spiritual, social, and political. Since the middle of the eighteenth century, that is, since the rise of a national German literature, the theatre has come to be regarded not so much as a place of entertainment but – in the phrase of Schiller – a 'moral institution', a platform where the vital ideas of the day as well as the timeless issues of human destiny are presented.

Germany has been the last of all the major European nations to develop a national literature in the full sense; its 'golden age' is the most recent – the late eighteenth and early nineteenth centuries. While England had its peak period in the Elizabethan age, France at the time of Louis XIV – that is, in a world far removed from our own – Germany's greatest minds lived and worked in a not so distant past. Goethe, in his old age, already saw the dim outlines of the world as we know it; his language is still regarded as the supreme model of German prose, his concept of personality as the living ideal of every educated German. All this has had a profound influence on the German approach to art, including the theatre. Although the average intellectual level of the German people is surely not higher than that of any other European nation, their appreciation of art-values is deeply coloured by their respect – genuine or affected – for '*Bildung*', for cultural education. One conspicuous sign of this is the wide interest taken in the theatre, and the large space allotted in the daily press to the discussion of plays and play-wrights.

Any account of German drama will inevitably present a more comprehensive picture of the social and historical back-ground than it would in other countries. While it is quite possible to give an outline of the more recent English theatre without touching on the wider issues of contemporary life, such a procedure would be impossible in the case of Germany. German drama, for the last two centuries, has been a faithful – perhaps the most faithful – mirror of the vital issues and currents in the nation's history. Any attempt to give a coherent account of modern German drama will therefore necessarily touch upon the main trends, spiritual, social, and political, of the period.

There can be no doubt where such an account will have to start. The birth of modern German drama is clearly fixed with the emergence of Naturalism in the 1890s, more precisely, with the first performance, in Berlin, of Gerhart Hauptmann's play *Vor Sonnenaufgang* in 1889. However, to appreciate the full significance of that event, it is necessary to sketch in outline the development of German drama up to that date.

There has been in Germany an almost continuous stream of drama since its inception with Lessing, in the middle of the eighteenth century. It was no doubt of vital importance for the course of German literature that its first eminent figure was above all a dramatist who was, moreover, keenly interested in the theory of drama as an art-form. Lessing's dramatic achievements were closely linked with the rise of the middle class, the *Bürgertum*; in his plays, its moral concepts and ideas, its self-assertion against the nobility, found their first clear expression. Thenceforth, the evolution of German drama was insolubly linked with the history of the *Bürgertum*, its triumphant rise, its crises, and its eventual disintegration.

The literary movement following on Lessing, known as *Sturm und Drang*, and foreshadowing, in its leading ideas, the French Revolution, found its signal expression once again in drama. Although its force was soon spent, and few of its dramatic achievements proved of permanent value, it left a deep and lasting mark. Time and again, in periods of violent upheaval, such as the *Junges Deutschland* of the 1830s, the Naturalistic movement of the 1890s, and Expressionism of the 1920s, German drama re-echoed the passion and vehemence of that outburst of youthful genius. And from its very midst arose the two greatest figures of German literature, Goethe and Schiller. The former poured the sum of his creative genius into a drama, *Faust,* and the latter was above all a dramatist. The twin peak of these two cast its shadow across the better part of the nineteenth century. The Romantic movement which followed the classical era was, as in every other country, not propitious to the creation of drama since it expressed itself, by its very nature, mainly in lyric poetry and narrative prose. However, on the fringe of the actual Romantic movement appeared a number of genuine dramatists – Kleist, Büchner, Grabbe – who carried on the tradition of high tragedy, taking their cue from Shakespeare. The literary movement of the 1830s, known as 'Young Germany', brought drama once more into contact with reality and the social issues of the day; its chief exponents, Laube and Gutzkow, were however comparatively insignificant.

German drama culminated, towards the middle of the

century, in Hebbel and Grillparzer – the one representative of Northern Germany, the other of Austria. These two can be regarded as the last direct heirs to the classical tradition as created by Goethe and Schiller. Their works are poetic dramas, mostly in blank verse, treating historical and mythological subjects in the grand manner. But although in form they look back to the classical age, their spiritual and psychological content points to the future, heralding the dawn of modern drama.

The century of German drama reaching from Lessing to Hebbel can be compared to any of the great epochs of world drama, the age of Shakespeare in England, of Racine and Corneille in France, and of Calderon and Lope de Vega in Spain. But owing to its later date and its totally different social conditions, it was of a very different texture and significance. While the great dramatic achievements of other nations were carried by a homogeneous society, and based on a firm set of values – the spirit of the Renaissance in England, the absolute monarchy in France, the Roman Catholic Church in Spain – classical drama in Germany lacked any such definite pattern of life. Instead, it was a creation of the isolated human mind; it lived and developed in a purely intellectual realm, divorced from its social environment. It was a late-comer, flourishing in a world that was no longer favourable to the creation of great drama. Perhaps this is one of the reasons why its impact was not as universal as that of the other major dramatic epochs. However, for the Germans it has the invaluable advantage of reaching to the verge of our own times, and of dealing with problems not so far removed from our own. In other words, Goethe, Kleist, or Büchner are in language and outlook much closer to the modern world than is Shakespeare or Racine.

After the death of Hebbel in 1863, it is true, the stream of drama seemed to come to an end. The following era coincided with the struggle for political unification and the rise of

Bismarck's empire. It seemed as though all creative energy was absorbed by the national aspirations and the accumulation of material wealth. The twenty-five years between the death of Hebbel and the appearance of Gerhart Hauptmann saw only one creative achievement of importance in the theatre: the music-drama of Richard Wagner, in whom Romantic ideals combined with the new age of national self-assertion. Apart from him, the German theatre passed through a singularly shallow period, punctuated by flimsy farces, sentimental domestic plays, and pseudo-classical blank verse histories in the vein of Schiller.

This stagnation came to an abrupt end with the appearance, in 1889, of Gerhart Hauptmann's *Vor Sonnenaufgang*. Of course, there were trends anticipating this event, both inside and outside Germany. But there can be few instances in the history of the theatre when the literary scene has been so radically transformed as it was by that first performance of an unknown author's first play. Not only did it introduce a new dramatist who for the next twenty years was to dominate the German stage – it also initiated an entirely new form of drama and opened up fresh fields for dramatic exploration.

Looking back to-day, it is still possible to recapture some of the excitement aroused by the advent of this new type of play, which seemed so perfectly in keeping with current ideas: materialistic philosophy, the awakening of social conscience, and the keen anticipation of a brighter age just round the corner. The period following on the rise of Naturalism cannot be compared, in terms of artistic accomplishment, with the century reaching from Lessing to Hebbel. But it is rich enough in new ventures and fascinating exploits in the dramatic field to warrant special study. And it has had its full share in the development of modern drama throughout the world. It is with the view of doing justice to this contribution to the drama of our time that this book has been written.

The period under review was one of violent changes in the political history of Germany. The comparative stability of the twenty-five years following the emergence of Naturalism was brought to an abrupt close by the First World War which led to the complete disruption of the social and political fabric of the country. The Weimar Republic, as it rose from the revolution of 1918, was in its leading ideas diametrically opposed to imperial Germany. But these ideas did not seem to be firmly enough rooted in the nation to have a lasting effect. The flimsy structure of the Republic, which was still based on what survived of the middle classes, was soon undermined by assaults from the extreme Left and Right. The economic slump of the early thirties brought the whole structure crashing to the ground, thus paving the way for Hitler. At a first glance, the triumph of National Socialism in 1933 looked like a resurrection of those forces that had been vanquished in 1918. But soon it revealed itself as what it really was – an entirely new social and ideological order. Its revolutionary impetus led straight to World War II, which ended in the second and even more complete defeat of Germany. The period that has elapsed since then, marked by the political division of the country, is still too fluid in its social and spiritual outline to present a clear picture.

These upheavals and vicissitudes are fully reflected in contemporary German drama. Styles and aesthetic doctrines follow one upon another with kaleidoscopic swiftness. The naturalistic movement was in its very essence critically opposed to the ruling powers of imperial Germany whose weaknesses it relentlessly exposed. This criticism was sharpened by acid satire in the plays of Wedekind and Sternheim. During World War I, it gained in revolutionary momentum until, after 1918, its full force was released in the shape of expressionist drama. When the storm of revolution had blown over, the drama reverted to a new realism, known as *Neue Sachlichkeit*, which was suffused with a sense of disillusionment and sober recognition of fact. However, side by side with this antagonistic, largely socialist or even communist trend, there ran a nationalist type of drama which foreshadowed the rise of National Socialism. The Nazi revolution of 1933 erased at one stroke, with a completeness unprecedented in history, all the cultural achievements of the republican era, including the drama.

The twelve years under the Nazis were marked by a conspicuous dearth of genuine dramatic production, in blatant contradiction to their claim of reviving the cultural life of Germany. The period following their collapse has so far not produced any notable dramatic author – with the exception of one or two established playwrights who have returned from exile.

This brief summary of the evolution of German drama during the past two hundred years shows clearly its peculiar instability. This characteristic accounts for both its strength and its weakness. Every generation, and indeed every individual playwright, had to create drama as it were anew. The chief reason for this was the absence of an established society, with its accepted values and traditions. In England, after the towering peak of Elizabethan drama, and the lesser heights of the Restoration, dramatic writing settled down to the portrayal of contemporary society. There is a direct line leading from the comedies of Congreve and Sheridan to the social satires of Wilde and Shaw. This continuity, much as it limited the scope of drama, provided individual authors with a ready mould into which they could pour their particular problems. It precluded, on the other hand, all those deeper issues that lie beyond the social plane and form the stuff of which great drama is made. This limitation is one both of content and form. The plane on which English drama has moved since the days of Congreve and Farquhar is that of reality, of everyday life; whenever it has ventured beyond these boundaries it has done so in a half-hearted fashion, only to return hastily to the safe ground of 'common sense'. This is one of the main reasons why English play-writing, for over two hundred years, has been so conspicuously poor in great drama.

German drama has developed along diametrically opposite lines. There is no society, no traditional pattern, no limitation of time or place. Every author faces as it were afresh the void from which to create his own world. Thus German drama ranges, unrestricted by conventions, over the whole field of human experience and imagination. Hence the instability, the diversity, the apparent anarchy of German dramatic literature. Hence, on the other hand, its richness, its untrammelled exploration of every sphere of human experience. Experiment is the very motive power of German drama. Anything is admissible if it be presented with sufficient force and originality; the sublime and the absurd live side by side and are often inextricably intertwined. The clash of passions and the unconstrained expression of the poet's 'message' frequently become a purpose in themselves. Lack of form is valued as a merit, signifying elemental dramatic power. Thence the German predilection for such 'demonic' dramatists as Kleist or Büchner; thence also their dangerous inclination to take mere vehemence for a sign of genius. It is hardly exaggerated to say that a play is liked in Germany for precisely those qualities for which it is disliked in England; and vice versa.

Of course, there are the great instances of classical balance in which the dissonance of passion seems to be resolved in harmony – Lessing, the mature works of Goethe and Schiller, and later, Grillparzer and Hebbel. But these brief moments of equilibrium were soon upset by a new eruption – the Storm and Stress, the Romantic movement, and more recently, Expressionism. It can easily be seen why in the German theatre genuine comedies are so few and far between. It is not owing to a 'lack of humour', as is so often claimed. But comedy requires dispassionate observation, common sense, strictly defined character – in short, realism.

In no other period are the peculiar characteristics of German drama so much in evidence as in the one we are concerned with here. For it was a period of upheaval and revolution, of deliberate negation of established values, and of a constant quest for new ones. These violent fluctuations had their repercussions on the drama, both in content and form. And although many of the plays written during these last seventy years have proved to be of merely passing value, the total impact of this period of theatrical history has been considerable. The Germans, with their love of experiment and their passion for carrying everything to extremes, have played their full part in the rise of modern drama all over the world.

Though this study concentrates on drama as a literary form it is necessary to say something about the pattern of theatrical life in Germany. For the drama is still-born without its realization on the living stage. The outstanding feature of the German theatre, compared with that of most countries, is its decentralization. While in England and France all theatres of importance are concentrated in the capitals, leaving the rest of the country to occasional 'try-outs' and touring companies, they are in Germany evenly spread throughout the whole country, down to middle-size and small provincial towns. The main reason for this is of course their origin in the court-theatres of the dukes and princes who vied with one another in artistic accomplishment. Thus such cities as Dresden, Mannheim, Weimar, Munich were focal points of theatrical life long before Berlin rose to the dominant position it held during the first third of this century. This decentralization continued even after 1918 when the numerous *Hoftheater* were converted into *Stadt-*, *Landes-*, or *Staatstheater*, i.e. theatres subsidized by the municipality or the state.

The wealth of theatrical life is due not only to historical factors: it could be maintained only through a keen and widespread interest in serious drama. This interest is undoubtedly a characteristic feature of the German people. Moreover, it is not limited to Germany, but extends to the other German-speaking countries, such as Austria, the German part of Switzerland and, up to 1945, the German minority in Czechoslovakia, with its first-rate German theatres in Prague and the smaller towns of Sudetenland.

This vast network of independent theatres, each with its own company and repertory, made it possible for any new theatrical venture to be carried swiftly to every part of the country; indeed, in many instances it was in a provincial centre that a new movement originated or a new dramatist made his name.

In the period under review, it is true, the capital took the initiative more and more. It was in Berlin that, in the early 1890s, the naturalistic movement won its first triumphs, promoted by the great producer and managing director of the Deutsches Theater, Otto Brahm. Similarly, the neo-romantic drama, although it had its origin and true home in Vienna, was carried to victory by Max Reinhardt, Brahm's pupil and successor, who dominated the German theatre for the next twenty years, raising it to an unprecedented level of perfection. The expressionist drama, too, had its centre in Berlin, though some of its main battles were fought in other cities, such as Frankfurt, Darmstadt, and Düsseldorf. The dominant role of Berlin continued in the Nazi era, only to come to an end in 1945. Since then, theatrical life has centred once more in the cities of Western Germany, Munich, Düsseldorf, Hamburg, Cologne, Göttingen, etc. Only quite recently has Berlin regained some of its former importance, especially through the striking productions of the 'Berliner Ensemble' in the Eastern sector.

This study concentrates on the drama as a literary form, touching on the wider issues of the theatre, including production and acting, only where necessary. Its main object is to illuminate a period in the history of German drama which was, if not equal to the great epochs of world drama, yet rich enough in bold ventures to hold its place in the theatrical history of our time.

Chapter One

NATURALISTIC DRAMA

I. ORIGIN AND PRINCIPLES

Throughout Europe, the eighteen-nineties were a period of literary ferment. The causes do not seem connected with any external events: outwardly, the social fabric which had grown out of the industrial revolution remained unshaken, and the steady material progress apparently unlimited. Moreover, the social unrest accompanying the early stages of the machine age seemed a thing of the past, and the rule of the middle class more secure than ever. Yet a sense of doubt and insecurity made itself felt as the century drew to its close. It was as though the mind registered the first shocks of the earthquake which was to bring down the whole social structure a quarter of a century later. As is usually the case, these doubts and premonitions first arose in the ruling social class, long before it was challenged from without. In other words, the middle class lost its complacency and self-assurance. Indeed, it might be said that every revolution takes its rise within the social stratum it is about to destroy.

The challenge to middle-class society and its intrinsic set of values came from two opposite quarters, which can best be indicated by the names of Marx and Nietzsche. The first stood for the revolutionary overthrow of bourgeois society, and its replacement by an entirely new social order; the second entailed a 'revaluation of all values', challenging the moral standards on which the middle classes were founded, and setting up the image of the strong and independent individual; the

23

first was collective and materialistic, the second individualistic and spiritual. Both these challenges made themselves increasingly felt towards the end of the century – the second somewhat later than the first – and helped to undermine the foundations on which the whole social structure was built.

In the field of literature, this process first became apparent in France. Ever since the Romantic movement had spent its force, literary taste had swung over to the other extreme – namely, realism. This implied not merely a new literary style but also the inclusion of a vast range of facts and problems which hitherto had lain outside the scope of creative imagination. The foremost literary form dedicated to this task was the realistic novel as it was developed by Maupassant, the Goncourts and, above all, Zola. Their creative achievements were supported by corresponding philosophical tenets which saw in material circumstance the prime factor shaping man's destiny. In particular, it was Taine's theories that exercised a powerful influence on the literature of the period. He applied scientific laws to the study of society and conceived man as a mere product of heredity and environment. Drama, it is true, had not caught up with these ideas. The French stage still cultivated the *comédie de mœurs*, the well-made play of Scribe, Sardou, and Henri Becque, which offered a measure of social criticism, but within a limited range and to no serious purpose. It was only with the dramatization of Zola's novel, *Thérèse Raquin*, in 1873, that the first play of a new type appeared on the stage.

Contemporary with this realistic movement in France there emerged the great Russian novels of Turgeniev, Dostoevsky, and Tolstoy. They, too, were realistic, but their realism sprang from deeper elemental sources. Instead of being the product of conscious aesthetic theories, they were deeply rooted in Russian life and imbued with Russian mysticism. Here, too, the greatest achievements were in narrative form. But soon the realistic portrayal of Russian life was transferred to the stage where it found its supreme fulfilment in Stanislavsky's productions of the plays of Tolstoy, Gorki, and Chekhov in the Moscow Art Theatre. In particular Tolstoy's sombre peasant drama, *The Power of Darkness*, and Gorki's *Lower Depths* made a strong impact on the German theatre.

The third, and probably the strongest, stimulus came from Scandinavia. It is a well-established fact that Ibsen's fame originated in Germany where he spent most of his voluntary exile. Technically, the social dramas of Ibsen were modelled on the French society play of Sardou and Dumas. But in their contents they opened up new vistas, attacking and exposing the hypocrisies and moral weaknesses of bourgeois society. In quick succession, the social plays of Ibsen's middle period appeared in the German theatre – *The Pillars of Society* in 1877, *A Doll's House* in 1880, *Ghosts* in 1887.

It is against this background that the rise of naturalistic drama in Germany must be viewed. Its full impact can be measured only against the complete stagnation of the preceding era. With the death of Hebbel, in 1863, the last impulse emanating from the classical age had spent its force. During the next twenty-five years, the German theatre contented itself mainly with the production of sentimental *Sittenstücke*, fashioned after the French *comédies de mœurs*, of flimsy farces, and of pseudo-classical iambic dramas in a patriotic vein. The most prominent exponent of the latter type was Ernst von Wildenbruch (1845-1909), who provided the stage with a host of blank verse dramas glorifying the German, and in particular, the Prussian past (*Die Karolinger*, 1881, *Die Quitzows*, 1888, *Heinrich und Heinrichs Geschlecht*, 1896, and others). As can be seen from the dates of his plays, his activities partly overlapped the rise of the naturalistic movement. In some of his later plays, in fact, he tried to adopt, not very successfully, the principles of Naturalism (e.g. *Die Haubenlerche*, 1890). His success, though striking at the time, was cut short by the triumph of realistic drama which was diametrically opposed to all he stood for. Apart from Wildenbruch, the German theatre fed on the day-to-day fare of light comedy, mass-produced by such prolific playwrights as Paul Lindau or the double-firm Blumenthal and Kadelburg (one of whose farces, *Im weissen Rössl*, later became world-famous in a musical adaptation as *White Horse Inn*). Perhaps only one play of that period deserves mention for its greater sincerity: Adolf Wilbrandt's *Der Meister von Palmyra* (1889), a philosophical drama on a Faustian scale, revolving on the theme of eternal life.

At the same time there were signs of a resuscitation of theatrical life. The impulse came, as so often in Germany, from a small provincial centre – in this instance, one of the miniature Thuringian principalities. Duke Georg of Meiningen, keenly interested in his court-theatre, had formed a model ensemble, devoted primarily to the revival of the classics in a realistic manner. Historical accuracy in décor and costume was carried to the extreme, and a new style of acting developed. By frequent tours these ideas were disseminated throughout the country, and an unprecedented standard of ensemble playing was set up. Another important step was the founding, in 1883, of the Deutsches Theater in Berlin, under the direction of Adolf L'Arronge. This theatre, run entirely on a private basis, was destined to become, under his successors Otto Brahm and, later, Max Reinhardt, the leading German stage – a position it held till the eve of the Nazi revolution. L'Arronge, himself a successful playwright, though of the old school, prepared the way by building up a highly trained ensemble, without paying much attention to the new naturalistic drama which was about to transform the scene. This task fell to the *Freie Bühne*, a private theatre club formed in 1889 by a group of writers under the leadership of Otto Brahm.

The naturalistic movement was more than a purely literary fashion; it had a distinct social and political bias, linked as it was with the rising power of Socialism. This connection is illustrated by the fact that in 1890, one year after the *Freie Bühne*, the so-called *Freie Volksbühne*, the 'free stage of the people', was founded in Berlin, which set itself the aim of winning over the broad masses to serious drama. 'Art shall belong to the people, and not be the privilege of one social class', its founder, Bruno Wille, proclaimed in his opening speech. This organization, working in close co-operation with the trade unions, was destined to grow into one of the most powerful factors of theatrical life in Germany, long after Naturalism had run its course. At the same time, the *Freie Bühne* continued its pioneering work for the new drama. When, in 1894, its leader Otto Brahm took over the direction of the Deutsches Theater, the naturalistic movement was as it were officially recognized. The ten years of his management, dedicated in the first place to the plays of Ibsen, Hauptmann, and Schnitzler, and supported by a splendid array of actors, must be regarded as one of the great periods of European theatre. It came to an end only when the impetus of realistic drama was spent and the reaction set in, led by Brahm's own disciple and successor, Max Reinhardt.

During the eighteen-eighties, the doctrines of realistic art had penetrated to Germany and prepared the ground. The two main centres were Berlin and Munich: in each city the new ideas were propagated by a literary review, *Die Gesell-schaft* in Munich, and *Die Freie Bühne* in Berlin (later renamed *Die neue Rundschau*, to this day one of the leading German periodicals). The dominant role soon passed to Berlin, whose keen intellectual climate was best suited to the development of the new art-form. Its principles were carried to the extreme, in keeping with the German love for theoretical consistency. Arno Holz, one of the champions of the movement, summarized its aim in his famous definition, 'Art has the tendency to revert to Nature'. And Otto Brahm, in a manifesto introducing the *Freie Bühne*, announced: 'The battle-cry of the new art is the one word – truth; and it is truth, truth in every walk of life, which we, too, are striving for and which we demand.' In these two pronouncements the tenets of consistent realism, or Naturalism, are clearly established. 'Nature', or 'Truth', was conceived as the faithful reproduction of a segment of reality, with particular emphasis on the cruder aspects of contemporary life, to the exclusion of any poetical adornment.

It was Arno Holz who, together with Johannes Schlaf, first applied these theories to creative writing. Their first experiments took a narrative form. In a volume *Papa Hamlet* (1889), published under the pseudonym Bjarne P. Holmsen (evidently in deference to the vogue for Scandinavian literature) they presented a series of studies describing, in minute detail, scenes from the Berlin slums. In some of them, mainly consisting of dialogue, the direct speech was printed in large and the descriptive passages in small type. From this it was only one step to the dramatic form. This final step the two authors took in their play, *Die Familie Selicke* (1890), which came to be regarded as the most consistent, though not the most artistically satisfying, instance of naturalistic drama.

The founding of the *Freie Bühne*, closely modelled on the Paris *Théâtre Libre*, provided the appropriate platform for the new dramatic movement. Significantly, the first work to be presented, in September 1889, was Ibsen's *Ghosts*. A few weeks later, the first play of an unknown native author carried the movement to victory – Gerhart Hauptmann's *Vor Sonnenaufgang*. Compared with the importance this event had in the history of modern German drama, the performance of *Die Familie Selicke*, in the following year, is to-day merely of academic interest. Yet it was this play which, in the view of the Berlin novelist and critic Theodor Fontane, a fervent champion of the movement, effected 'a complete break with all previous stage productions, not excluding Ibsen'. Despite its cosmopolitan affiliations, the movement had a strong nationalist flavour. In an introductory note, the two authors claimed that their work was 'the most German play our literature possesses'.

Neither in form nor content does the play bear out this claim. *Die Familie Selicke* portrays the drab life of a poor Berlin family living in constant terror of the drunken father. The action is almost static. Throughout the first two acts, the youngest child lies dying at the back of the room. The elder daughter, who is in love with a young clergyman, rejects his proposal of marriage, unable to free herself from the sordid environment into which she has been born. The play ends as it began – in hopeless fatalism. Of far greater importance than this indifferent plot is the consistent application of all the formal principles of naturalistic drama: the elimination of theatrical conventions such as soliloquies, asides, dramatic suspense and surprise, effective climaxes and 'curtains', the renouncement of any poetic embellishment and the minute reproduction of everyday speech, down to its slightest inflections.

Die Familie Selicke was to remain the only dramatic product of Arno Holz' and Johannes Schlaf's co-operation. Soon after, their ways separated; neither of them achieved another real success. Schlaf produced, among others, a starkly realistic play, *Meister Oelze* (1892), whereas Holz wrote, in collaboration with O. Jerschke, a successful play about school life, *Traumulus* (1904), centring on the pathetic figure of an idealistic schoolmaster, a kind of German counterpart to Mr. Chips. His more ambitious project to write a dramatic cycle picturing Berlin society at the turn of the century resulted in three rather indifferent plays, *Sozialaristokraten* (1896), *Sonnenfinsternis* (1908), and *Ignorabimus* (1912).

Any new spiritual impulse, any innovation in form and technique, soon finds its realization in one or several outstanding personalities. Thus German Naturalism found its

fulfilment in two pre-eminent playwrights, Gerhart Hauptmann and Hermann Sudermann. These two, who appeared
almost simultaneously on the literary scene, and whose
names were for some time closely linked, were soon found to
be of very unequal stature. While Sudermann's fame declined
almost as swiftly as it rose, Hauptmann's grew steadily throughout the whole span of his life.

II. HERMANN SUDERMANN

Hermann Sudermann was born in East Prussia, in 1857.
Although he spent much of his life in Berlin, which forms the
background to some of his best-known plays, he reverted
time and again in his writings to his native province and its
ruling Junker class. His first play, *Die Ehre* (Honour), produced
in the Berlin Lessing Theater in the autumn of 1889, only a
few weeks after Hauptmann's *Vor Sonnenaufgang*, brought
him instantaneous fame. It was, in fact, the first undisputed
triumph of the new realistic drama in Germany. Only gradually was it realized that its success was not due to any novel
dramatic technique or content but to the clever exploitation of
the conventional devices of the well-made play. *Die Ehre*
centres on the time-honoured contrast between rich and poor,
which is here vividly illustrated by the juxtaposition of
Vorderhaus and *Hinterhaus*, i.e. the front and back part of
a Berlin residence. The former is the home of a wealthy
business man and his family whereas the latter is occupied by
the family of one of his employees. The play opens with the
return of Robert, the poor man's son, from a long absence
overseas, and his discovery that his younger sister has been
seduced by the son of his employer. When he calls him to
account the father offers to settle the matter with a large sum.
While Robert's family are quite prepared to accept the
money, he proudly refuses it and challenges the seducer to a
duel. His challenge is not accepted on the ground of his

inferior social status. As he leaves the house defiantly, he is joined by the rich man's daughter who has all along been in love with him. The whole play revolves on the concept of 'honour' – or rather, the clash between two or more concepts, as they appear on different social levels. As Count Trast, a kind of *raisonneur* and mediator between the two hostile camps, puts it to Robert: 'Each caste has its own honour. Unhappy the man who has broken with his caste without having the courage to break with his conscience too.' On the surface, *Die Ehre* is a drama of social protest. Robert flings his defiance in the face of the rich: 'We work for you, we give our sweat and our heart's blood for you. At the same time you seduce our sisters and our daughters and pay off their disgrace with the money we've earned for you!' However, it soon became evident that Sudermann's challenge was not to be taken seriously. As in all his subsequent plays, he merely exploited the ideas of the age for theatrical purposes. His very first work revealed both his strength and his weakness. Fundamentally, Sudermann's technique derived from the French *pièce à thèse* of Dumas and Sardou. All the well-worn devices – soliloquies, asides, the *coup de théâtre* – are there. His plots are artificially contrived with the sole object of theatrical effect; his characters are the stock-types of the sentimental domestic play. But these devices he skilfully infused with the ideas and problems of the new drama – a fusion which for some time deceived both critics and public.

Sudermann's second play, *Sodoms Ende* (1890), has for its central figure an artist who is corrupted through his contact with society – the frivolous, dissipated society of the Berlin *nouveaux riches*. (The symbolic title refers to a picture he has painted in his better days, depicting the destruction of Sodom.) He has an affair with a cold-hearted, ambitious society woman who for the sake of appearances intends to marry him off to her niece. He in turn is loved by an innocent young girl who drowns herself when she learns of his amorous entanglements. When the body is brought to the artist's studio he attempts to sketch it and dies of a haemorrhage. Once again, Sudermann contrives his main conflicts by contrasting two social sets, the artist's humble parents and former friends who want to recall him to his better self, and the depraved upper class which ruins him. And again, the playwright's ambition to present a realistic picture of contemporary Berlin society is thwarted by his addiction to theatrical effect and melodrama.

The next play, *Heimat* (Home, 1893, better known outside Germany under the name *Magda*), was Sudermann's greatest success. This was largely because it provided a rewarding part which was played by Duse, Sarah Bernhardt, Mrs. Patrick Campbell and other prominent actresses of the period. Magda, a celebrated prima donna, on a chance visit to her native town, calls at her parents' house which she left as a young girl under dramatic circumstances. She is confronted by her father, a retired officer, the typical coarse and honest father of the old domestic drama. He is prepared to forgive her on condition that she marries the man he has appointed for her. As it happens, this man was her first lover, from whom she has a child. On realizing the full extent of her immorality, the outraged father points a pistol at his daughter, but is saved from the worst by a timely heart-failure. The free morals of artistic libertinage are effectively contrasted with narrow bourgeois conventions. At the climax of the play, Magda, the 'woman with a past', flings her defiance in her father's face: 'If you give us freedom, don't be surprised if we use it!' – to which he retorts with righteous indignation: 'This is the spirit of rebellion which now pervades the world!' Basically, the conflict is that of the traditional domestic melodrama, clothed in modern trappings.

Perhaps the most genuinely convincing of Sudermann's plays is *Fritzchen*, the second of three one-act plays published under the title *Morituri* (1896). It is the brief and poignant episode of a young lieutenant on the eve of a duel which he feels will be fatal for him. On the way he visits his home to bid farewell to his parents and his fiancée. While his father knows the truth, his mother remains ignorant to the end: watching him from the window as he goes to his death, she proudly tells of a dream in which she saw her son at the side of the Emperor – a perfect instance of Sudermann's sense of dramatic irony.

With the first of the three one-act plays, *Teja*, showing the last king of the Goths on the eve of his death in battle, Sudermann ventured for the first time into history. The result was as unsatisfactory as was a later, more ambitious essay in biblical drama, *Johannes* (1898), in which he tried to present the story of John the Baptist in terms of realistic drama. Even less successful was an attempt at medieval legend, cast in rhyming couplets, *Die drei Reiherfedern* (The Three Heron Feathers, 1899). Sudermann remained at his best when he kept to his own plane, that of contemporary Berlin society, as he did in *Es lebe das Leben* (The Joy of Living, 1902), a drama of adultery set against the background of political intrigue. He reverted to his native East Prussia in such plays as *Glück im Winkel* (The Vale of Content, 1895) and *Johannisfeuer* (Midsummer Madness, 1900). The latter pictures, in a terse and well-constructed action, the conflict between Christian morality and primeval pagan instincts which find vent in the wild celebrations on midsummer night.

In his later plays (*Sturmgeselle Sokrates*, 1903, *Stein unter Steinen*, 1905, and others), Sudermann tried again and again to recapture his earlier successes. The fierce opposition he encountered on the part of the professional critics drove him to an embittered counter-attack which still further injured his case. By the turn of the century, his fame had faded; his name became a byword for cheap theatrical effect and melodramatic cliché. When he died in 1928, he had long outlived his time.

This change of fortune was largely due to the leading dramatic critic, Alfred Kerr, who from the first had exposed his work to ridicule. Much as his criticism was vitiated by personal rancour, it contributed greatly to emphasizing, by comparison, the superiority of Sudermann's contemporary, Gerhart Hauptmann. It is curious that outside Germany Sudermann's success has generally surpassed Hauptmann's: it is usually the second-rate which is most easily transferred into a foreign medium. Sudermann is at best another Pinero; whereas there is really no parallel to Hauptmann.

III. GERHART HAUPTMANN

October 20th, 1889, when Hauptmann's 'social drama' *Vor Sonnenaufgang* was performed at a literary matinée of the *Freie Bühne*, is generally regarded as marking the birth of naturalistic drama in Germany. There are few instances in the history of literature when the beginning of a new epoch can be fixed to a day, as it was in this case. The young author who faced the storm roused by his challenging play was then twenty-seven years old. He was born in a small town in Silesia, the son of a hotel proprietor. Throughout his life, the people and the landscape of his native province were a vital stimulus to his creative work. So also was the countryside round Berlin, where he made his home as a young married man. It was here, in the little lake-side village of Erkner, that he came into contact with the pioneers of Naturalism, among them Arno Holz, with whom he founded a literary club under the name of *Durch* (Through). It was to Holz, 'the most consistent realist', that he dedicated his first play. Like Holz, Hauptmann first used the naturalistic style in narrative form: in 1887, he wrote two stories, *Fasching* (Carnival) and *Bahnwärter Thiel* (Signal-Man Thiel). Set in the landscape of his immediate neighbourhood, these tragedies of simple country-folk are told with acute psychological insight and a sure sense of atmosphere. A narrative quality is still evident in the detailed descriptive stage directions of his early plays.

Vor Sonnenaufgang (Before Sunrise) is set in a family of Silesian farmers who have suddenly grown rich through the discovery of coal deposits on their land. Demoralized by their new wealth, they have given themselves up to drink and every conceivable vice. Into this setting steps the hero of the play, Alfred Loth, an idealistic social reformer. The rich farmer's daughter, Helene, the only one untouched by the moral depravity of her people, falls in love with him, seeing in him her saviour. As his eyes are gradually opened to the appalling state of affairs, he shrinks from the possible effects of the laws of heredity, and renounces her. In her despair, Helene kills herself. This play is in many respects the work of a beginner. Moreover, it is the only play of Hauptmann in which the theories of Naturalism are fully applied, both in technique and content. Yet it surpasses in sheer dramatic impact any play of the other naturalistic playwrights. Its emphasis on the crude and hideous aspects of contemporary life is relieved by some striking poetic touches, as in the charming love scene between Loth and Helene. When challenged on this point by an orthodox naturalist, Hauptmann replied, 'Can I help it if nature is also beautiful?'

The theme of heredity also underlies Hauptmann's second play, *Das Friedensfest* (Reconciliation, 1890), sub-titled 'a family catastrophe'. The terse action unfolds on a single evening – Christmas eve – in the living-room of a middle-class family. The occasion is a family reunion in which the father and two sons, who have left home years ago after a violent quarrel, once more face one another. Despite all attempts at a reconciliation, their deep-rooted enmity breaks out anew, and the father has a stroke. However, the sombre gloom of the play is lit with a ray of hope when the younger son's fiancée stands by him, encouraging him to break the vicious circle of guilt and retribution in which he feels himself caught.

Hauptmann's third play, *Einsame Menschen* (Lonely Lives, 1891), centres on the problems of marriage. If *Das Friedensfest* was to a certain extent influenced by Ibsen's *Ghosts*, *Einsame Menschen* shows an affinity to *Rosmersholm*. It deals with the struggles of a 'problem character' (*problematische Natur*) in conflict with the conventions of his time. The central figure, Johannes Vockerat, a young writer keenly interested in modern scientific ideas, is married to a woman intellectually inferior to him. The marriage is endangered by a girl student from Russia who shares his intellectual interests. He asks her to stay in his house; but their belief in a purely Platonic relationship presently turns out to be a delusion. Unable to extricate himself from his predicament, Vockerat drowns himself in the lake. In this play, the consistent naturalistic form gives way to a wider dramatic conception in which psychological insight and the subtle recreation of atmosphere play a greater part. It was the first work of Hauptmann's to reach a wider public, and the first that carried his name beyond the German borders.

But it was with his next play, *Die Weber* (The Weavers, 1892), that he gained his most resounding success and accomplished what is indisputably the masterpiece of naturalistic drama. Drawing on his childhood impressions of Silesian village life, he depicts the rising, in the 1840s, of the Silesian weavers, put out of work by the introduction of machinery. There is no individual hero. In five acts, the gathering force of the rebellion is pictured, carried by a teeming crowd of sharply profiled characters, each of whom is no more than a voice in a tremendous chorus. The dull despair of the beginning eventually finds vent in a violent outburst when the weavers invade the manufacturer's house. But the rising is quelled by the soldiers called in to restore order. This play, which was at first banned by the censor, has been taken from the start as a revolutionary drama and exploited for political purposes. It is in fact nothing of the sort. Hauptmann, in spite of his early socialist affiliations, was never concerned with the propagation of social doctrines. *Die Weber*, as all his works, was inspired by a deep compassion for human suffering – the mainspring of his creative imagination. More poignant than the physical plight of the famished weavers is their inarticulate spiritual urge, rooted in their simple Christian faith.

This religious impulse is even more evident in another drama dealing with a social uprising, *Florian Geyer* (1896). In this vast pageant of the sixteenth-century German peasant war Hauptmann applied the naturalistic technique for the first and only time to historical drama. In a prologue and five long acts, filled with a crowd of more than a hundred characters, he presents a comprehensive picture of the peasants' rebellion, or rather of its final phase – its brutal suppression by the nobility. In true naturalistic fashion, dramatic climax and external action are studiously avoided; the events are merely reflected in interminable discussions and arguments. Yet the total impact is that of compelling tragedy. As in *Die Weber*, the emphasis is laid on a multitude of small characters who interweave like so many minute strands in a vast colourful tapestry; but here there emerges the single figure of their leader, the 'black knight' Florian Geyer, who, a renegade from his own class, has sided with the peasants and dies for their cause. This drama, which at its first performance proved a failure – the first for Hauptmann after an uninterrupted series of triumphs – was recognized in its true stature only after 1918, when defeat had awakened the German public to its sombre message.

Between these two great social dramas Hauptmann turned for the first time to comedy. In *Kollege Crampton* (1892) he presented a comedy of character, portraying a Falstaff type – a teacher of art who ruins his career through his addiction to drink but is saved from utter corruption by a devoted pupil. Of far greater importance was the comedy *Der Biberpelz* (The Beaver Coat, 1893) which has come to be recognized not only as one of Hauptmann's most outstanding works but as one of the rare comic masterpieces in German literature. The play is set in a village near Berlin and has as its central character a washerwoman, a devoted wife and mother, who increases her meagre livelihood by petty theft. The comic turn arises from the fact that the official who is in charge of the investigation neglects his duty, since he is preoccupied with hunting down political suspects (the period is towards the end of Bismarck's rule, at the time of the anti-socialist laws). This figure, the local magistrate Wehrhahn, has come to be the epitome of bureaucratic narrow-mindedness and conceit. However, for all its political satire, the chief merits of the comedy lie in its ingenious characterization, the coming-to-life of a whole community and, above all, the masterly portrait of the shrewd and down-to-earth heroine, 'Mother Wolffen'.

Nearly ten years later, Hauptmann wrote a sequel, *Der rote Hahn* (Conflagration, 1901), which centres on the same two principal characters. Now, however, the colours are somewhat darker; the heroine is involved in a more serious fraud, and the play ends with her death, just as the net is about to close on her.

The year 1893, which saw the first performances both of *Die Weber* and *Der Biberpelz*, was also marked by a very different type of play, the dream-poem *Hanneles Himmelfahrt* (The Assumption of Hannele). Now for the first time Hauptmann in part abandoned the naturalistic style. What was at first decried as a 'betrayal' of the movement was presently recognized to be the opening-up of deeper creative sources which had flowed beneath the surface of Hauptmann's work and which were gradually to sweep him in entirely new directions. In fact, Hauptmann still conformed fully to the naturalistic manner in this moving little play about the dying girl who is rescued from the village pond and who, in the squalid workhouse to which she is taken, experiences in her delirium the bliss of paradise. The realistic plane is abandoned and the language elevated to verse only in the feverish hallucinations of the child. Realism and poetry are here perfectly integrated – more perfectly perhaps than ever again in Hauptmann's work.

From then onwards, these two trends of his creative mind ran for a long time side by side, occasionally merging but more often unconnected and finding expression in works of a very different type. Far from turning his back on Naturalism in which he had gained his first triumphs, it was now that Hauptmann wrote some of his most compelling plays, using the naturalistic technique for the creation of human character. This applies above all to his two dramas of Silesian village life, *Fuhrmann Henschel* (Drayman Henschel, 1898) and *Rose Bernd* (1903). In these works the exact reproduction of a whole social milieu is subordinated to the building-up of one central character. They are in fact genuine tragedies moulded in the naturalistic form. The protagonists of both these plays are passive – an essential characteristic of most of Hauptmann's heroes and heroines; their tragedy springs not from action but from suffering. This suffering is not imposed on them by external circumstance but has its source in their own characters, which lead them to inescapable doom. 'I have just stumbled into it', mutters Henschel, the good-natured drayman who has been tricked into an unhappy marriage with his housekeeper, a heartless, domineering woman. *Rose Bernd*, on the other hand, is the drama of a hot-blooded country girl who falls an easy prey to the men of the village and is driven in the end to kill her illegitimate child. Her tragedy, too, is one of helpless entanglement brought upon her by the blind force of instinct.

The underlying philosophy of both these plays – as of all Hauptmann's works – is determinism; but their driving force is that of all great tragedy – pity. 'That girl – what she must have suffered!' runs the final line of *Rose Bernd* – a comment that might be applied to most of Hauptmann's characters.

Michael Kramer (1900), one of the most intimate of Hauptmann's works, is an artist's tragedy centring on the conflict of father and son. The special problems of the artist formed a favourite theme in literature around the turn of the century. In Hauptmann's play, this theme assumes an intensely personal flavour. The figure of Michael Kramer, like that of the earlier play *Kollege Crampton*, is modelled on an art master at the Breslau academy where the author had studied during his adolescent years. Kramer's son, who is infinitely more gifted than he, suffers from a physical deformity which drives him to vicious hatred of his fellow-men. Humiliated by his unhappy infatuation for a barmaid, the son takes his own life. In the final act, the father, watching over his son's body, pours out his heart to a friend in what is virtually one long soliloquy. In this scene – one of the most intensely moving Hauptmann has written – the realistic plane is once again transcended: the individual case gives rise to a general meditation on the significance of suffering and the final triumph of love. Even the language, though realistic on the surface, changes imperceptibly to a rhythmical pattern touching on verse.

In another artist's drama, *Gabriel Schillings Flucht* (Gabriel Schilling's Flight, 1906), Hauptmann resumes the theme of his earlier play *Einsame Menschen* – the man torn between two women – a theme that recurs repeatedly in his work. This play is set on an island in the Baltic where the dramatist used to spend the summer. The wide expanse of the sea, the luminousness of the landscape form an unchanging background. For all its realistic detail, the play has a quality of unreality and translucence which raises it above the naturalistic plane. It also is free of the doctrinal zeal that informs the earlier piece, *Einsame Menschen*, and concentrates on the psychological interplay of the main characters. Once again, the central figure, a painter who seeks refuge on the island from a hopeless emotional entanglement, finds the only solution in suicide. And a friend, watching as the body is recovered from the sea, makes the final comment, 'If Schilling has really fled – no, don't let's go after him like hounds!'

The last of Hauptmann's distinctly naturalistic plays is one of his most arresting – *Die Ratten* (The Rats, 1911). Here the two aspects of his dramatic art, the faithful reproduction of a social milieu in a multitude of sharply defined characters, and the unfolding of a single human drama, are perfectly blended. The action is set against the background of a Berlin tenement, with its noise and squalor. The main plot concerns a mason's wife who has adopted a child and clings to it with frantic love, pretending it is her own. When, in the end, the child is taken from her, she throws herself from a window. Intertwined with this tragedy of thwarted mother-love run several sub-plots. A retired actor, who gives dramatic lessons in the attic, extols the superiority of high-flown classical tragedy over the modern realistic school. Yet all along a genuine human drama unfolds as it were under his very nose. In this way, the play presents not only one of the most striking examples of naturalistic drama but also its theoretical foundations – and this, incidentally, just at the moment when Hauptmann was to abandon Naturalism for good.

As already indicated, the sequence of naturalistic plays up to *Die Ratten* was interspersed, from *Hanneles Himmelfahrt* onwards, with plays of a very different type in which the realistic plane was partly, or wholly, abandoned for poetic and symbolic subjects. Hauptmann was frequently rebuked at the time for yielding, in these poetic verse plays, to the symbolist or neo-romantic movement which began to supersede

Naturalism. Only in the light of his later development did it become clear that these works formed no less an essential part of his nature than the realistic ones – that both were in fact merely two aspects of the same creative impulse.

The first wholly poetic play was *Die versunkene Glocke* (The Sunken Bell, 1896) which, along with *Die Weber*, came to be Hauptmann's most resounding success. Curiously enough, it is the one which, of all his works, has dated most quickly. For all its personal sincerity and poetic beauty, its period character is perhaps most evident. It is an artist's drama, picturing the aspirations and mental conflicts of a creative artist in purely symbolic and poetic terms. The tremendous popular appeal of the work was largely due to its use of German folklore and fairy-tale. The central conflict, that between Christianity and paganism, symbolized by the church in the valley and the sun temple on the heights, was in tune with the period in which the impact of Nietzsche made itself increasingly felt. Once again, the hero, the bell-founder Heinrich, is torn between two women, his down-to-earth wife Magda and Rautendelein, the elfin spirit of the hills, who inspires him to new creative heights. She is the prototype of a long line of bewitching young girls who play so great a part in Hauptmann's later work.

None of Hauptmann's poetic dramas can compete in popular appeal with *Die versunkene Glocke*, though some of them are artistically more satisfying, especially when, like *Hanneles Himmelfahrt*, they grow from a closely defined realistic level. This is also the case in *Schluck und Jau* (1900) which develops the age-old theme of the poor man made rich for one day. Here the story is enacted in the familiar Silesian setting, and the experience is shared by two tramps, one a coarse drunkard, the other gentle and good-natured. Each reacts in a different way when he finds himself transferred to a knightly court by the caprice of a nobleman, and endowed with unlimited power. In the end, they are restored to the roadside where they were first found, and look upon the whole adventure as a dream. The dependence on Shakespeare is evident: it is even accentuated by the language, the alternation of colloquial speech for the tramps, and blank verse for the nobility. This is, incidentally, the first of several plays in which Hauptmann took his cue from Shakespeare.

Reality and poetry are perfectly integrated in the fairy-play *Und Pippa tanzt!* (And Pippa Dances, 1906), perhaps the most entrancing of Hauptmann's poetic plays, although it never shared the popular success of *Die versunkene Glocke*. Like so many of his works, it is set in the Silesian mountains, drawing on their local legends and folklore. It is a winter's tale, lit with the dazzling whiteness of the snow-capped peaks, and ringing with the tinkle of icicles. The action starts in the realistic setting of a mountain inn, frequented by woodcutters and glass-blowers; it ends in the snow-bound abode of a mythical wizard high on the peaks. Pippa is a bewitching dancing-girl, daughter of an Italian who has strayed into this northern world from Venice. She is carried off by a half-savage glass-blower, 'old Huhn', who keeps her imprisoned in his lonely hut. But a wandering apprentice, Michael Hellriegel – a figure hailing straight from the world of German fairy-tale – frees her from her captivity and escapes with her over the mountains, in a romantic longing for the South, the native land of Pippa. Caught in a snow-storm, they find shelter in a kind of mountain observatory belonging to the magician Wann. Here a silent but embittered fight for the girl ensues between the three men – the wise old sage, the young ap-prentice, and the uncouth glass-blower who has pursued them. In the end, Pippa dances in spite of Wann's warning, and falls dead as a Venetian glass breaks in Huhn's hand. The sage remains alone, resigned to his spiritual life, while Michael, blinded by the snow, sets out on his journey to the South, believing Pippa is still beside him. 'It may after all come to pass,' says Wann as he puts him on his way,

> 'that you will have to sing and play here and there at people's doors. But don't lose heart. First, you have the key to the palace, and when it grows dark, Pippa will carry this torch before you; and then verily you will come where peace and joy await you. Only sing and play bravely, and do not doubt!'

The action of the play is set on several levels simultaneously. But there is a general trend from the realistic to the symbolic plane. Its symbolism is open to various interpretations. Pippa may stand for Beauty, or the Ideal, or man's unfulfilled longing. The antagonism of Wann and Huhn has something in it of Prospero and Caliban, that is, man at his highest and his lowest level; but it is Michael, the poet and dreamer, who eventually attains the ideal – if only in his imagination. In this figure, with its subtle connotations of Grimm and the Romantics, Hauptmann has personified something like the dream-image in which the German likes to see himself.

In several of his poetic dramas Hauptmann turned to medieval legend. The first, and probably the most accomplished, was *Der arme Heinrich* (Henry of Aue, 1902), based on a medieval German epic by Hartmann von der Aue. In Hauptmann's hands, the story of the knight who is stricken with leprosy in the full vigour of life, and is cleansed through the selfless devotion of an innocent maid, assumes a wider symbolic significance. *Kaiser Karls Geisel* (Charlemagne's Hostage, 1908), another legendary play, deals with an episode in the life of Charlemagne. The ageing emperor falls passionately in love with a young Saxon harlot and is only brought back to his royal duties when his chancellor has her poisoned. *Griselda* (1909) is based on the old tale of the nobleman who marries a peasant girl and tests her love by taking her children from her. In Hauptmann's version the story is given a pathological turn:

the nobleman's action is dictated by an obsessive jealousy of his own child. All three plays, as so many others of Hauptmann, turn on erotic obsessions, and the power they hold over man for good or ill.

Until about 1912, realistic and poetic plays, or those uniting both styles, went side by side in Hauptmann's dramatic work, with the former predominating. *Die Ratten* was not only his last clearly naturalistic drama but the last important product of Naturalism. Thus it marked the end of an epoch both in the development of this dramatist and in German literature generally. From then onwards, Hauptmann's writings moved in a very different direction, carrying him to new and unexplored fields. The works of this second period were no longer of decisive importance for the development of German drama; nor were they noticeably influenced by the changing styles and literary fashions that grew up around him. Yet so great was his authority that it secured him a dominant position in the German theatre up to his death in 1946. In two of his later plays, he reverted once more to realism without, however, resuming the strictly naturalistic technique. *Dorothea Angermann* (1926) is expressly set in the 1890s, the time of his youth. It is the drama of a young girl who falls a victim to her instincts and is driven by her overbearing father, a prison chaplain, to marry the brute who seduced her. The second play, *Vor Sonnenuntergang* (Before Sunset, 1932), is of greater importance. Its title, referring explicitly to his first drama, *Vor Sonnenaufgang*, denotes the end of the epoch which Hauptmann himself had inaugurated. The play centres on the love of a man of seventy (the author's own age) for a young girl, and the rebellion of his grown-up children when he proposes to marry her. The outcome is tragedy.

With the exception of these two realistic plays, Hauptmann's later dramatic work consisted almost entirely of verse plays. He received a powerful stimulus from his immersion in ancient Greek mythology. The journey to Greece he had undertaken in 1907 proved a turning-point in his creative development comparable to the Italian journey in Goethe's. Its first fruit was *Der Bogen des Odysseus* (The Bow of Odysseus, 1914), a drama of Ulysses' return to Ithaca and his vengeance on the suitors, rich with the glowing colours of the Mediterranean landscape.

The Great War and the social and moral anarchy that followed in its wake drove Hauptmann into an ever deepening despair of mankind. This mood is poignantly reflected in two plays which appeared almost simultaneously at the end of the war: the first, *Der weisse Heiland* (The White Saviour, 1920), deals with the conquest of Mexico by the Spanish. The author's sympathies lie wholly with the natives, above all with the tragic figure of their emperor, Montezuma. He portrays him as a dreamer who sees in the conquest the fulfilment of an ancient prophecy, and whose faith is basely betrayed by the brutal cynicism of the conquerors. The second play, *Indipohdi* (1920), set on an ocean island, is inspired by Shakespeare's *The Tempest*. Its central figure is Prospero, in whom Hauptmann embodies his philosophy of pessimism and renunciation of the world. The characters of Caliban and Ariel are omitted, and the shipwrecked company is led by Prospero's own son who rises in revolt against his father. In the end, the sage ascends a volcano to seek death in the crater, bidding farewell to the world and to his own magic powers. His final soliloquy ends with the words, '*Ich fühle dich, ich sinke in dich, Nichts!*' (I feel thee, I sink into thee, nothingness!).

Undoubtedly, this work was intended by the dramatist to be his own valediction to life. However, he was to live for another quarter of a century – years of ceaseless production in every field of literature, dramatic, epic, and narrative. The rise of the Nazis did not perceptibly affect his creative work which developed along its own consistent lines. In the late thirties, he published two more plays based on medieval legend, *Ulrich von Lichtenstein* and *Die Tochter der Kathedrale* (The Daughter of the Cathedral), both in 1939. His most arresting dramatic work of that period was once again inspired by Shakespeare, *Hamlet in Wittenberg* (1935). Hauptmann had long been fascinated by the figure of Hamlet; he had even attempted, if not very convincingly, to re-edit and complete Shakespeare's drama in translation. In his own play, he traces the story of the prince back to his student days at Wittenberg, thus providing a kind of full-scale prelude to Shakespeare. Advancing the time of action to the sixteenth century, he places Hamlet in the Wittenberg of the Reformation and shows him in disputation with Luther's friend, Melanchthon. The play ends with the arrival of messengers from Elsinore, announcing the death of the king . . .

Hauptmann's last dramatic work, written during the war years 1940-1944, is a cycle of four plays dealing with the doom of the House of Atreus. The first and the last, *Iphigenie in Aulis* and *Iphigenie in Delphi*, centre on the tragic figure of Iphigenia, her sacrifice at the hands of Agamemnon and her expiatory death to redeem the curse on her family. The connecting link is formed by two one-act plays, *Agamemnons Tod* (Agamemnon's Death) and *Elektra*, treating the murder of Agamemnon and the vengeance of Orestes. The whole work is infused with a sense of inexorable doom and of man's surrender to evil – a reflection of the war years during which it took shape.

In surveying the work of Gerhart Hauptmann down to his death in 1946, we have far overstepped the limits of naturalistic drama. It soon became evident that this dramatist who with his early plays had carried Naturalism to victory, abandoned it as soon as it failed to satisfy his artistic purposes. At the end of his long career, he arrived at dramatic forms diametrically opposed to his beginnings. Thus he mirrored in his own creative evolution the course European drama took during his life-span. Nevertheless, it is the naturalistic plays of his earlier period, ranging from *Die Weber* to *Die Ratten*, which seem to remain most alive in the German theatre of to-day. In these, he proved his singular faculty for creating characters from minute observation, and endowing them with a life of their own. In his hands, Naturalism was not an end in itself but a means to convey his poetic insight into human nature. 'This is not accuracy; this is intuition', as Alfred Kerr, one of his foremost champions, defined it. In spite of his apparent vacillation between many types of drama, realistic, poetic, social, historical and legendary, his entire work springs from a single apperception of man, a deep compassion for humanity, its sufferings and longings.

IV. SOME MINOR PLAYWRIGHTS

In most literary movements, one or two pre-eminent figures are accompanied by a number of lesser writers each of whom adds his individual note to the period. Thus, in the case of Naturalism, the early achievements of Sudermann and Hauptmann soon called forth a whole crowd of minor talents who responded to the challenge of the new dramatic style – usually with only one or two successful works.

The most noteworthy of these was undoubtedly Max Halbe (1865-1944), a native of West Prussia, a former province of Eastern Germany with a considerable Polish population. After a series of less successful plays touching on such topical problems as free love and socialism, he achieved his greatest success with *Jugend* (Youth, 1893). Set in the author's native province, it is the simple love story of two young people, Hans and Ännchen, which runs its tragic course within two summer days. The friction between Germans and Poles, and the narrow-minded zeal of a Catholic priest, serve as a sombre foil to their idyll. The current doctrine of heredity is emphasized in frequent references to the girl's mother who, like her, came to

1. HAUPTMANN, *Die Weber*. Berlin, 1921

2. WEDEKIND, *Erdgeist*. Berlin, 1902 (Reinhardt)

grief through her passionate nature. In the end a half-wit, who is also in love with Ännchen, shoots at her lover in a frenzy of jealousy and kills her instead. What made the success of this play was not so much the new technique employed but the folk-song quality, the nostalgic evocation of youth and love which goes to the heart. Halbe never contrived to follow up that early success. Of his many subsequent plays, perhaps only *Mutter Erde* (Mother Earth, 1897) deserves mention. It is set in the same East German borderland which forms the background to most of his plays, and extols the regenerating powers of the soil. The hero is torn between two women who stand for the city and the country respectively. Returning to his parental estate after many years of town-life, he discovers that he has missed his true vocation, and failed to marry the right girl. Since his wife, a sophisticated woman from Berlin, refuses to let him go, he chooses death with his former love. The issue of Hauptmann's *Einsame Menschen* is here as it were reversed: it is the simple, unsophisticated woman who wins over the intellectual 'modern' type; the outcome, in either case, is tragedy.

Another of the minor naturalistic playwrights was Georg Hirschfeld (1873-1935), whose main success was *Die Mütter* (The Mothers, 1896). This play develops two stock themes of the period, the contrast between middle and lower classes, and the problem of the artist in conflict with his environment. The hero, a young composer, leaves his comfortable bourgeois home to live with a working girl. However, he finds that the sordid environment is incompatible with his creative work. Unable to face up to the strain he returns home hoping to reconcile the girl to his mother. But she, although expecting a child from him, proudly rejects his offer. The vital scene, the confrontation of the two women, is curiously evaded, and the unstable character of the hero fails to evoke sympathy. Hirschfeld's next play, *Agnes Jordan* (1898), presents the somewhat oversentimentalized life-story of a woman who stays with an unloved husband for the sake of her children.

Naturalistic drama, which had started as a literary revolution, presently settled down to the routine of conventional stage realism: by the turn of the century, it had lost its distinction as a clearly defined literary form. What had first been hailed as an opening-up of new regions for dramatic treatment, was soon seen to have its limitations. The naturalistic approach, with its insistence on photographic accuracy and on the dominant power of external circumstance, touched merely the surface reality of things, while ignoring man's deeper spiritual forces. In due course, this neglect produced a violent reaction in the shape of the neo-romantic, or symbolist, movement which gave full rein to colour, poetry, and imagination.

Chapter Two

NEO-ROMANTIC DRAMA

I. THE AUSTRIAN TRADITION

It is a curious coincidence that at the very moment when
Naturalism was triumphant in Northern Germany, around
1890, a literary movement sprang up in Vienna which was its
precise opposite, and which was eventually to supersede it.[1]
Nor was it merely accidental that this movement had its
origin in Vienna. Ever since Berlin had emerged, in the eighteenth century, as the Prussian capital, the German-speaking
countries had as it were two focal points. While Berlin eagerly
absorbed every new literary fashion, the imperial city, with its
ancient traditions and its heritage of many races, kept aloof
from the intellectual movements of Germany proper. The
great battles of the literary scene had been fought and won far
from Vienna; the classical age of Goethe and Schiller and the
Romantic movement had barely touched it. In one field only
did it rank supreme – in music. The great upsurge of musical
genius ranging from Haydn and Mozart to Schubert signified
for Austria what the poetic achievements of Lessing, Schiller
and Goethe were to Northern Germany. While the German
public was roused by *Emilia Galotti*, *Götz von Berlichingen* and

---

[1] The movement in art and literature which swept most European countries at the
turn of the century has been variously labelled Symbolism, Impressionism, and Neo-
Romanticism. Though these terms are by no means synonymous, they apply to
different aspects of the same aesthetic phenomena. 'Neo-Romantic' is the term most
used in Germany in connection with the drama; but it must be borne in mind that at
any rate the prose plays of Schnitzler and his followers do not strictly fall into this
category.

Wallenstein, the Austrian audiences hailed *Figaro*, *The Magic Flute* and *Fidelio*. Literary life was strictly controlled by the two dominant powers (which were in fact one), the Church and the imperial court.

Nevertheless, the theatre occupied a high place in the cultural life of the southern capital. The Burgtheater, founded in the 1770s as one of the earliest national theatres, although closely linked to the court, soon attained the rank of a leading German stage – a position it has held to the present day. But its repertory, for lack of indigenous talent, was at first exclusively devoted to the German classics and to the great drama of other nations, above all Shakespeare and Calderon. Only in the nineteenth century did Austria produce a literary figure of more than local importance, Franz Grillparzer (1791-1872). His work continued, in a somewhat attenuated form, the classical humanism of the Weimar era, though with a distinct Austrian flavour. Apart from Goethe and Schiller, Grillparzer drew his inspiration from Shakespeare and the Spanish drama of Calderon and Lope de Vega, to which the Austrian theatre has always felt a close affinity. His plays, ranging from Greek mythology to subjects from Austrian, Spanish, Bohemian and Hungarian history, reflect the rich cultural heritage of the Habsburg Empire. With his over-sensitive and hypochondriac nature, embittered by constant squabbles with the imperial censorship, Grillparzer presents a typical facet of the Austrian character. His somewhat pedestrian blank verse is equally remote from the sublime perfection of Goethe's as from the rhetorical sweep of Schiller's. His glorification of the simple pleasures of life, as opposed to the fickleness of worldly power – the basic theme of so many of his plays – may also be considered a typically Austrian trait.

Side by side with the Burgtheater, with its classical repertory of high tragedy, there flourished the popular theatres on the fringe of the city, devoted to the *Volksstück*, the popular comedy in local dialect. The division between high tragedy and popular suburban comedy marks the Vienna theatre to the present day. It is in the latter that the theatrical genius of the people, their passion for laughing at themselves, has found expression. While Grillparzer's lofty dramas edified the nobility and upper middle classes, Ferdinand Raimund (1790-1836) and Johann Nestroy (1802-1862), with their dialect *Volksstück*, delighted the hearts of the common people. Significantly, both these playwrights were in the first place actors, closely linked with the practical life of the stage. Raimund's *Zaubermärchen* (magical fairy-plays) represent the genuine Austrian contribution to the Romantic movement. Their origin, however, reaches far back into the eighteenth century, to the Viennese tradition of *Zauberstücke*, one of which gained immortality through its music – Mozart's *Magic Flute*. The interweaving of everyday reality with a supernatural sphere of spirits, who influence the lives of men for good or ill, characterizes all Raimund's plays. His praise of a simple and contented life, the final triumph of good over evil, of common sense over conceit, gratified the hearts of his unsophisticated public. Nestroy's comedies and farces are considerably more pointed, more caustic in their social challenge. He abandoned the supernatural sphere and concentrated on the realistic depiction of Viennese life and society. As in the plays of Raimund, the comic song (*Couplet*) forms an essential ingredient of Nestroy's comedies. Their inexhaustible wit springs from the local Viennese language which he kindled into a blaze of baroque exuberance.

It is on Raimund's and Nestroy's dialect *Volksstücke* that the plays of Ludwig Anzengruber (1839-1889) were based. He, too, started his career as an actor, touring the provinces with small companies. Though Viennese himself, his plays are set, almost without exception, among the Tyrolean peasants. His psychological insight far exceeds that of his predecessors, and his very themes imply a challenge to society. In his comedies – *Der Pfarrer von Kirchfeld* (1870), *Der Kreuzelschreiber* (1872), *Der G'wissenswurm* (1874), etc. – he still retains the old tradition of the *Couplet*; but in his serious plays he completely eliminates that remnant of the traditional *Volksstück*. Among these, *Das vierte Gebot* (The Fourth Commandment, 1878), set in the suburbs of Vienna, rises to the level of serious realistic drama; it received full recognition with its performance, in 1890, at the Berlin *Freie Bühne*.

Naturalism did not sweep Austria with the force of a literary revolution, as it did Northern Germany; it grew organically from the local tradition of the realistic *Volksstück*. Though tinged with social criticism, it was free from the revolutionary momentum of its German counterpart. Moreover, it was limited almost exclusively to the realistic depiction of peasant life. In short, it formed merely a side-line to the main course of Austrian writing where the naturalistic movement never gained a real foothold.

Anzengruber found his legitimate successor in Karl Schönherr (1867-1943) whose particular achievement was the portrayal of Austrian peasant life in a terse and vigorous style. Unlike Anzengruber, he was himself a native of Tyrol, and closely connected throughout his life with the mountain people of that province. After a number of plays (*Der Bildschnitzer*, 1900, *Sonnwendtag*, 1902, *Karrnersleut'*, 1904, etc.), he reached full maturity in his two dramas *Erde* (Earth, 1908) and *Glaube und Heimat* (Faith and Home, 1910). The central character of *Erde* is an old peasant who refuses to die. Rooted in the native soil from which he draws his strength, he asserts his vitality against his aspiring heir and smashes the coffin his son has made for him. *Glaube und Heimat*, as the title indicates, deals with the conflict between religion and patriotism. Set at the time of the counter-reformation, it depicts the struggle of a group of Tyrolean peasants who refuse to be brought back to the fold of the Roman Church. *Weibsteufel* (Devil Woman,' 1914), enacted between three characters only, centres on a peasant woman who by sheer sensual vitality outlives two men, her husband and a young lover. During the First World War, when the author's homeland was threatened by Italian invasion, Schönherr contributed to the patriotic drama of those years his play *Volk in Not* (A People in Distress, 1915) which describes the rising of the Tyrolese against Napoleon under their national hero, Andreas Hofer. In a later play, *Der Judas von Tirol* (1928) he turned again to that cherished idol of Tyrolean patriotism. During his later years, Schönherr's sense for theatrical effect and terse dramatic action degenerated into routine; such plays as *Es* (It, 1923) or *Der Armendoktor* (The Panel Doctor, 1925) did not add essentially to his stature. When he died in 1943, he had long outlived his own reputation.

II. ARTHUR SCHNITZLER

Like many other European capitals, Vienna experienced during the 1890s a wave of creative activity. It had its own particular colour, revealing the Austrian spirit once more in all its facets before the empire was shattered into fragments. This wave carried a large number of minor talents but reached its peak in two pre-eminent figures, Arthur Schnitzler and Hugo von Hofmannsthal. Unlike their German counterparts who worked as isolated individuals or in rival literary cliques, the Viennese writers lived in close personal contact. Moreover, they were carried by a firmly established society, held together by common traditions and highly receptive to artistic achievement. This society, persisting almost unchanged right down to the cataclysm of 1914, found its faithful reflection in the plays of Arthur Schnitzler. Hofmannsthal's work encompasses the whole of the Habsburg Empire, with all its historical and spiritual associations, and much more besides; Schnitzler's is specifically Viennese and is confined to a definite period and a definite social class. Consequently his work faded when this society ceased to exist, whereas Hofmannsthal's kept growing in stature, independent of the period from which it sprang.

Schnitzler's society is the upper middle class, including its higher and lower fringes – aristocrats, artists, professional men. The lower classes scarcely intrude into this circumscribed province, and when they do it is without harsh conflict. They are the petty bourgeois of the Vienna suburbs, simple artisans who watch without envy or resentment the glittering spectacle enacted by the favoured. The principal, indeed, the only point of contact is in the erotic sphere, that is, between the simple *Mädchen aus dem Volke*, the 'girl of the people', and the man of higher social standing who uses her as a pastime. This motif, recurring in many of Schnitzler's works, appears in his very first play which brought his name before the public in 1891 – *Anatol*. This sequence of seven scenes contains the best, and almost the whole, of Schnitzler: in fact, he rarely transcended it in substance and range. The scenes represent the amorous adventures of a young Viennese philanderer, a man-about-town, who styles himself a 'light-hearted melancholic'. Anatol, introspective, idle, sensitive, cultivating his varying *Stimmungen*, became the prototype of a whole generation, the embodiment of the Viennese *fin de siècle*. He relishes his own morbidity: 'There are so many diseases and only one health.... One must always be just as healthy as the others – but one can be ill quite differently from anyone else!' His foil and partner is Max, a more level-headed rationalist and cynic, who serves as the *raisonneur* of the play: their conversations, sparkling with pointed aphorisms, form the backbone of the seven scenes, each of which is devoted to one of Anatol's love-affairs. Many of Schnitzler's favourite motifs are struck; in two or three variations, there is the type of the *süsses Mädel* – the simple girl from the Vienna suburbs, at once easy-going and sentimental.

It is characteristic of the close contact existing between the Viennese writers that this first work of Schnitzler was introduced by verses signed 'Loris' – none other than Hugo von Hofmannsthal, then seventeen years old. These verses, with their precocious mixture of self-conscious melancholy and refined elegance, strike the keynote of the whole generation:

> *Eine Laube statt der Bühne,*
> *Sommersonne statt der Lampen,*
> *Also spielen wir Theater,*
> *Spielen unsere eignen Stücke,*
> *Frühgereift und zart und traurig,*
> *Die Komödie unsrer Seelen,*
> *Unsres Fühlens Heut und Gestern,*
> *Böser Dinge hübsche Formel,*
> *Glatte Worte, bunte Bilder,*
> *Halbes, heimliches Empfinden,*
> *Agonien, Episoden . . .*

> For our stage a summer house,
> For our lights the summer sun,
> This is how we play at theatre,
> Play our trivial little pieces,
> Sad and tender and precocious,
> Play the comedy of our souls,
> Past and present of our feelings,
> Pretty words for wicked things,
> Facile phrases, coloured pictures,
> Half-felt and concealed sensations,
> Agonies and episodes . . .

Arthur Schnitzler, born in 1862, was the son of a famous Vienna physician. He, too, studied medicine and established himself as a practitioner and editor of a medical journal. He developed a keen interest in psychiatry and published a thesis on the hypnotic treatment of neurosis. After the success of his third play, *Liebelei* (1894), he gave up his profession to devote himself entirely to writing. However, his medical interests left deep traces in his literary work. Owing to his close association with the teachings of Freud, he was one of the first to explore the workings of the 'subconscious' in literature, though more fully in his prose writings than in his plays. His main theme, retold in countless variations, is the relationship between the sexes, ranging from fatal passion to playful flirtation, with all its associated emotions, jealousy, hatred, frustration and ecstasy. Often, he contrasts the transient *affaire* with the *grande passion*. The most poignant presentation of this contrast is undoubtedly *Liebelei* (Light o' Love). Christine, another of Schnitzler's *süsse Mädel*, takes her own life when she learns that her lover has fallen in a duel for another woman. The hero, Fritz, is a more sincere version of Anatol, the amorous adventurer. Not only Schnitzler but many of the Viennese writers of the period were fascinated by the figure of the 'adventurer' whose prototype they saw in Casanova. Indeed, the literary portraits of the notorious eighteenth-century gallant, both in drama and in prose, are innumerable. Schnitzler himself introduced him twice, in a play *Casanova in Spa* (1919), and in one of his most accomplished stories, *Casanovas letztes Abenteuer* (Casanova's Last Adventure). It is easy to see why that generation was so strongly attracted by the adventurer-type – the man who merely plays with life, incapable of surrendering himself wholly to a deep and genuine emotion: he was the epitome of 'impressionist man' – the man who lives only in the moment and for the moment, conscious of the transience of all things, and wholly given up to fleeting 'impressions'. In Schnitzler's work, the theme is struck with the light touch of comedy in *Anatol*; it recurs in the sombre tones of tragedy in a later play, *Der einsame Weg* (The Lonely Road, 1903). Von Sala, one of the principal characters, is Anatol grown old, an *homme à femmes* on the decline, nostalgically savouring bygone pleasures, who once more tries to recapture his waning youth by proposing to a girl less than half his age. His final wisdom is resignation: 'Even if a train of Bacchantes accompanies us – we all go the downward way alone.' Sala has his counterpart in his friend Julian, an ageing bachelor like himself, who seeks a belated purpose in life by claiming a young man whom he believes to be his illegitimate son; he, too, is rejected. More compelling than the slight action of the play is the impalpable atmosphere of nostalgia and autumnal decay enveloping it, and the final realization of irrevocable loneliness the two men have reached. *Der einsame Weg* reveals the defect of most of Schnitzler's full-length plays: lack of dramatic unity and a tendency to dissolve into a multitude of loosely joined episodes. Another play of this type is *Das weite Land* (The Wide Country, 1910), which presents a broad picture of Viennese society on the eve of the First World War.

It has been said that Schnitzler was the Austrian Ibsen. His field is contemporary middle-class society; his method its realistic depiction. As with Ibsen, his dramatic technique frequently consists in the gradual revelation of the past, the successive unfolding of past errors and past guilt. However, Schnitzler's approach is as different from Ibsen's as is the soft and music-haunted air of Austria from the cold and austere Norwegian world. His method is not analytical dissection and the relentless quest for truth but gentle understanding and resigned acceptance of human foibles. In some of his early plays, it is true, he chastises social prejudice and hypocrisy – the arrogance of the officer caste in *Freiwild* (Fair Game, 1896), or class prejudice in *Das Vermächtnis* (The Legacy, 1897); but his main province is the erotic sphere – the unceasing war of the sexes. He has reduced this war to its crude essentials in his play *Der Reigen* (The Round, 1900), since made famous through its French film version *La Ronde*. Its ten scenes, each enacted by a different couple and culminating in the act of love, present a comprehensive picture of all classes, seen from one angle only; it is, as it were, the erotic counterpart to the medieval dance of death.

Only once, in his play *Professor Bernhardi* (1912), did he completely ignore sex and treat a topical social issue which was close to his heart – anti-Semitism. Schnitzler set it in the milieu he knew best, the medical sphere. Professor Bernhardi, the head of a large Vienna hospital, has prevented the priest from attending a dying girl, aware that the full knowledge of her impending death would hasten the end. This sets in motion an ever widening circle of intrigue and political controversy in the course of which Bernhardi is dismissed from his post and even sent to prison. The play presents a penetrating study of Vienna society shortly before the outbreak of war, with the political and ideological cross-currents which finally led to its disintegration.

Schnitzler rarely overstepped the limits of his special province. His only historical play, *Der junge Medardus* (1909), pictures in fact the same society, projected a century back into the Napoleonic era. It shows once again a cross-section of Vienna, encompassing all classes from the aristocracy to the small suburban craftsmen. And it is significant that his hero, who has set himself the task of assassinating the French emperor at Schönbrunn, is involved in a passionate love intrigue which eventually thwarts his purpose. Perhaps the most personal touch in this sprawling historical drama is the episode of the 'very old man' who, accompanied by his little great-grand-daughter, appears in every act, dispassionately watching the historic events unrolling before his eyes.

Although Schnitzler took for granted the pre-war Viennese society, with its moral code and accepted set of values, he was well aware that its carefree existence was doomed. Once

he revealed the abyss which lay beneath its shining surface –
in the one-act play *Der grüne Kakadu* (The Green Cockatoo,
1898), set on the eve of the French Revolution, at the very
moment when the graceful world of the Rococo drew to its
close. Some Paris aristocrats gather nightly in a sordid tavern
where their lust for sensation is gratified by ragamuffins dressed
up as cut-throats. But the play suddenly becomes reality –
the drawn dagger really kills the duke, the masks fall, while
outside in the streets the mob storms the Bastille. . . .

This brilliant little play touches on one of Schnitzler's
central themes – the contraposition of illusion and truth,
of play and reality. Several of his most pointed one-act plays
turn on this very problem: in *Stunde des Erkennens* (Hour of
Recognition), the wife of a celebrated actor, watching him
inadvertently in an unguarded moment, suddenly sees through
his insincerity, and turns from him; in *Die letzten Masken*
(The Last Masks), a ham-actor and a petty journalist, dying
in a hospital ward, suddenly in the face of death realize the
futility of their lives; in *Literatur*, two former lovers, meeting
after some years, discover to their dismay that each has written
a novel, incorporating their mutual love-letters, thus turning
their feelings into 'literature'; and so on. Every time the
vanity of false emotions is confronted with the truth of life.
This basic motif Schnitzler has formulated succinctly in his
one-act verse play *Paracelsus* (1897): the famous physician and
alchemist who, for a short moment, has played with the lives
and fortunes of three ordinary people, voices his ultimate
insight in these closing words:

> *Mit Menschenseelen spiele ich. Ein Sinn*
> *Wird nur von dem gefunden, der ihn sucht.*
> *Es fliessen ineinander Traum und Wachen,*
> *Wahrheit und Lüge. Sicherheit ist nirgends.*
> *Wir wissen nichts von andern, nichts von uns;*
> *Wir spielen immer, wer es weiss, ist klug.*

I play with human destinies. A purpose
Is only found by him who looks for it,
Waking and dreaming merge one in another
Like truth and falsehood. Certainty is nowhere.
We know naught of the others nor ourselves;
We're always playing – he who knows is wise.

The world of Schnitzler vanished in the cataclysm of the
First World War. During the following thirteen years (he
died in 1931) he wrote only three more plays all of which
retrace ground covered more effectively in earlier works. *Die
Komödie der Verführung* (The Comedy of Seduction, 1924)
follows the usual erotic entanglements of an upper-class set
on the eve of the war. *Der Gang zum Weiher* (The Walk to
the Lake, 1925), a verse play, is fraught with an autumnal
mood of resignation, while the last, *Im Spiel der Sommerlüfte*
(In the Playing Summer Breezes, 1930) recalls nostalgically a
distant summer in the countryside near Vienna. Nothing could
show more clearly how Arthur Schnitzler had outlived his
own time than these three post-war plays which are no more
than faint reflections of a past irretrievably lost. But this past –
the last twenty-five years of pre-war Vienna – has found its
faithful and lasting mirror in his whole work.

Besides Schnitzler, the last decade of the nineteenth century
saw the rise of a considerable number of lesser playwrights
who followed in his wake. Among these, Hermann Bahr
(1863-1934) was probably the most notable. Most of his
numerous plays – about eighty in all – are undistinguished.
Perhaps only one deserves mention as a witty society comedy,
Das Konzert (The Concert, 1909). Enacted by four characters,
it centres on a celebrated pianist inclined to amorous escapades;
he is recalled to the fold of matrimony by his clever wife who
contrives to rouse his jealousy. Bahr's importance derives less
from his own plays than from his critical activity, promoting
the work of others. He was one of those figures, indispensable

to literary life, who untiringly and selflessly mediate between creative achievement and the public. His versatility became almost proverbial: with equal enthusiasm he flung himself into each successive literary fashion. In Berlin, in the early nineties, he made himself the herald of Naturalism, editing the literary review of the *Freie Bühne*. A few years later, in Paris, he discovered the symbolists and decadents of the *fin de siècle* and associated himself with the writings of Mallarmé, Maeterlinck, and Claudel. These literary tendencies he introduced to the young Viennese writers; it was Bahr who coined the name *Jungwien* (Young Vienna) for them. After some more transmutations, his restless mind found a haven in the Roman Catholic Church and the art of the Baroque in which he saw the spiritual fountain-head of Austrian culture.

III. HUGO VON HOFMANNSTHAL

The plays of Schnitzler, Bahr and other Viennese writers, such as Taddeus Rittner, Raoul Auernheimer, and Felix Salten, move on the whole within the conventions of the realistic theatre. The real challenge to Naturalism came from the authors who defied these conventions and aimed at the rebirth of poetic drama. In contrast to the everyday speech of Naturalism, they resorted to rich and mellifluous verse; for the drab gloom of the former, they substituted colour, music, and fantasy. Above all, they turned their backs on the social reality of the present day and focussed their attention on the inward life of the individual, his subtle moods and emotions. They showed a marked predilection for myth and legend, and for the more colourful periods of history, ancient Greece, the Middle Ages, the Italian Renaissance. Since their own creative faculties were lyrical rather than dramatic, they contented themselves, more often than not, with re-interpreting existing works, especially of the Greek, Spanish, and seventeenth-century English dramatists. They infused the old plays with modern psychological problems, and clothed them in luxurious verse.

German literary historians, always keen to classify groups and movements, labelled these writers 'Neo-Romantics', though they showed little more than a superficial resemblance to the German Romantics of the early nineteenth century. This label seems particularly inadequate for their most outstanding figure, Hugo von Hofmannsthal.

Among the dramatists of the last decades of the Austrian Empire, Hugo von Hofmannsthal is without doubt the most prominent, and the one whose stature has steadily grown since his death in 1929. The appearance of the young Hofmannsthal on the literary scene of Vienna, in the early nineties, caused something of a sensation. His contemporaries never tired of recalling their amazement when those exquisite little verse plays and literary essays, signed 'Loris', equally striking by their perfection of form and maturity of thought, were found to be written by a boy of seventeen who was still a pupil at a Vienna Gymnasium. 'I had the feeling', related Arthur Schnitzler, who was his senior by twelve years, 'that for the first time in my life I had encountered a born genius.'

Hofmannsthal was born in 1874, the son of a well-to-do Viennese banker; in his veins mingled the blood of several races, South-German, Italian, and Jewish: thus this brilliant youth seemed to embody the multiform cultural heritage of Austria. He was at once acclaimed as the mouth-piece of a rising generation that pitted its ideals of beauty and sensitive refinement against the harsh naturalism whose intellectual centre was Berlin. Hofmannsthal became the Austrian counterpart to such writers as Swinburne, Maeterlinck, Mallarmé, Barrès, and D'Annunzio; to most of these he devoted penetrating essays which revealed his gift for entering into the artistic achievements of others. His cosmopolitan mind was equally at home in ancient Greece, in the Italian Renaissance, in Elizabethan England, in seventeenth-century France, in the Spanish

3. VOLLMOELLER, *Das Mirakel*. Dortmund,
1927 (Reinhardt)

4. HOFMANNSTHAL, *Das Salzburger grosse Welttheater*.
Berlin, 1933 (Reinhardt)

Baroque as well as in the great periods of his native Austria. His faculty of assimilating and re-interpreting the spirit of bygone ages and peoples was to have a profound effect on his dramatic work.

Along with his literary criticism, which throughout his life formed an essential part of his writings, his creative genius first found expression in lyric poetry and particularly in a series of small verse plays, not actually intended for the stage. Some of these – e.g. *Der Tod des Tizian* (The Death of Titian, 1892), *Das kleine Welttheater* (The Little Theatre of the World, 1897) – are scarcely more than lyric poems divided among several characters; others – *Der Tor und der Tod* (Death and the Fool, 1893), *Die Frau im Fenster* (The Woman at the Window, 1897) – are in fact lyrical monologues. All of them dwell in a realm of sublime beauty and precocious introspection, consciously aloof from material reality.

> *Altkluger Weisheit voll und frühen Zweifels,*
> *Mit einer grossen Sehnsucht doch, die fragt.*

> Full of precocious wisdom, early doubt,
> And yet with a deep, questioning longing.

These lines from the prologue to one of the playlets strike the note common to all. Their dominant theme was one which was to recur in many of Hofmannsthal's mature works, namely, the transitoriness of life and its constant closeness to death. This theme is poignantly realized in the longest and most famous of the playlets, *Der Tor und der Tod* (1893). It is virtually one long lyrical soliloquy of a young nobleman, Claudio, who in the face of death comes to realize that he has failed truly to live his life. Death, in the guise of a fiddler, summons the shadows of his misspent life, his mother, his friend, the girl he has deserted: in the hour of death, Claudio experiences in a flash the true import of life.

All the central figures of these early lyrical plays, Claudio, the young disciples of Titian, the emperor in *Der Kaiser und die Hexe* (The Emperor and the Witch), the young lovers in *Der weisse Fächer* (The White Fan), are incarnations of the poet's own precocious youth. Looking back on that first phase of his poetic evolution, Hofmannsthal liked to call it 'pre-existence' – a glorious but precarious state of premature insight, in which he achieved perfection through deliberate detachment from life. He saw all his subsequent writings as so many ways of surmounting that state and of reaching 'existence', i.e. a full understanding of life with all its challenges. This process was accompanied by a painful spiritual crisis the poet underwent in his middle twenties, from which he emerged a mature man. What led to this crisis was his longing for a deeper and fuller acceptance of reality. Life, from which he had shrunk because of its harshness and cruelty, he now came to recognize as a task to be faced and accomplished. Hofmannsthal stepped as it were from the ivory tower of his self-centred youth into the world at large. In his private life, too, this was a turning-point: in 1901, he married and made his permanent home in Rodaun near Vienna, taking upon him the responsibilities of a husband and father. The transformation was evident also in a change of literary form: he abandoned the lyric poem and the short verse play that had won him his early fame, and developed step by step the full-length poetic drama which steadily expanded in range and dramatic pitch. More and more, he turned his attention to the living stage.

It is fascinating to follow this process in the poetic plays Hofmannsthal wrote, in quick succession, at the turn of the century. Though drawing their subjects from a wide variety of sources, they all revolve around the theme that was closest to his heart – man's success or failure to face the challenge of life, whatever shape it may take. *Der Abenteurer und die Sängerin* (The Adventurer and the Prima Donna, 1898) has as its central character once again that favourite figure of the Viennese writers, Casanova. The plot is drawn from an episode in his memoirs in which the ageing adventurer, on his return to Venice, meets a former mistress, a great singer who has a son by him and is now married. As in so many of Hofmannsthal's works, Venice is the city of beauty, of amorous adventure, a symbol of life's entanglements. What was a trivial incident in the adventurer's life has shaped the woman's destiny: through her love, she has become the great artist she is. – *Die Hochzeit der Sobeide* (Zobeida's Wedding, 1899) has an oriental setting. It is the story of a poor girl who marries a wealthy elderly merchant for her parents' sake. When, on the wedding-night, she confesses that she is in love with a poor man, the husband lets her go to join her lover. But she finds him in the arms of a harlot and, not knowing where to turn, ends her own life by throwing herself from a tower. – *Das Bergwerk von Falun* (The Mines of Falun, 1899) is based on a tale by E. T. A. Hoffmann. This play was only partly published during the author's lifetime and performed for the first time as late as 1951. More than any other work, it reveals an affinity to the Romantics. Yet, in Hofmannsthal's hands, the story assumes a new significance. Elis, a young miner betrothed to a country girl, succumbs to the magic of the Mountain Queen who one day appears to him down the mine; on the eve of his wedding, he disappears for ever into the mountain. The symbolism is obvious: the realm of the spirit proves stronger than the daylight world of reality and draws the hero into its spell.

It was perhaps the fascination of its setting more than anything else which induced Hofmannsthal to turn Otway's *Venice Preserved* into his first full-length tragedy, *Das gerettete Venedig* (1905). Following in outline the action of the original, he deepened the psychological motivation and recast the dialogue in his rich, melodious verse. More important was Hofmannsthal's approach to Greek mythology as a source of inspiration. Already as early as 1893, he had made his first step in this direction by recasting Euripides' *Alkestis*; but this attempt was still conceived in the purely lyrical vein of that early phase, and scarcely intended for the stage. Now, however, stimulated by his experience of the living theatre, he wrote two full-length verse plays on Greek mythological subjects, *Elektra* (1903) and *Oedipus und die Sphinx* (1905). His approach to the ancient myths is very different from that of German classicism: by-passing the Periclean age, he turns to the archaic period. He ignores the religious significance of the stories and concentrates on their psychological, or even pathological, interpretation. The terseness of action and clash of passions are carried to the utmost pitch in *Elektra*. Agamemnon's daughter has renounced her womanhood for the single aim of avenging her father's murder – an aim she pursues with the violence of one possessed; when the deed is done (not by her, it is true, but at her instigation) she breaks into a dance of frenzied triumph and falls dead. It was with *Elektra* (produced, as most of his plays, by Max Reinhardt in Berlin) that Hofmannsthal gained his first real theatrical success, even before it was set to music by Richard Strauss.

Oedipus und die Sphinx, providing a kind of prelude to Sophocles' drama, marked the end of what may be called the second phase in Hofmannsthal's development. Soon after, he ventured in two new directions, comedy and opera. From then on, these two theatrical forms went side by side with his serious drama. In his comedies, Hofmannsthal came closest to what he was aiming at, the portrayal of 'life' and all it implies. Comedy, as he defined it in one of his self-interpreting notes, was *das erreichte Soziale* – the attainment of the social (as distinct from the purely individual) sphere. Hofmannsthal's comedies are throughout in prose, and often in Viennese dialect. Yet they spring from the same poetic source as his serious plays, never stooping to the level of mere entertainment. They follow in the tradition of Molière, Goldoni, and the native Austrian comedy. In fact, Hofmannsthal translated or adapted three of Molière's plays, *Le Médecin malgré lui*, *Les Fâcheux*, and *Le Bourgeois Gentilhomme*. His first completed prose comedy (after a fragment, *Sylvia im Stern*) was *Cristinas Heimreise* (Cristina's Journey Home, 1909). The plot is once again based on the memoirs of Casanova; this time, however, he is not the ageing adventurer (as in *Der Abenteurer und die Sängerin*) but the dashing youth in the prime of life. Again, the setting is Venice, at any rate in the opening act. Florindo (as he is renamed), always on the look-out for new amorous adventures, is struck by the charms of a strange young girl he sees embarking in a gondola. On the spur of the moment, he joins her on her journey home. On the way he succeeds in spending a night with her in a roadside inn. The next morning, unwilling to commit himself to a lasting alliance, he takes his leave, entrusting the girl to the care of a middle-aged sea captain, a sturdy, warm-hearted man who eventually marries her. In these two figures, the light-hearted philanderer and the man of constancy, Hofmannsthal embodies once again two attitudes to life. But Florindo is not merely a callous rake: he lives fully and passionately in the moment and for the moment. Yet in the depths of his heart he is aware that life's supreme value lies beyond his reach: 'There is not one in a thousand [he says to the captain] who senses that what makes life worth living lies beyond this point – in marriage! in the happiness of unshakable trust!'

It is the same idea that lies at the core of Hofmannsthal's second prose comedy, *Der Schwierige* (The Difficult Man), completed as late as 1918. This is, in fact, the only one of his plays set in the immediate present, that is, in post-war Vienna. But the social plane on which it moves is an anachronistic relic of the pre-war world, the Austrian aristocracy. It is as though Hofmannsthal wanted to set up a monument to a way of life at the very moment when it ceased to exist. The central idea is once again *Treue* (fidelity), or more precisely, a man's transformation from an adventurer to one who recognizes in constancy life's greatest value. Count Bühl, an Austrian aristocrat to his fingertips, in previous days had dreaded the very thought of being tied down in a permanent relationship. But the war and its continual threat of death have wrought a change in his attitude. He has come to recognize 'necessity' as a sacred principle; and necessity, applied to the relations between the sexes, expresses itself in marriage.

> The same necessity [so the Count philosophizes] also exists between man and woman; where it prevails the one is drawn to the other, there is forgiveness and reconciliation and staying together. And then there may be children, and there is marriage and a sanctuary, despite everything.

With this newly gained insight, he eventually plucks up courage to propose to the girl he imagined as his wife at the moment of mortal danger, when he lay buried alive 'out there'. The language of this subtle play is couched in the inimitable accent of the Viennese aristocracy whose peculiar charm is caught with loving sympathy. *Der Schwierige* is undoubtedly Hofmannsthal's best comedy. It was followed, some years later, by *Der Unbestechliche* (The Incorruptible Man, 1923), a comedy of a more conventional kind. Its leading character is an officious butler who runs his master's love-affairs and shrewdly restores his somewhat shaky marriage – a figure Hofmannsthal designed with an eye to the great Austrian comedian Max Pallenberg.

Any account of Hofmannsthal's comedies would be incomplete without including his two comedies for music, *Der Rosenkavalier* (1911) and *Arabella* (1933), the first and the last of his operatic libretti for Richard Strauss. *Der Rosenkavalier*, the most widely known of all Hofmannsthal's works, is set in the golden age of Vienna, the reign of Maria Theresia.

In its four principal characters – the ageing Marschallin, the coarse, philandering Baron Ochs, the young nobleman Octavian, and Sophie, the innocent young girl straight from the convent – the spirit of the epoch is recaptured in an inimitable way. The same is true (though perhaps not to the same extent) of *Arabella*, a deliberate attempt to repeat the success of *Der Rosenkavalier*. Its period is the 1860s, and its social setting an impoverished middle-class family. The action turns on two sisters, the younger of whom, for reasons of economy, is brought up as a boy.

Hofmannsthal's work for the operatic stage, extending over more than twenty years as it does, constitutes not merely a side-line but an essential part of his creative achievement. What led him to opera was partly an intuitive awareness that his poetic capacities would find their full realization in music. Moreover, his basic conception of the theatre as a festive institution, aloof from everyday life, found its fulfilment in opera, an art-form combining poetry, music and movement in a single whole. In this conception he felt himself heir to a tradition which had its roots in the Baroque, and which was most fully alive in Austria and South Germany.

> Drama and opera are essentially one [he writes] – high tragedy and opera, separated only in the abstract, merging in the seventeenth-century Baroque theatre, are in fact inseparable.

From this insight sprang Hofmannsthal's preoccupation with opera and his collaboration with Richard Strauss. In the six operatic works resulting from this collaboration the Austrian theatre returned, as it were, to its fountain-head. These works reflect the two distinct forms in which opera first emerged, namely, mythological serious opera, on the one hand, and realistic comic opera, on the other. The former is realized in *Elektra*, *Die ägyptische Helena*, and *Die Liebe der Danae* (completed after the poet's death by Joseph Gregor), the latter in

Rosenkavalier and *Arabella*, while *Ariadne auf Naxos* (1912) presents an ingenious device to combine the two. This opera, originally designed as an operatic divertissement to follow Molière's *Bourgeois Gentilhomme*, and later expanded into a separate work, is artistically the most satisfying, though not the most popular, of Hofmannsthal's libretti. In it his basic antimony is once again personified in the two contrasting characters of Ariadne and Zerbinetta, the one faithful unto death, the other flippant and inconstant. The subtle irony of the solution lies in the fact that Ariadne, while believing she embraces death, wakes to a new love in the arms of Bacchus. The idea of 'fidelity' also lies at the core of *Die ägyptische Helena* (Helen of Egypt, 1928), in which Helen, after her return from Troy, resists a new temptation before she is truly re-united with Menelaus. Of all his libretti, *Die Frau ohne Schatten* (The Woman Without a Shadow, 1919) is probably the most complex in range and depth of thought, though marred by an excess of symbol and allegory. It follows in the old Viennese tradition of the *Zaubermärchen*, which bore its finest flower in Mozart's *Magic Flute*. In a fantastic 'Empire of the South-Eastern Isles', two couples are contrasted, one royal and one of humble birth. These four characters, passing through various temptations and trials, attain a higher level of understanding and love. By self-denial and self-humiliation, the Empress (who is the central character) gains her full status as a human being and a wife. This work, which occupied Hofmannsthal and Strauss during the First World War, was first performed in 1919 in Vienna.

The dissolution of the Austro-Hungarian Empire, in 1918, deprived Hofmannsthal of the mainspring of his creative powers. But unlike Schnitzler, he was not content to dwell nostalgically on the past. On the contrary, he experienced, during the last decade of his life, a resurgence of creative energy. Only one year after the end of the war, he founded, together with Max Reinhardt, the Salzburg Festival which was to perpetuate the best of the dramatic and musical heritage of Austria. The centre-piece of the annual festival was from the outset, as it has remained to this day, his re-creation of the old morality play of *Everyman*. With his *Jedermann* (1911), Hofmannsthal entered a new phase, transcending the aesthetic and psychological plane of his early plays and creating a religious drama of universal appeal. His version is enriched by a sequence of scenes showing Everyman's earthly life and culminating in a lavish banquet at the height of which Death appears to summon him. Thus his final agony and contrition are set against the foil of his worldly life, re-echoing the poet's early lyrical play, *Der Tor und der Tod*, but now within the firm frame of the Christian faith.

The dance-of-death theme also underlies *Das Salzburger grosse Welttheater* (The Salzburg Great Theatre of the World, 1922), which was specially designed for the Salzburg Festival as a counterpart to *Jedermann*. This drama is based on Calderon's *El gran teatro del mundo*. The basic idea, that the world is a stage and life a play enacted to the glory of God, is in the true Baroque tradition. The allegorical figures who perform this play – the King, the Rich Man, Beauty, Wisdom, the Peasant and the Beggar – are lifted from Calderon's drama. In Hofmannsthal's hands, the Beggar's part is greatly expanded and has topical implications: he challenges the order as established by God, in words that echo communist ideas. He is prompted by Satan, who appears in the guise of a Doctor of Law and Logic, invoking the 'natural equality of man'. But as the Beggar raises an axe against the King, he is struck by a sudden light; he realizes that his deed would upset the divine order. Not through violent usurpation, but by acquiescence (*Einverständnis*) in the place allotted to him, man attains true freedom. When Death summons the players one after another from the stage, the Beggar is the only one who follows gladly, to be set above the others by the judgment of God. In Hofmannsthal's version, the ageless Christian ideas, as contained in Calderon's play, are fused with contemporary social issues. Hofmannsthal, deeply aware of the powers arising in the post-war world, threatening the very foundations of European civilization, unequivocally puts forward his ideal of a hierarchic society based on Christian concepts. *Das Salzburger grosse Welttheater* presents this ideal in an allegorical and static form; *Der Turm* (The Tower, 1925), his last and most comprehensive work, unfolds it in fluid dramatic action, on a half-realistic, half-symbolic plane. This work, too, is inspired by a play of Calderon's, *La vida es sueño*, which had occupied him at various stages of his life. It was only after the experience of the war and the revolution that he remoulded it into a new and independent work.

In essence, *Der Turm* is a political drama, encompassing the main trends of political thought through several centuries of European history. The scene is 'a kingdom of Poland, rather of legend than of history'; the period 'a past century in its atmosphere similar to the seventeenth'. The central character is Sigismund, a prince who has been held captive in a tower by the king, his father. All the characters are at the same time exponents of political ideas. The king stands for absolute monarchy based on Divine Right; Julian, a nobleman and guardian of the prince, for the feudal order. Each of them in turn tries to use Sigismund for his own ends, and each is killed in the ensuing war. Eventually the power falls to the mob under their despotic leader, Olivier, the very embodiment of destruction and evil. He, too, tries to use Sigismund for his own selfish purposes, but the prince ignores him and goes his way Among the poor and suffering he finds his true followers who acclaim him as *Armeleutekönig* – king of the poor. In the saintlike figure of Sigismund, Hofmannsthal has embodied his idea of true kingship: he is man at his most sublime, unsullied by any contact with the world, purified by martyrdom, 'a quintessence of the supreme terrestrial forces'. His attempt to set up his kingdom is, however, doomed to failure: within sight of his goal, he is poisoned by Olivier. Yet the final message is not one of frustration: at his death-bed there appears a delegation from the orphans who have escaped the ravages of war, led by their chosen *Kinderkönig* – the children's king. Paying homage to Sigismund, he pledges himself to carry out his vision: 'We have built huts and keep fires burning in the forge and beat the swords into ploughshares. We have given new laws, for the laws must always come from the young.'

Two years later, in 1927, Hofmannsthal published a second version of the drama in which the Children's King is eliminated and the ending is one of unrelieved tragedy. It is the upstart Olivier, the exponent of brute force, who now emerges triumphant, while Sigismund dies, on his lips the words which now conclude the play: 'Bear ye witness that I have been here though none has recognized me.' It seems as though Hofmannsthal, at the end of his life, became more fully aware of the darkness which was to engulf his world a few years later.

The literary fame of Hugo von Hofmannsthal has steadily grown since his death. After the enforced neglect his work suffered during the Nazi régime, he has come to be regarded as one of the leading figures in modern German literature. In the spiritual vacuum of post-war Germany, his personal integrity, the moral values implicit in his work, and his keen awareness of tradition and historical continuity, have proved an unfailing source of inspiration and re-orientation. His fame, however, is based no less on his work as an essayist and poet than on his dramatic achievements. Of all his plays (apart from his operatic libretti) perhaps only *Jedermann* and the comedy *Der Schwierige* have found a permanent place in the theatre. As a playwright, Hofmannsthal lacked the elemental power of the born dramatist; despite the fascination the theatre held for him, he remained at heart what he had been at the outset – a poet. He drew his inspiration not so much from life as from letters; his plays are, almost without exception, derivatory, that is, adaptations and re-creations of existing works of world-literature. Moreover, his creative energies were thwarted by a fatal inclination towards introspection and self-analysis. His path is strewn with innumerable fragments, and even his completed works often exist in more than one version. During his lifetime, he suffered under the overwhelming impact of his early fame which obscured his later achievements. Only gradually the works of his maturity came to be seen in their right perspective: far from being the half-hearted endeavours of an aesthete to gain a foothold on the stage, they stand out as the last link in a great theatrical tradition.

IV. OTHER NEO-ROMANTIC PLAYWRIGHTS

The circle of Viennese poets and playwrights constituting the neo-romantic movement was rich in talent. Next to Hofmannsthal, Richard Beer-Hofmann was perhaps the most prominent figure. Born in 1866, he was eight years senior to Hofmannsthal to whom he was bound in a life-long friendship. Owing to his slow and painstaking method of work, his literary output was remarkably small: his fame is founded mainly on two plays which appeared nearly twenty years apart, one at the beginning of the century, the other after the First World War. The first, *Der Graf von Charolais* (The Count of Charolais, 1904), was at once hailed as one of the most successful dramatic achievements of its time. Like Hofmannsthal's *Das gerettete Venedig*, written in the same year, it is based on a seventeenth-century English play, *The Fatal Dowry* by Massinger and Field. This choice of subject was typical of the neo-romantic taste for the dramatists following in the wake of Shakespeare, with their emphasis on high-pitched sentiment and violence, and their blazing rhetorical verse. Beer-Hofmann recast the old play in his florid language, endowing the characters with a subtle psychology rather out of keeping with their time. He failed to overcome the structural flaw of the original – its lack of dramatic unity. The first half of his drama centres on the gallant young count who, to satisfy his dead father's creditors, pledges himself as a hostage and is saved by the president of the court who pays his debts and gives him his daughter in marriage; whereas the second part turns on the infidelity of the wife, her abduction to a disreputable inn, and her ultimate remorse and suicide. It is this female character, Désirée, that has undergone the most marked transformation: in the old play, she is a wanton ready to deceive her husband from the start; with Beer-Hofmann, she is a pure and loving wife, momentarily yielding to the advances of a practised seducer. This conception raises her final repentance and self-destruction to a higher moral level. The modern poet has not attempted to inform the drama with a deeper philosophy: his characters are helpless victims of uncontrollable forces. This acquits them of any moral responsibility for their actions.

> '*Es*' *trieb uns – treibt uns – Es! Nicht ich – nicht du!*
>
> 'It' drove us – drives us. It! not I – nor you!

Thus the hero sums up the events when the drama has run its course.

Beer-Hofmann's second major work, *Jaakobs Traum* (Jacob's Dream, 1918), though written for the greater part before the war, proved one of the major theatrical successes of the early post-war years. The play was designed as a prelude to a biblical trilogy on the life of King David, which remained uncompleted. It pictures, in a single act with a short introductory scene, Jacob's celestial vision as he spends a night under the open sky at Beth-el, culminating in the Lord's promise to raise his seed above the peoples of the earth. The language has still the rich splendour of neo-romantic drama; but the play is infused with a new spirit which points to the fundamental change German drama underwent in the intervening years. The purely psychological and impressionist approach is discarded; instead, there is a distinct trend towards transcendental issues. The religious content of the play, its fervent diction, its culmination in a universal 'message' – in this instance, the elevation of the Jewish race to God's chosen people – all this marks the influence of Expressionism which by this time had made itself felt in German drama. The central scene, Jacob's dream, in which the well and the stone begin to talk, the archangels appear in their glory, and the voice of God announces His message, has a purely visionary character.

Of the trilogy on King David, to which *Jaakobs Traum* was to be a prelude, only the first part, *Der junge David* (Young David), appeared in print in 1934. Meanwhile, however, the interest in this type of drama had waned and political events had changed the face of the theatre. Beer-Hofmann was forced to leave Austria after its seizure by the Nazis in 1938; he emigrated to the United States, where he died in 1945 at the age of seventy-nine.

Of the other poet-dramatists who followed in the wake of Hofmannsthal, only two achieved major successes on the stage, Ernst Hardt (1876-1947) and Karl Gustav Vollmoeller (1878-1948). Both, though German by birth, made their main impact on the Austrian stage. Both at one time belonged to the circle of the poet Stefan George under whose domineering influence Hofmannsthal, too, had fallen in his youth; like Hofmannsthal, they aspired to transfer the decorative verse of George to the theatre. Their choice of subject-matter was almost wholly confined to medieval legend and the Italian Renaissance. In their plays, indulgence in highly rhetorical and flowery verse mingled with a tendency towards the morbid and the macabre. These two elements characterize Ernst Hardt's *Tantris der Narr* (Tantris the Fool, 1908), his greatest theatrical success. The author paraphrases the medieval saga of Tristan and Isolde, concentrating on the love-lorn knight's marriage to a second Isolde, and his return to the court of King Marke in the guise of a jester, unrecognized by everybody except his dog. Two other plays of Ernst Hardt, *Gudrun* (1911) and *Schirin und Gertraude* (1913), founded alike on medieval legends, failed to achieve a similar success.

Karl Gustav Vollmoeller made his name as a playwright with a Renaissance drama, *Catharina, Gräfin von Armagnac* (1903), rich in sensational incident and morbid eroticism. Its dramatic climax – the heroine directing her passionate addresses to her dead lover's head – echoes Wilde's *Salome* which had just gained its triumphant success on the German stage. Another play, *Der deutsche Graf* (The German Count, 1906) introduced once again that cherished figure of impressionist drama, Casanova. In his later career, Vollmoeller turned to pure mime, renouncing the spoken word and relying solely on visual splendour. His *Mirakel* (1911), in the spectacular production of Max Reinhardt, won international fame: its story is based on the medieval legend of the love-sick nun who elopes from the convent and on her return finds the Holy Virgin has taken her place as doorkeeper. As this development bears out, neo-romantic drama, in its later stages, insisted more and more on external accessories, and presently degenerated to a mere vehicle for the lavish display of colour and scenic effect. A Gothic cathedral erected in a circus arena, or in the monster hall of London's Olympia – this was in fact the end of a movement which had started as an inspired reaction to the drabness of Naturalism. The first shot of the 1914 War shattered an artificial world which had completely lost touch with life.

It was perhaps with the conscious intention of coming to

grips with reality, while at the same time passing beyond its confines, that another Austrian, Anton Wildgans (1881–1932), created his peculiar form of drama, trying to get the best of both worlds. After starting as a lyric poet of a rather conventional neo-romantic type, Wildgans made his first appearance on the stage with a terse realistic court-room play in one act, *In Ewigkeit Amen* (For Ever and Ever Amen, 1913). These two trends, the lyrical and the realistic, merged in his three major dramatic works, *Armut*, *Liebe*, and *Dies Irae*. All three were written during the First World War and thus stood at the turning-point between two epochs and two modes of literary expression. They clearly bear the imprint of that time of transition, mingling as they do two, or rather three, heterogeneous styles, the naturalistic, the neo-romantic, and the expressionist. Their structural pattern is identical: the characters, set in a well-defined social milieu, at first move on a realistic plane; at moments of high emotional pitch the language rises to verse; finally, in the closing acts, the drama transcends the confines of reality and is lifted to a symbolic level on which the theme of each play is viewed in its timeless aspects. In these closing acts, which culminate in an emphatic 'message', Wildgans clearly approaches Expressionism. The very titles of the plays point to their universal significance. A further device, adopted with the object of emphasizing the symbolic import of the action, is the introduction of Latin designations for the single acts, such as 'actus quasi prooemium', 'actus mysticus', and especially for the symbolic fifth acts – 'requiem con sordino', or 'quasi epilogus sub specie aeternitatis'. This fusion of three different levels, though striking at the time, proved unconvincing in the long run; for instead of blending into a single whole they follow one another with a painful jerk. There is really no artistically satisfying transition from the extreme naturalism of the beginning to the ecstatic symbolism of the end.

Armut (Poverty, 1915), the first play, demonstrates the demoralizing effect of poverty on a suburban family. In order to procure some money to help her sick father, the daughter offers to give herself to a lodger who is their only source of income. The adolescent son acts as a kind of mouthpiece for the author: it is he who, in the symbolic fifth act, hurls in soaring verses his accusations against the hard-heartedness of man and the scourge of poverty, while the undertaker haggles over the cost of the funeral.

In a similar way, *Liebe* (Love, 1916) probes into the problems of marriage. The central characters are a married couple who feel their love has died in the course of the years. Both seek momentary diversion – the man with a prostitute, the woman with a friend of her husband, a musician who has just arrived from overseas and brings with him the tang of adventure. Both shrink, in the last moment, from committing adultery. The closing scene shows them in their matrimonial bedroom, voicing their emotions in a pompous duologue. Again, the individual case is raised to a 'universal' level. The husband points to the millions who suffer the same afflictions:

> *Wir, nicht wir nur, Anna! Lenk du den Blick hinaus*
> *In die vergehende Nacht, in geisterndes Sternenlicht!*
> *Siehst du die Dächer an Dächern, und Fenster an Fenstern dort?!*
> *Lass das Gemäuer versinken, das Nachbar von Nachbar trennt!*
> *Und tausendmal tausend Betten wie unsere,*
> *Unabsehbar im Dämmer, sind hingereiht!*
> *Und in den Betten die Menschen, leidend am selben Leid!*

> Not we alone, Anna! Send your glance out
> Into the fading night, the shimmering light of stars!
> Do you see roof upon roof, window upon window there?
> Let the walls fall that separate neighbour from neighbour!
> And a thousand thousand beds like ours
> Ranging along in the twilight!
> And in the beds are people, suffering the same grief!

These two plays, though written during the war years, still belong in subject-matter and mood to the pre-war world. The third, *Dies Irae* (1918), shows the impact of its own day: it deals with a topical theme that held a dominant place in the German post-war theatre, the conflict between father and son. It is also more clearly expressionist in character than its predecessors. Again the scene is laid in a Viennese middle-class family, and the characters are drawn in realistic detail. Hubert, the eighteen-year-old son, is clearly developed from the son in *Armut*: hypersensitive, morally unstable, and torn between his parents who live in an unhappy marriage. In this fatal conflict, he eventually chooses suicide as the only possible solution. No social or ideological issues are involved in the antagonism between father and son, which is kept within the personal sphere. These wider issues are, however, raised by the son's friend, Rabanser. Being an orphan, he feels himself untrammelled by social conventions and tries to rouse Hubert to open revolt against his parents. In the concluding 'actus mysticus', he appears as 'choragetes', summoning the father to the day of judgment and making him responsible for the son's death. He claims to speak for the multitude of the unborn: 'I am but the voice of millions who have perished from the crime of procreation!' Finally, a 'chorus puerorum et adolescentium' takes up the challenge, accusing the fathers of forsaking their children. The last verses glow with undiluted expressionist ecstasy:

> O, die den Menschen zeugen
> Nicht um des Menschen willen,
> Ihrer die Schuld!

> Those who engender man
> Not for the sake of man,
> Theirs is the guilt!

This was the nearest any Austrian dramatist of the neo-romantic school came to Expressionism, which at that time was sweeping the German stage. Like Naturalism, the expressionist movement of the post-war era never gained a real foothold in the Austrian theatre, which by its very nature was deeply conservative and firmly set in a native tradition wholly different from the German.

This tradition even survived the dissolution of the Habsburg Empire. In the small Austrian Republic, the recollection of its former glory was still a vital force. Hofmannsthal lived for another decade, producing some of his most essential works. Beside him, and partly under his guiding influence, there appeared a number of younger writers who continued, in one way or another, the line of Austrian drama. The most prominent figure among these was Max Mell (1882-   ), a Styrian by birth. His two main sources of inspiration were the Christian faith and the *Laienspiel*, the amateur village stage, with its age-old tradition of religious play-acting. Following the lead Hofmannsthal had given with his *Jedermann*, Mell wrote three plays on religious themes, cast in simple rhymed verse: *Das Apostelspiel* (The Apostle Play, 1922), *Das Schutzengelspiel* (The Play of the Guardian Angel, 1923) and *Das Nachfolge-Christi-Spiel* (The Play of the Imitation of Christ, 1927). The first is the most poignant: two tramps, intent on breaking into a farm and killing its inhabitants, are moved to give up their plan by the naïve faith of a peasant girl who takes them for two wandering apostles. In his later development, Mell extended his range and aimed at high tragedy on classical lines. *Sieben gegen Theben* (Seven Against Thebes, 1932) revives the story of Oedipus' children, the fraternal strife of his two sons and the self-immolation of Antigone. The two succeeding works show Mell rather under the influence of national socialist ideas. *Das Spiel von den deutschen Ahnen* (The Play of the German Ancestors, 1935) is of the 'blood-and-soil' type of drama, though on a superior level: a young farmer is

83

dissuaded from selling his land by an apparition of his ancestors. During the Second World War, Mell wrote a play in two parts, *Der Nibelungen Not* (1944), an Austrian counterpart to Hebbel's dramatization of the medieval German epic. His latest work, *Jeanne d'Arc* (1957), is yet another version of the well-worn theme.

The neo-romantic movement was, of course, not confined to Austria. It was in fact part of a general movement which made itself felt in almost every European country, be it under the name of Impressionism or Symbolism. Although it had sprung up, in its particular Austrian form, as a reaction to Northern German Naturalism, it soon affected Germany. As a matter of fact, it was on the Berlin stage that the Viennese playwrights, above all Hofmannsthal, had their first decisive successes. For here Max Reinhardt, himself an Austrian by birth, provided in his Deutsches Theater the foremost platform for their works. Just as Otto Brahm, with his meticulously realistic stage-productions, had carried the naturalistic drama to victory, Reinhardt (who had started as an actor under his direction) fulfilled the aspirations of the new poet-dramatists. His secession from Brahm in 1902, and the establishment of a theatre of his own, marked the opening of a new chapter in the history of the German theatre. When, in 1905, he took over the Deutsches Theater as Brahm's successor, the new form of drama was firmly established. The twenty-eight years Reinhardt directed the Deutsches Theater, making it the leading stage in Germany, mark one of the richest periods of German, and perhaps of world theatre. In his later development, especially after the First World War, his versatile genius responded to new trends of dramatic art, even to Expressionism. He outgrew the limitations of the conventional stage and explored every possibility of scenic representation, from intimate theatre to mass-spectacle. But his heart was with the generation he had helped to victory, the neo-romantic and symbolist playwrights of the beginning of the century. Reinhardt brought to the sophisticated German capital a southern breeze, a dazzling display of colour, light, music, fantasy. For him the stage was not merely a faithful mirror of reality but a magic world radiating its own light. 'The world is merely reality, but its reflection [in the theatre] has infinite potentialities', Hofmannsthal wrote in an essay, *The Stage as a Dream-Image*, evidently with the theatre of Reinhardt in mind. It was quite consistent that these two, Hofmannsthal and Reinhardt, jointly called into being the Salzburg Festival: in it they saw the realization of their conception of the theatre as a festivity, uniting all the arts in a single whole.

In Germany, Neo-romanticism produced no single outstanding dramatist. There were, however, some lesser playwrights who responded to the vogue for poetic drama, apart from the two already mentioned, Ernst Hardt and Karl Gustav Vollmoeller. Eduard Stucken (1865-1936) drew his inspiration from the medieval mystery play and the aesthetic symbolism of Maeterlinck. His plays, cast in archaic, highly decorative verse, were chiefly derived from the Arthurian legend: *Gawân* (1902), *Lanzelot* (1909), *Merlins Geburt* (Birth of Merlin, 1913), and *Tristram und Ysolt* (1916). Other playwrights combined reality and fantasy in various ways. Among these, Schmidtbonn and Eulenberg, both natives of the Rhineland, were the most noteworthy. Carl Schmidtbonn (1876-1952) won his greatest success with his first play, *Mutter Landstrasse* (Mother Highroad, 1901, first produced by Reinhardt in 1904), a modern version of the parable of the Prodigal Son, in which the son is rejected by his unforgiving father and cast out to wander the highroad. Schmidtbonn treated the theme once more in *Der verlorene Sohn* (The Prodigal Son, 1913), this time in its biblical setting and with the original happy ending. His other plays deal for the most part with medieval and classical subjects. *Der Graf von Gleichen* (The

85

Count of Gleichen, 1908) has as its central figure a crusader who returns with a Saracen slave girl and tries in vain to reconcile her to his wife; the outcome is tragedy. *Der Zorn des Achilles* (The Wrath of Achilles, 1909) is a forceful dramatization of the Homeric story, written in free verse. Of his later plays, only *Die Fahrt nach Orplid* (Journey to Orplid, 1922) attracted some interest: dealing with a group of emigrants who turn their backs on war-ravished Europe, it reflects the escapist mood of the immediate post-war years.

The other Rhenish playwright, Herbert Eulenberg (1876-1949) had a much wider range and a surer sense of the theatre. His plays, aglow with uncontrollable violence and bizarre fantasy, are clearly modelled on Jacobean drama and the German *Sturm und Drang*. His heroes are dreamers and eccentrics who give free rein to their passions and thus clash headlong with social convention. *Anna Walewska* (1899), his first play, deals with the incestuous love of a Polish count for his daughter. *Leidenschaft* (Passion, 1901) is a tense drama about a girl who falls wildly in love with a dissolute young officer, follows him to his garrison and, when she realizes his worthlessness, kills herself. Eulenberg's romantic strain found vent in such plays as *Münchhausen* (1900), a kind of German Cyrano, and *Ritter Blaubart* (Bluebeard, 1905). Some of his later works have a contemporary setting – *Alles um Liebe* (All for Love, 1910), *Alles um Geld* (All for Money, 1911), and *Belinde* (1912) – each of them turning on violent conflicts of loyalty.

The year 1914 put an end to this whole world of dream and fantasy which was no more than an afterglow of nineteenth-century drama, uncommitted to the real issues of the age. The vital challenge to that age, in terms of drama, came from quite a different quarter.

Chapter Three

SOCIAL SATIRE

I. FRANK WEDEKIND

That remarkable era of artistic and intellectual ferment, the 1890s, saw the emergence of yet another type of drama, which ran side by side with the naturalistic and the neo-romantic. It was not carried by any movement nor was it founded on any conscious aesthetic doctrine. It was, for the time being, the creation of one solitary figure, Frank Wedekind. Yet it proved, in the long run, to be of greater consequence for the development of German drama than any other type of play.

In 1891, Wedekind's first full-length play, *Frühlings Erwachen*, was published, though it did not have its first public performance until 1906. Wedekind was born in 1864; his father was an ardent German liberal and supporter of the 1848 revolution, who had turned his back on Germany and, after some vagrant years overseas, settled in Switzerland. The son was educated in Zürich where he first earned his living as publicity agent to a commercial firm. It was here that, in the late eighties, he came into contact with a group of socialist writers which included the young Gerhart Hauptmann. Between these two, an instinctive antipathy grew up from the outset, which was acerbated by Wedekind's assertion that Hauptmann had misused his personal confidence when writing his play *Das Friedensfest*. He retaliated with a satirical comedy *Kinder und Narren* (Children and Fools), later renamed *Die junge Welt* (The Young World), in which he ridiculed the naturalistic method of photographic realism. But it was with

Frühlings Erwachen (Spring's Awakening) that Wedekind produced his first vital work, initiating, as it turned out, a new type of drama. It is a tragedy of adolescence – the first of a long line of plays dealing with the problems of young people, and their rebellion against the world of adults. The play centres, with unprecedented candour, on the sexual problems of puberty. A boy and a girl, both of school age, are drawn together and succumb to their passion as they meet in a hay-loft at harvest time. The girl becomes pregnant and dies from the abortion her parents force on her. Wedekind lays the blame on the narrow-mindedness of the schoolmasters and the moral cowardice of the parents who shrink from enlightening their children on the facts of life. No less revolutionary than the content of the play is its style. At first glance, it seems realistic; in fact, it is written on two different levels. The language of the young people has a lyrical quality which re-echoes the drama of *Sturm und Drang* and of Georg Büchner (who had just been rediscovered). These influences are unmistakable in the very form of the play – the breaking-up into a sequence of short scenes and the emotionally heightened speech of the young.

In blatant contrast, the language of the adults is matter-of-fact, and that of the schoolteachers in particular is reduced to downright imbecility; their very names – Fliegentod (Flydeath), Zungenschlag (Tonguestroke), Hungergurt (Hungerbelt), and so on – are pure farce. At the crucial staff-meeting which is to decide the boy's fate, most of the time is spent on an argument as to whether the window should be open or shut. Finally, in the concluding churchyard scene, the realistic plane is altogether abandoned: as Melchior, the boy, stands at the girl's grave, a school friend who has shot himself for failing an examination steps from behind his tombstone and tempts him to follow his example. Melchior is saved from suicide by a 'Masked Gentleman' in tails and top-hat who persuades him to choose life as the better alternative. In this figure Wedekind the moralist makes his first appearance.

The scorn Wedekind poured on the German school was aimed at society at large. This school for him was merely the most conspicuous product of the hypocrisy and moral coward-ice of the age. The critical exposure of middle-class morality had of course set in with the social plays of Ibsen and Haupt-mann. Yet both these dramatists proceeded as it were from an objective view-point, shaping their characters with impartial care and presenting even the objects of their criticism as human beings in their own right. Not so Wedekind. He portrayed the world deliberately out of focus; his characters are either over or undersized. The targets of his scorn are mere carica-tures, soulless automata in a grotesquely distorted world.

The vantage point from which Wedekind attacked middle-class morality was not a new social class (the working class never came within his range) but a cosmopolitan set of artists, crooks, adventurers, libertines, in short, the outcasts of society who reject its accepted standards and conventions. These are the apostles of his fundamental creed – the gospel of sexual freedom and physical vitality.

The elemental force of sex and its antagonism to a society hemmed in by hypocritical conventions: this is the central theme of all Wedekind's plays. But never again did he express it with such sympathetic insight and tenderness as in *Frühlings Erwachen*.

After spending several years in Paris (where he met Strind-berg, whose second wife, Freda, later became his mistress), Wedekind made his permanent home in Munich. Towards the end of the century, the Bavarian capital had become, along with Berlin and Vienna, a cultural centre with a distinct physiognomy of its own. Its Bohemian set of artists indulged in untrammelled *joie de vivre*, pouring scorn on philistinism in every sphere of life. One of the focal points of this attitude was the satirical review *Simplizissimus* in which Wedekind took a leading part. It was here in Munich that the idea of the *Überbrettl*, the 'super-cabaret', was born: on its platform Wedekind recited his cynical ballads about seduced girls, murdered aunts, and the delights of free love, accompanying himself on the guitar. Throughout his life, he was drawn to the lower fringes of the theatrical world, circus, music-hall, and variety. This passion left its mark on his dramatic production, with its love for the garish and the grotesque. The prologue of his second and most famous play, *Erdgeist* (Earth Spirit, 1894), appears in the guise of a circus manager, complete with top-hat and tails, cracking his whip and firing a pistol into the audience. This prologue, frequently impersonated by the author himself (who later took to acting the principal parts in his plays) serves as a kind of herald of Wedekind's artistic creed. He sets out by deriding the naturalistic drama of the time:

> *Der eine Held kann keinen Schnaps vertragen,*
> *Der andre zweifelt, ob er richtig liebt,*
> *Den dritten hört ihr an der Welt verzagen . . .*

> One hero cannot stomach any brandy,
> Another doubts whether he's really in love,
> A third you hear despairing of the world . . .

– words obviously aimed at the early plays of Hauptmann. By way of contrast, he is going to show '*das wahre Tier, das wilde, schöne Tier*' (the true, savage, beautiful beast). Mankind is a menagerie in which woman is the serpent, embodied by Lulu, the central figure of the play. *Erdgeist* and its sequel, *Die Büchse der Pandora* (Pandora's Box), completed seven years later, are Wedekind's most startling and most significant dramatic achievements. Their highly melodramatic action revolves around Lulu, the personification of woman, as the author sees her, soulless, callous, driven only by her animal instincts, leading man after man to his ruin. The first play ends with Lulu shooting her third husband – 'the only man,' she remarks, 'I have been in love with.' In the second play, her career takes a turn for the worse. She is now in Paris, in the company of freaks, crooks and perverts, including a Lesbian countess who is desperately devoted to her. Finally, she ends up as a prostitute in the East End of London, and is disembowelled, in a squalid attic, by Jack the Ripper.

This macabre ending seems to contradict Wedekind's advocacy of a life of unrestrained sexual licence. In fact, the rebel against middle-class morality was at heart a fervent moralist: sincerity and travesty were inextricably mixed in all he wrote. This peculiar mixture became increasingly evident in his subsequent plays. More and more, he concentrated on his own role as an artist, mingling self-advertisement with self-pity, and hiding the wrath of the prophet behind the grin of the jester. The central figure of *Der Marquis von Keith* (1900) is an upstart and swindler who collects vast sums for a fraudulent project. Through his superior intelligence and utter recklessness, he subjects men and women alike to his will. His philosophy of life is one of pure cynicism: 'Morality', he declares, 'is the best business in this world', and 'sin the mythological term for bad business'. However, his scheme misfires: before the project materializes, his victims call him to account and expose the fraud. Facing arrest, he considers suicide. But a cheque, presented in the nick of time, offers him a different way out. Weighing the pistol and the cheque in his hands, he takes his leave with the cynical comment, '*Das Leben ist eine Rutschbahn*' (Life is a switchback).

Wedekind's scorn is not directed at the impostor whom he presents with patent admiration, but at a society which succumbs to his spell, and whose moral standards match his. The theme recurs in *Karl Hetmann*, or *Hidalla* (1904). Here, however, it is raised to a more serious level; the central character is clearly a self-portrait of the author. Like the Marquis of Keith, he suffers from a physical deformity but is endowed with a superior intellect. He, too, pursues a project with the purpose of enhancing the joy of living: he has founded an 'International Society for the Breeding of Human Thoroughbreds', the members of which must pledge themselves to unlimited promiscuity within the society. The irony lies in the fact that Hetman himself, owing to his physical imperfection, is excluded from membership. He comes into conflict with the authorities and is thrown into prison. After his release, his former associates turn against him and declare him insane. Eventually, when a circus manager offers him a job as a clown, he realizes the futility of his fight and hangs himself.

The autobiographical touch is equally evident in *König Nikolo*, or *So ist das Leben* (Such is Life, 1901) – the only one of Wedekind's major plays set in a legendary past. A fairy-tale king has been dethroned by a common upstart and goes into exile, accompanied only by his daughter. He is forced to take on various degrading jobs and, eventually, joins a company of strolling players where he acts the part of the king. He is seen by the usurper, who is so impressed by his acting that he offers to make him his court jester. On the steps of the throne, vainly trying to prove his identity, he collapses and dies. The usurper-king orders his burial in the royal tomb, with the final comment: 'History shall not say that I have made a king my court jester!' This highly melodramatic story is yet another of Wedekind's self-revelations: like his player-king, he felt himself an exile from human society, stooping to play the jester while his true worth remained unrecognized.

Wedekind's later works are little more than variations on earlier themes. An unmistakable weakening of his creative power is accentuated by an excess of startling incident and a growing indulgence in moralizing. In *Tod und Teufel*, or *Totentanz* (Dance of Death, 1905), a white slave trader is challenged by a missionary lady who tries to save a victim from his clutches; but in the end she herself is won over to his maxim that sensual pleasure is 'the only unclouded happiness our earthly life offers us'. *Musik* (1906) is a weird play about a young singing pupil who falls a victim to her dissolute music teacher, whereas *Zensur* (1907) is a long-winded diatribe against censorship, in which the author once again portrays himself in the figure of a harassed writer. *Schloss Wetterstein* (Wetterstein Castle, 1910) illustrates, according to the author's preface, Wedekind's views on marriage and the family. A mother marries the man who has killed her first husband in a duel, whilst her daughter follows the way of Lulu and ends up as a prostitute.

Perhaps the most noteworthy of the later plays is *Franziska* (1911), subtitled 'a modern mystery play', in which Wedekind aimed at presenting something like a female counterpart to *Faust*. The sequence of scenes roughly follows Goethe's drama. Franziska, a young girl of good family, is persuaded by a worthless rake, Veit Kunz, to elope with him and explore to the full the pleasures life has to offer. Kunz, true to his model, Mephistopheles, pledges himself to serve her on condition that she will belong to him after a given time. A Berlin tavern, thronged with debauched revellers, corresponds to Auerbach's Cellar; there is a ducal court at which Franziska and Kunz take part in an allegorical masquerade. Eventually Franziska discloses to Kunz that she is pregnant and leaves him cheated out of his due reward – like Mephistopheles. In the end, we find her in a rural idyll with her little boy, enjoying the simple pleasures of motherhood. Whether this ending is pure irony or whether it implies a renunciation of Wedekind's satanism, remains an open question.

With *Franziska*, Wedekind's actual work as a dramatist came to an end. What followed did not add anything new to the picture of the author. In two blank verse dramas, *Simson*

(1913) and *Herakles* (1917), he merely reiterated his old themes under a mythological guise. Both plays hinge on the conflict of the sexes, and both heroes, the biblical and the Greek, succumb to the sensual power of woman. A dramatic chronicle *Bismarck* (1916) was plainly stimulated by the patriotic spirit of the war years. Wedekind died in 1918. The revolution, and the abolition of literary censorship that accompanied it, brought a notable revival of his work. Wedekind was rightly acclaimed as a forerunner of expressionist drama.

Of all his plays, probably only the first two, *Frühlings Erwachen* and *Erdgeist*, stand a chance of survival, owing to their spontaneous dramatic impact. Nevertheless, the importance of Frank Wedekind for the development of German drama cannot be overrated. With his plays, a fresh breeze seemed to blow into the stuffy atmosphere of the late nineteenth century. Though much of his writing was actuated by an impish desire to shock and to startle, he was at heart a zealous moralist. This contradiction underlies all his work. He proclaimed the 'emancipation of the flesh' as the universal cure for all social evils; yet most of his characters, both men and women, who live up to that message, come to a sordid end. He exalted physical perfection – 'the savage, beautiful beast' – yet it is in fact the intellectually superior, the Hetmans, von Keiths and Casti Pianis, who wield power over their fellow-men and women. Wedekind's obsession with sex and the hold it gives woman over man seems, at a first glance, to have much in common with his contemporary, Strindberg. However, his approach was in fact the reverse. For Strindberg, sex was the original sin, and woman the instrument of Satan from whom he sought salvation on his road to Damascus; for Wedekind, sex itself meant salvation from the drabness of life. Strindberg hated woman for the power she exercises over man; Wedekind glorified her courage in following her natural instincts. More important than the substance of Wedekind's philosophy of life was the fact that he made his plays vehicles for a 'message', and that he created characters to proclaim it, regardless of dramatic probability. He saw his task not in portraying reality as it is, but in distorting and overdrawing it with the deliberate intent of conveying this message. By this method, Wedekind distinguished himself clearly both from the naturalist and the neo-romantic playwrights of his time. As it turned out, his conception proved to be the most vital for the development of modern German drama.

The effect of Wedekind's dramatic method was not immediately perceptible. His type of drama seemed too closely linked to his own eccentric personality to generate a movement or a 'school'. It is only in a certain sharpening of social criticism, and in the prevalence of satirical comedy, that the influence of Wedekind on the contemporary theatre may be traced. This is true of two playwrights, both of them Bavarians with an outspoken anti-Prussian bias, Ludwig Thoma (1869-1921), a contributor to *Simplizissimus*, and Josef Ruederer (1861-1915), whose *Fahnenweihe* (Presentation of Colours, 1894) was a hilarious satire on Bavarian village life. Two favourite targets for criticism recur in the German theatre at the turn of the century – the military caste and the school. Several plays set out to expose the arrogance of the officer class, at the same time trading on the popularity of garrison life on the stage. The most successful of these was *Rosenmontag* (1900) by O. E. Hartleben; it was followed by Herbert Eulenberg's *Leidenschaft* (Passion, 1901) and A. Beyerlein's *Zapfenstreich* (Reveille, 1903). In a similar way, the school figured in a large number of plays at the time. Unlike the many English plays set in public schools, their German counterparts present a biting criticism of obsolete educational methods, despotic schoolmasters and the sexual frustration of adolescents. Wedekind's *Frühlings Erwachen* opened a long line of school plays among which Otto Ernst's *Flachsmann als Erzieher* (Flachsmann as Teacher,

1900) and Arno Holz' *Traumulus* (1904) were the most success-ful. They were followed, after the First World War, by the numerous plays on rebellious juveniles which held so prominent a place in expressionist and post-expressionist drama.

All the plays mentioned hardly count for more than isolated achievements of secondary playwrights. The first outstanding figure who can be regarded as the true successor to Wedekind was Carl Sternheim.

II. CARL STERNHEIM

The pungent attack on middle-class morality which had been launched by Wedekind was carried a step further by Carl Sternheim (1878-1942). Unlike Wedekind, Sternheim dis-pensed with explicit moralizing and contented himself with satire pure and simple. Of all German playwrights, he was the only one who concentrated almost exclusively on comedy. He claimed for himself the role of a 'modern Molière': like Molière, he aimed at holding up the mirror to the ruling class of his age – in his case, the German bourgeoisie on the eve of the First World War. This he did in a cycle of comedies written in the years immediately preceding 1914 to which he gave the general title *Aus dem bürgerlichen Heldenleben* (From the Bourgeois Hero's Life). Three of these comedies, *Die Hose*, *Der Snob*, and *1913*, form a sequence, tracing the rise of a bourgeois family through three generations; in others, the same characters recur several times, giving the whole a deliber-ate dramatic coherence. These characters are not so much individuals as types – a distinct anticipation of expressionist drama. The motives underlying their actions are the same throughout – greed, class prejudice, ruthless ambition; their whole lives centre on money and social advancement. Even the non-bourgeois types, such as the members of the working class or the nobility, have adopted the materialistic concepts of the middle class which thus gives its stamp to the whole age.

Sternheim's most striking method of debunking bourgeois mentality is his artificially contrived language. This language is far removed from everyday speech: it is a calculated device designed to expose the insipidity of bourgeois values. This it does with the aid of deliberate bathos, spurious romanticism, misquotations from Wagnerian opera and student songs, and clichés from newspaper leaders. This diction, with its inverted constructions and staccato sequences, was another anticipation of expressionist technique. In Sternheim's comedies it was used solely for satirical purposes; its emotional and poetic potentialities were fully developed only by his successors, especially by Georg Kaiser.

Sternheim's first two plays, *Don Juan* and *Ulrich und Brigitte* (both 1909), were still of the neo-romantic type and showed no trace of his peculiar style. It was with *Die Hose* (A Pair of Drawers, 1909) that he produced his first typical bourgeois comedy. The whole action, set in a stuffy German provincial town, is based on a trivial incident – a minor clerk's wife loses her drawers in broad daylight in the street. This mishap induces two passers-by, a poet and a hairdresser, to take up lodgings in the lady's house, with the avowed purpose of making advances to her. The real hero, however, is the husband, Theodor Maske, who makes good use of the addition to his meagre salary: he finds himself at last in a position to start a family. This Theodor Maske is the very prototype of the bourgeois as Sternheim sees him: unimaginative, materialistic, self-centred, and callous. He becomes the progenitor of a whole line of 'Maskes' (the very name has a satirical tinge); in a later play, *Der Snob* (1913), Sternheim follows up the story of his son, Christian Maske, a social upstart. He has been coached in all the refinements of high society by his mistress, but ruthlessly dismisses her when a friend, Count Palen, offers him a business partnership. Moreover, in order to conceal his humble origins, he pays off his parents and sends them abroad. In short, Christian coldbloodedly subordinates every human affection to his social career. Eventually, he crowns his ambitions by marrying the count's daughter. On the wedding-night, he implies that he is really the illegitimate son of a nobleman, and thus her equal by birth. All along, the author's sympathies evidently lie with his hero who, with his unscrupulous egotism, has a curious fascination of his own.

This is even more evident in the third play of the sequence, *1913*. Here we find Christian Maske at the top of the ladder: he is now knighted 'Freiherr von Buchow' and master of the biggest industrial concern in the country. Of his three adult children (he is now a septuagenarian) two are utterly worthless and degenerate, exclusively concerned with the latest English fashions, whereas his eldest daughter is a ruthless business-woman, and in every respect his true successor. The struggle between these two, father and daughter, forms the main plot of the play; in the end, the father outwits the daughter by joining the Roman Catholic Church – with the sole object of thwarting an arms deal she has contracted with the protestant Dutch government. In the flush of victory, he dies of a stroke. The title of the play, *1913*, has a prophetic ring: written in the winter 1913/14, it presents a striking picture of German society on the brink of the First World War. The capitalist system is carried to the extreme; materialism and the struggle for power dominate life. Christian Maske, the very embodiment of the era, recognizes that its end is at hand: 'When the peak of a system has been reached the possibility of a change is always imminent.' He almost longs for the revolution that will over-throw the world he himself has helped to create: 'After us the collapse,' he prophesies, 'we are ripe!' His own secretary secretly conspires with a revolutionary agitator who propounds anti-capitalistic theories. The play ends in a grotesque mas-querade, a kind of ghostly dance-of-death of a society doomed to extinction.

These three plays thus portray, in satirical distortion, the ascendancy of the German middle class through three generations, from the narrow provincialism of the Bismarck era to the ruthless plutocracy on the eve of World War I. In his other comedies, Sternheim expanded this picture in various directions. *Die Kassette* (The Money Box, 1912) has as its central figure a schoolmaster, Krull, who is ready to sacrifice his wife and daughter to his greed. The plot hinges on a money box containing the fortune his aunt has promised to leave him on her death. For the sake of this box, in which he sees 'a symbol of traditional middle-class wealth', he neglects his wife and hazards his daughter's honour. The irony lies in the fact that all along the coveted money has been maliciously bequeathed to the Church. Sternheim's indebtedness to Molière's *L'avare* is obvious. However, as always, he is not concerned with the portrayal of an individual character or of a timeless human vice but with the satirical depiction of a social stratum, the lower middle class, in what he considers its salient characteristic – avarice.

Bürger Schippel (1912), perhaps Sternheim's best comedy, deals once again with a social upstart – this time a proletarian who becomes a '*Bürger*'. The setting is the usual one – a provincial German town, with its philistinism and petty intrigues. An amateur vocal ensemble, formed by four typical *petits bourgeois*, have lost a member and are in desperate need of a substitute as they are about to perform before His Highness the resident prince. The only eligible candidate is a working-class man, Schippel. The latter, however, claims full social equality in recognition of his services; moreover, he asks to marry the sister of one of the three, and is refused. The girl starts a romantic love-affair with the prince (complete with balcony, moonlight, and abduction) and is then offered to Schippel, to cover up the consequences. Flushed by his newly gained self-respect, it is now his turn to refuse. Finally he gets involved in a duel with a rival. Having grazed his opponent by a chance shot, he is declared the victor and fully accepted as a respectable member of the middle class. Gleefully, Schippel congratulates himself in his concluding words, 'You are *Bürger!*'

As is evident from this outline, Sternheim does not credit the lower classes with superior moral standards: their one and only ambition is to attain middle-class respectability. This cynical view also underlies the comedy *Tabula rasa* (1917) which may be considered the logical conclusion to the whole series. Though of little value as a play, it is the only one to touch on problems of social revolution. The central character is an employee at an industrial plant who, for rather obscure reasons, plots against the management by calling in two social-ist agitators, one an advocate of peaceful evolution, the other an extremist. Eventually he comes to the conclusion that any revolution 'must unfailingly restore the gods it destroys', and proclaims self-centred individualism as his gospel. This is the only place in Sternheim's work where some sort of positive ideal is indicated. However, it is inconsistent with the character who pronounces it, and it is too vague to carry conviction. Nor did Sternheim follow it up in any of his later plays.

When, in 1918, the revolution actually overthrew the social order Carl Sternheim had satirized in his comedies, his own work had more or less come to an end. The plays he wrote after the war (*Die Marquise von Arcis*, 1919, *Oscar Wilde*, 1925, etc.) had no bearing on topical issues. Only once did he attempt a social satire on the scale of his earlier plays – in *Die Schule von Uznach* (The School of Uznach, 1926) which ridicules German post-war youth, with its cynical disillusion-ment and its affected disregard for all moral standards. The setting is a 'progressive' girls' school where the pupils seek 'self-expression' in dance and unrestrained sexual licence. The sub-title of this play, *Die neue Sachlichkeit* (The New

Matter-of-factness) was the name given to the literary movement which superseded Expressionism in the middle twenties. It was Sternheim's last major success. Driven into exile by the rise of Hitler, he died in Brussels in 1942.

Carl Sternheim belongs essentially to the last phase of Wilhelmine Germany. The main target for his satire was the *Bürgertum* which, in his view, had ceased to have any cultural function and was engaged solely in the accumulation of wealth. His fight, he pronounced in one of his theoretical essays, was 'against the soullessness of the bourgeois soul'. 'Man has allowed matter to gain power over him, instead of imposing on it his own mind and heart.' His method was purely destructive; he had no positive values to set against the false gods he relentlessly exposed in his comedies, save that of unscrupulous egotism and self-realization at any price. However, his importance for the evolution of modern German drama was considerable. His hectic staccato diction, known as 'telegram style', quickened the pace of the action; his reduction of characters to social types clearly foreshadowed the technique of expressionist drama. Though not an expressionist himself, he was one of the principal forerunners of the movement. It needed the war and the disintegration of the social fabric to release its full force.

Chapter Four

EXPRESSIONIST DRAMA

I. ORIGIN AND PRINCIPLES

The literary movement known as Expressionism covered roughly the period 1910 to 1925. It coincided with the two main events of that period, the First World War and the revolution which followed in its wake. It has often been described as the reflection, in the sphere of art and literature, of the social and spiritual upheaval wrought by these events. Yet certain trends of an unmistakably expressionist character preceded the war by several years. This clearly proves that the cataclysm of the war cast its shadow back in the apparently calm and stable pre-1914 world: the imminent catastrophe was registered in the realm of the mind before it happened in reality. However, the movement attained its full momentum only as a result of the war, that is, in the years 1917 to 1920; after this, with the return of a certain measure of social stability, it gradually subsided.

The principal forerunners of Expressionism in the field of drama were, in Germany, Frank Wedekind and Carl Sternheim. Another important impulse came from abroad – from August Strindberg. Viewed as a whole, the plays of the Swedish dramatist present an evolution from Naturalism to Symbolism. His early plays, such as *The Father* (1887) and *Miss Julia* (1888), are plainly realistic, whereas in his final phase (*After the Fire, The Pelican, The Spook Sonata,* 1907) reality is resolved into a realm of symbol. Strindberg's true essence transcends these classifications. His fundamental impulse is a religious one, though he formulates it only in his later works in terms of orthodox Christianity. His writings revolve around timeless issues of good and evil, of guilt and atonement. They are centred in the solitary individual, or more precisely, in the author's own self which permeates them from beginning to end. All the other characters, indeed the whole material world, exist only as reflections of this self. The pre-eminent example is his trilogy *The Road to Damascus* (1898-1901). In this work, the chief formal principles of expressionist drama are for the first time clearly applied: firstly, the reduction of the characters to mere types, named by general terms such as the Stranger, the Beggar, the Doctor; secondly, the unfolding of the action in a succession of scenes, denoting stages of the central character's development towards a spiritual goal; thirdly, the identification of the author with his central figure, the Stranger, who on his road of martyrdom passes through every form of mental agony until he attains redemption in the Christian faith. There is no antagonist equivalent to the hero: all the other characters are merely projections or embodiments of his inner struggle. Thus *The Road to Damascus* stands as the prototype of expressionist drama long before this actually came into being.

Another of Strindberg's plays which exercised a powerful influence on expressionist drama was *A Dream Play* of 1902. Here the action unfolds on a purely fantastic plane where the laws of causality are suspended and the logic of dream alone prevails. The characters split, double, multiply, merge into one another. The incidents are related to a transcendental background: the play opens with a dialogue between the god Indra and his daughter, who pleads for permission to descend to earth, roused by compassion for suffering mankind. This celestial prologue is a device frequently recurring in expressionist drama. The isolated scenes of *A Dream Play* are realistic, but their realism is always related to a spiritual plane.

This dual level is another essential feature of Expressionism.

It was mainly from these two sources, represented by Wedekind and Sternheim on the one hand, and Strindberg on the other, that the expressionist movement in the theatre derived its most powerful impulses. Wedekind and Sternheim contributed through their pungent satire on bourgeois society, Strindberg by introducing the supernatural into the world of reality, and by placing his own self in the centre. The merging of these two currents produced the expressionist drama.

Any attempt to define the basic principles of Expressionism must take account of the fact that the movement was not confined to literature but affected every sphere of thought and creative activity, including philosophy, music, and the visual arts. It is in this wider context that the emergence of Expressionism about 1910 must be viewed.[1]

The expressionist movement must first and foremost be seen as a violent reaction against the conceptions of life and art which dominated the latter part of the nineteenth century, and which found their literary expression in Naturalism and Impressionism. Much as these two differed in their aim and style, they were nevertheless two aspects of a single world concept. For all their emphasis on emotions and mood, the Impressionists still conceived man as being ruled by 'matter' – no longer perhaps by crude material conditions but by the subtler influences of colour, perfume, and melody.

In contrast to this, Expressionism emphasized the supremacy of the spirit over matter. Man was no longer a product of his environment, driven by forces beyond his control, but he was

[1] The first application of the term 'Expressionism' is a matter of controversy among literary historians. According to R. Samuel and R. H. Thomas (*Expressionism in German Life, Literature and the Theatre*, 1939) it was the art critic W. Worringer who first used the term 'Expressionists' in a review on paintings by Cézanne, van Gogh, and Matisse, published in 1911. J. Bithell (*Modern German Literature 1880–1950*, 1959) attributes the first application of the term to Otto zur Linde who used it, in the same year 1911, with reference to a group of poets associated with his literary review, *Charon*.

himself the driving agent, capable of transforming the world according to his vision. It is not the world that fashions man; it is man who fashions the world. Both the faithful portrayal of reality and the pursuit of aesthetic values for their own sake were renounced for unrestrained 'self-expression'. This extreme subjectivism found its most congenial medium in lyric poetry; but it soon forced its way into the theatre. Expressionist drama, especially in its early stages, betrayed its descent from lyric poetry – a heritage it never fully outgrew. Its very language was poetical – not in the sense of traditional verse drama but as a form of expression suited to its intensely emotional emphasis. Expressionism forged its own language – or rather, every expressionist writer coined his personal idiom, from the inarticulate ejaculations of August Stramm to the crisp precision of Georg Kaiser. In this process, grammar and syntax were ruthlessly overthrown, articles eliminated, sentences clipped, new words created. In some extreme instances, the dialogue was reduced to bare exclamations; the ecstatic cry was the ultimate mark of expressionist diction. Once again, the German indifference to tradition, the passion for daring experiment, favoured this break with every known dramatic form. Yet in spite of its excesses to the point of absurdity, the German expressionist theatre imparted to European drama a new and powerful impulse, the repercussions of which can be felt to this day.

The expressionist movement was carried by a new generation born in the 1880s and 90s. Almost without exception, its protagonists went through the holocaust of the 1914–1918 War from which they received their decisive creative impulse. More often than not, their contribution was limited to a single significant work, after which they spent themselves in fruitless repetitions or succumbed to the more profitable temptations of the routine theatre. If they survived, their literary careers – and, in many instances, their lives – were cut short by the rise of Nazism in 1933. In dealing with their works, we leave the realm of artistic accomplishment and find ourselves in a welter of experiments, of fervent aspirations, which only in a few instances were crowned with success. Yet so powerful was the impulse that activated them, so urgent the message they had to convey, that it carried even the lesser talents along and won them momentary fame.

The task facing these young writers was, indeed, incomparably more difficult than was that of the older generation. They lacked any scale of values to build upon; they awoke into a crumbling world, and chaos was their life-element. From out of that chaos they created the form (if form it can be called which by its very nature was formless) which alone seemed apt to reflect their vision.

In the course of its existence, Expressionism underwent various significant changes. In the years prior to the war, it bore the stamp of extreme subjectivity, indeed of anarchy. The lone and isolated individual strove to give expression to the full life he craved. The expressionist plays written before 1914 were mainly personal dramas, depicting the struggle of a man to break away from his everyday environment in order to live his life to the full. Yet even at that early stage, a social note was struck. In contrast to the preceding neo-romantics, the expressionist writers showed a marked tendency to face the ugly aspects of modern civilization – the big city, the machine, the drudgery of mechanical labour, the plight of the working class. All these appeared as symptoms of a corrupt and evil world from which 'expressionist man' strove to break away in his quest for a higher form of existence. Almost from the outset, an apocalyptic feeling, a premonition of impending catastrophe took possession of the expressionists. It frequently culminated in visions of a universal war which would engulf the present world, and from which a new world, governed by love, would arise. There are some remarkable instances of prophecy in the war poems of Georg Heym, Ernst Stadler, Franz Werfel, all written between 1912 and 1914. In the field of drama, Carl Hauptmann's *Krieg* (1912) foreshadowed the war in an uncanny way.

This vision of impending war was often linked with the idea of revolution. Thus a political momentum entered expressionist writing, an 'activist' trend with distinct social and revolutionary tendencies.[1] Originally, this revolutionary impulse was not directed towards any definite programme or social class. But as its antagonism was from the outset turned against bourgeois and capitalist society, the future it visualized soon took the shape of a socialist or, in its extreme form, communist order, and the social class on which it fixed its hopes was the proletariat. Nevertheless, the connection between the expressionist movement and the political struggle of the working class must be considered a secondary factor. It became effective only with a certain group of expressionist writers, such as Ernst Toller, Ludwig Rubiner, Johannes R. Becher. Viewed as a whole, Expressionism was essentially a spiritual movement aiming at the moral regeneration of man, and unrelated to any specific social programme.

When war actually broke out, it created the chaos the expressionists had beheld in their vision. From out of this chaos arose the cry for reconciliation and human brotherhood. In this way Expressionism began to veer towards social issues which had originally been foreign to it. The conflict between the individual and the community emerged, in fact, as one of the fundamental issues of the whole movement.

Expressionism thus evolved two basic types of drama: in one, the hero (identical with the author's self) held the stage from beginning to end, while the real world faded into

[1] The revolutionary character of pre-war Expressionism is evident in the very names of its representative reviews and periodicals, e.g. *Die Aktion* (1910), *Der Sturm* (1910), *Revolution* (1912). The actual term and programme of *Aktivismus* originated from Kurt Hiller in 1915.

insubstantial symbols; in the other, the central figure was confronted with social reality, depicted in its multiform modern aspects – home, factory, police, office, prison, war, etc. In the latter case, the hero strove to impress his message upon the world and either succumbed, or contrived to transform society by the force of his appeal. Between these two poles, expressionist drama vacillated, now accentuating the lone individual in his quest for self-fulfilment, now the problems of social transformation. However, a distinct trend is evident throughout the whole period: before 1914, expressionist drama stressed the subjective side; it gathered more and more social momentum under the impact of the war and culminated, about 1918, in the revolutionary drama. This trend can be traced in many of the writers concerned.

II. EARLY EXPRESSIONISM

It is characteristic of the close interrelation between Expressionism in art and in literature that among the pioneers of expressionist drama were Oskar Kokoschka (1886-   ), the painter, and Ernst Barlach (1870-1938), the sculptor. Kokoschka's *Mörder, Hoffnung der Frauen* (Murderer, Hope of Women, 1907) was probably the first attempt at drama in the expressionist manner, depicting, as do most of his writings, the perennial struggle between the sexes, usually in a mythical setting and in a violent, explosive diction. His second play, *Der brennende Dornbusch* (The Burning Bush, 1911) is enacted in a modern setting. But reality is here resolved into a sequence of vague and fleeting images. The action revolves around two lovers, defined merely as The Man and The Woman, who in a series of ecstatic duologues and soliloquies pass through every degree of passion, of torment, and of rapture. The characters surrounding them are reduced to an anonymous chorus of men and women. Already the essence of Expressionism is dimly perceptible: the two main characters attain, through pain and suffering, a higher and purer level of existence. The climax is accentuated by the threefold cry of the chorus, 'I believe in the resurrection within myself!' In his later plays, such as *Hiob* (Job, 1917) and *Orpheus und Eurydice* (1918), Kokoschka treated mythological subjects in the same extreme manner, without fresh development.

Kokoschka's literary achievement is hardly more than a side-line to his work as a painter. Ernst Barlach, on the other hand, presents one of the rare cases of an artist who expressed himself with equal force through two different media. Both his plays and his sculptures are suffused with the same spirit, blending a heavy and earth-bound realism with a mystical, religious ecstasy. His true source of inspiration was Gothic art, which the Expressionists regarded as one of the mainsprings of their spiritual fervour. Barlach was born and bred in the plains of north-west Germany, bordering on the North Sea; the heavy skies and brooding mists of his native land are always present in his work. His characters seem unable to emerge from the misty twilight which envelops them. Yet they grope, in their ponderous way, for spiritual self-fulfilment. This peculiar blend of realism and mysticism, interspersed with grotesque elements, characterizes his very first play, *Der tote Tag* (The Dead Day) of 1912. The action centres on a mother and a son who live in 'a vast hall', filled with perpetual twilight. The mother strives desperately to keep the son under her sway and to prevent him from maturing to manhood. She even kills and buries the magic steed his unknown father has sent him. But the son is driven by an irrepressible urge to find his father, the source and mainstay of his spiritual life. In the end it becomes clear that his father is spirit, is God. In this strange myth, pervaded by a vague and rather obscure symbolism, Barlach's innermost creative impulse, the 'search for God', already forms the dominant theme. In his later plays, the realistic element becomes more clearly defined: there is a more detailed depiction of the settings and the characters drawn from his immediate homeland. In *Der arme Vetter* (The Poor Cousin, 1918), probably his most convincing play, a young man, a dreamer and visionary tormented by doubts, detaches himself from his petty and narrow-minded fellow-men, in a mystic quest for God and the true meaning of life. In the end he commits suicide, but by this very act rouses a young girl, who chances to cross his way, to break with her former existence and to devote herself to a life in the spirit. *Die echten Sedemunds* (The True Sedemunds, 1920) is a caustic satire on the microcosm of a small town, its philistine inhabitants with their trivial conflicts and their apathy towards any higher spiritual appeal. In *Der Findling* (The Foundling, 1922) a diseased child is left to die by the roadside. All the passers-by refuse to pick it up, seeing in it a symbol of their own wretchedness and guilt, till eventually it is saved by two young lovers and reveals miraculous healing powers. The deep-rooted Christianity that informs all Barlach's works, finds full expression in *Die Sündflut* (The Flood, 1924) which revolves, within the traditional story of the Flood, around the timeless issues of sin and redemption. God is seen wandering through the vice-ridden world in the guise of a beggar. In the end he comes to realize that not even the Flood can purify mankind, since good and evil are inherent in the very nature of man.

In his last important drama, *Der blaue Boll* (Blue Boll, 1926), Barlach resumed the manner of his earlier plays, mingling the grotesque with the mystical. Boll is a robust country squire, earth-bound and self-confident, given to food and drink, who, through a series of strange experiences, undergoes a complete transformation. He breaks the chains of his narrow existence and sets out to seek the spiritual meaning of life and 'give birth to a new Boll'.

Barlach's plays, though never wholly successful, held a

peculiar fascination of their own. It emanated not so much from their action (which is negligible) as from their immanent poetic power and brooding atmosphere, lit up by flashes of bizarre humour. Barlach stands as one of the pre-eminent exponents of what may be called the mystic or religious type of expressionist drama. Although he produced plays right through the whole period up to 1933 (when the rise of the Nazis silenced him as it did so many others) his work was scarcely affected by outside events. His concerns were the timeless issues of human existence, the triumph of the spirit over the encroaching materialism of our age.

The same is true, though perhaps to a lesser degree, of the plays of Franz Werfel (1890-1945). If Barlach's mysticism was rooted in Christian concepts, Werfel's had its source in the Jewish faith. Like Rilke and Kafka, he was a native of Prague with its peculiar mystical traditions. He first became known as a lyric poet of a distinctly expressionist type. His early lyrics, collected in *Der Weltfreund* (1911), *Wir sind* (1913), *Einander* (1915) and *Gerichtstag* (1919), proclaimed, in dithyrambic verse, the message of all-embracing love. They were at once received as the clarion-call of a new generation and a new ethical interpretation of life.

Werfel serves as a good example of the close connection between lyric poetry and drama, characteristic of early Expressionism. His first play, *Die Troerinnen*, written shortly before the outbreak of war and published in 1915, is a re-creation of Euripides' *The Trojan Women*. In a preface to the play, the poet elucidates his approach to ancient Greek drama. He points to the analogy existing between the present age and that of Euripides, both of which are marked by 'the shrill cries of dying individualism'. In man's growing sense of moral responsibility he apprehends signs of an 'impending revolution'. The quest for the moral import of life indicates the dawn of a new religious faith.

These remarks illuminate the spirit in which the expressionists approached mythological subjects. The revival of mythological drama, ancient Greek as well as biblical, was a salient feature of the movement. But their approach was quite different from that of the classicists or the neo-romantics. What they sought was the ethical and religious message inherent in Greek drama and in biblical legend, the embodiment of universal ideas in characters of superhuman stature. Expressionism was focussed on the timeless and unchanging essence of man, not his incidental attributes of period and place. At the same time, the mythological subjects served as a medium to convey a topical message.

Werfel's play follows closely the action of Euripides' drama, cutting out some parts and elaborating others. Impassioned soliloquies, terse dialogues and choral lyrics are cast in his own exuberant verse. Hecuba, the hapless queen of Troy, holds the stage from beginning to end. Together with Cassandra and Andromache, she laments the vanished glory of the city and their own fate. But through her experience of suffering and humiliation, she rises to a new conception of ethical values: 'And yet being good is more than being happy!' Exalted by this newly gained insight, she conquers her desire to perish with Troy and decides to endure her captivity to the bitter end:

> *Seht her, so nehme ich*
> *Mein Leben an die Brust und trag's zu Ende!!*

> Behold ye, thus I take
> My life unto my breast and bear it to the end!

The message implicit in the play, the vivid depiction of a nation's fall from the height of power to the humiliation of defeat, made an immediate impact on its publication in 1915. *Die Troerinnen* was received as the first manifestation of a revolutionary spirit defying the war.

Werfel's most important contribution to expressionist drama

was the 'magic trilogy' *Der Spiegelmensch* (The Mirror Man, 1920). This poetic play is enacted in a setting of a vaguely oriental character. The central figure, Thamal, is a kind of modern Faust, embodying Man in the widest sense. Weary of life, he has withdrawn to a monastery, where he is told by the abbot that he is not yet mature enough to renounce the world. The drama presents his spiritual development through various phases of his life. He is seen in violent conflict with his father whose death he causes by sheer will-power. He then appoints himself leader of the people, inciting them with glowing promises of wealth and happiness. All along, he is accompanied by his mirror-image, a kind of Mephistophelean *alter ego*, embodying his lower instincts. At a later stage, he gives himself up to trial and of his own free will takes death upon himself, in order to atone for his wrongs. As he empties the cup of poison, the mirror-image rejoins the mirror which is transformed into a window revealing a vision of pure and perfect life. This drama can be regarded as a kind of summary of the leading motifs of Expressionism, presented in abstract symbols. It was deemed worthy of performance at the Vienna Burgtheater – one of the few instances of expressionist drama in Austria.

Werfel's next play, *Bocksgesang* (Goat Song, 1921), showed a distinct advance towards a more realistic form: the scene is laid in a country district beyond the Danube, among Slavonic peasants. The action turns on an uprising of the landless peasants against the wealthy landowners. This uprising has a deeper meaning: it implies the challenge of man's primeval instincts to the established order. In a kind of religious frenzy, the crowd worships an uncouth monster, half ram, half man, that has emerged from the woods. The rebellion is crushed, and the leaders are executed. The monster perishes in the burning woods, but the daughter of a wealthy peasant bears a child from it: the challenge of the nameless crowd is as it were perpetuated. Despite its mystical and remote content, the drama reflects the emotional upheaval of the period.

Schweiger (1922) has a contemporary and, on the surface, realistic setting. Like *Der Spiegelmensch*, it treats of a man's dual personality, his vacillation between good and evil, his yearning for salvation. The hero, a respectable citizen venerated by his fellow-men, is discovered to have committed a murder. When his memory of the crime is revived by a psychiatrist, he is plunged into a terrible conflict which eventually drives him to suicide. The wider significance of the case is emphasized by a priest who sees in his crime a manifestation of Satan: 'I can smell the smoke of a hidden conflagration hanging over our age.' But evil, he continues, is merely an instrument of divine mercy: 'The blacker the evil, the greater man's readiness for grace!' The root of all evil is man's innate loneliness from which only the power of love can save him. For Schweiger, this redeeming love is embodied in his wife; only when she forsakes him, does he fall back into the abyss of his lower self. The attempt to capture the apocalyptic mood of the period in this somewhat pathological case-history is rather unconvincing.

The struggle between evil and the divine force in man's soul remained the dominant theme in Franz Werfel's writings. Following the general trend in German drama, he presented this theme in his later works within the framework of a definite historical situation. His greatest theatrical success was *Juarez und Maximilian* (1924), the tragedy of the hapless Austrian archduke who finds himself emperor of Mexico, and is defeated by events he is powerless to control. Two later plays, permeated by Werfel's religious mysticism, proved less successful on the stage: *Paulus unter den Juden* (Paul Among the Jews, 1925) deals with the conflict between inspired prophecy and orthodox religion among the early Christians, while *Das Reich Gottes in Böhmen* (The Kingdom of God in Bohemia, 1930) unfolds a vast picture of the Hussite movement in the author's homeland. Roused by the challenge of Nazi persecution, which forced Werfel to leave Germany, he glorified the unconquerable strength of the Jewish race in a verse play, *Der Weg der Verheissung* (The Road of Destiny, 1936), performed in New York in a spectacular production by Max Reinhardt. The same theme, treated humorously, underlies Werfel's last play, *Jakobowsky und der Oberst* (Jacobowsky and the Colonel, 1944). It deals with an episode of the French collapse of 1940: a Jewish refugee contrives, by his superior intelligence and ingenuity, to take an anti-Semitic Polish officer with his French mistress through the German lines to the coast and safety.

Apart from this slight play, Werfel devoted the last years of his life in America exclusively to novels. Among these, *Das Lied der Bernadette* (The Song of Bernadette), prompted by his perilous escape from France in 1940, won him international fame. In it, and in some later novels, the mystical and spiritual impulse of Expressionism found its last, belated outlet.

The plays of Barlach and Werfel represent what may be called the mystic or religious type of expressionist drama. Although they could not have been written at any other time, they do not deal directly with the social issues of the period but with timeless problems of human existence. It is in the single work of a young author that we have the first expressionist drama in the full sense of the term – *Der Bettler* (The Beggar, 1912) by Reinhard Johannes Sorge (1892–1916).

The protagonist of this 'dramatic mission' is the Poet – in other words, the author himself, who reveals within the play his innermost conflicts and aspirations. He sees himself as the pioneer of the 'new drama' which addresses itself not to a select few but to the masses:

> *Es wird*
> *Das Herz der Kunst: aus allen Ländern strömen*
> *Die Menschen alle an die heilende Stätte*
> *Zur Heiligung, nicht nur ein kleines Häuflein*
> *Erlesener!*

It will be
The soul of art. From all countries
Mankind will throng to the healing-place
To be sanctified – not merely the select few!

He is carried away by visions of a glorious future for mankind:

Meere! Neu-Meere! Nie betretene Küsten!
Menschen! Licht-Menschen! Nie geliebte Liebe!

Oceans! New oceans! Never trodden shores!
Men! Men-of-light! Love never loved!

The real world the Poet has to face is represented in a
series of tableaux – newspaper readers in a café, streetwalkers,
and the like – contrasting crudely with the Poet's dream world.
The form of these tableaux points the way for the entire
expressionist drama. The characters are not individually
differentiated but simply numbered as First Listener, Second
Reader, etc. They are merely interchangeable types, speaking as
single voices or combining in chorus. They are not at all
life-like but are distorted into caricatures or demonically
enlarged. In the last act, against an acoustic background of
military music and cheering crowds, the Poet breaks into an
interminable monologue expressing utter revulsion and culminating in the cry, 'Everything is evil!' The only one to join
the hero in his revolt against everything and everybody is the
Girl, who accompanies the Poet through all his mental struggles
and in the end merges with him in a kind of *unio mystica*.

The central part of the play is devoted to the domestic drama
of the hero (who in these scenes is called the Son) and his
parents. Here a dominant theme of expressionist drama appears
for the first time, the conflict between father and son. Expressionism was in the first place the revolt of a new generation
against the old one. The father, as the personification of the
established order, constituted the chief obstacle to the aspirations of the young. It was in the revolt of son against father,

culminating in attempted or actual parricide, that the revolutionary impulse of expressionist drama first found vent. (In this, the expressionist movement bears a striking resemblance to the *Sturm und Drang* of the 1770s which was also fomented by the revolt of a new generation against the established order.)

In Sorge's play, the theme assumes a peculiar form: the father is depicted as being insane. However, his insanity is merely an accentuation of his particular view of life. He is by profession an engineer and indulges in fantastic technical projects. He, too, dreams of the future happiness of mankind, but in terms of scientific progress and mechanical achievement. The son, on the other hand, abhors the father's scientific interpretation of life: he aims at a spiritual and moral regeneration. Eventually, he releases the father from a futile existence by poisoning him. He commits the deed at the express wish of the father and regards it, without the slightest remorse, as conforming to the laws of nature.

As may be judged from this outline, Sorge's play is, from the literary viewpoint, immature in the extreme. Yet in the history of German drama it has its place as the first clearly expressionist play in which the seeds of all subsequent achievements are latent. It remained the only notable work of the author who was killed in Flanders in 1916, at the age of twenty-four.

Another expressionist playwright who emerged before 1914 was Paul Kornfeld (1889-1942). In his first play, *Die Verführung* (The Seduction, 1913) the antagonism between rebellious youth and society is carried a step further. Here the principal characters bear individual names, only the secondary ones are anonymous – a Schoolmaster, a Lady, a Poet, etc. The dialogue is throughout in prose, though of an exalted quality, far removed from ordinary speech. In an introductory essay, the author laid down some directions for the acting, typical of expressionist concepts in general. The actor, Kornfeld wrote, should not merely be an 'imitator' striving to 'fake reality'; instead, 'he should venture to open his arms wide, as he would never do in life. . . . He should abstract . . . from the attributes of reality and be nothing but an exponent of ideas, of emotions, or of fate!' The central character, with the telling name Bitterlich, is once again the author's mouthpiece. His attitude to life is a Werther-like *Weltschmerz* to which he gives vent in endless soliloquies and impassioned outbursts. Realizing the futility of life and the viciousness of men, he abandons himself to despair: 'Stupidity remains the same, vulgarity remains the same, my fate remains the same, there is nothing but chaos – chaos in all eternity!' This universal *taedium vitae* is sharpened by a deep revulsion against his own time and class, their materialism and narrow-mindedness. His disdain for contemporary society culminates in the actual murder of a man he has never met before, but in whom he sees an embodiment of the 'spirit of the age'. This symbolic murder forms the pivot of the action. Bitterlich is arrested and thrown into prison. On this occasion, the functionaries of the State, policemen, prosecutors, prison-guards, who were to play so vital a part in expressionist drama, appear for the first time in their typical grotesque forms. In the isolation of the prison cell Bitterlich feels happy, since he is at last freed from the 'real world' and allowed to live his inward life to the full: 'No more do I wish to see anything real, but only believe in what grows in my mind, regarding everything else as an illusion!' However, he is tempted to face the world once more by a young girl, Ruth, who persuades him to escape and seek happiness in love. But society, which Bitterlich has challenged with his murder, takes its revenge. One of its members (actually, his brother-in-law) takes retribution into his own hands and kills Bitterlich by slowly poisoning him.

All subtler differentiation of character, all plausibility of plot are here ignored for the sake of self-expression at any price. The drama ceases to be a work of art in its own right and serves merely as a vehicle for a message. This is even more evident in Kornfeld's second play, *Himmel und Hölle* (Heaven and Hell, 1919). In contrast to the bleak pessimism of *Die Verführung*, this post-revolutionary play culminates in the fervent promulgation of new ethical values and in the redemption of man through love. Superficially viewed, it depicts a mere domestic tragedy, revolving round an unhappy marriage. But the action and the characters have a wider significance. The dialogue rises at times to verse, moulded in duets and trios of an almost operatic character. The drama fluctuates between extremes of emotion, between good and evil, sin and atonement. A cryptic figure, named Jacob, acts as a kind of commentator and *raisonneur*. Moved by compassion for suffering mankind, he feels himself drawn towards all who are in distress. In his utter dejection, he yearns for the end of all life: 'An end! May everything cease! May man vanish! May the earth die out!' From this nihilism he is, however, gradually converted when he witnesses the self-sacrificing love of a woman for her husband. He comes to realize that God embraces even him, the embodiment of 'eternal protest'. At the close, female spirits announce, in hymnic verses, the gospel of Love which has the power to transform the earth into a paradise.

After the decline of Expressionism, Kornfeld turned with some success to comedy of a bizarre type, as in *Kilian und die gelbe Rose* (Kilian and the Yellow Rose, 1926). He died in a concentration camp in Poland, in 1942.

The most outstanding of pre-war expressionist plays was undoubtedly *Der Sohn* (The Son, 1914) by Walter Hasenclever (1890-1940), which came to be regarded as the dramatic manifesto of the young generation. With regard to form, Hasenclever's play kept to more traditional lines. It is in five well-constructed acts, the dialogue being in straight, though intensely dramatic prose, with blank verse for the hero's monologues. The principal characters are nameless types, the Son, the Father, the Friend, and the whole work is fired by an unmistakably expressionist passion. 'We are only alive in ecstasy: reality would embarrass us!' the Son proclaims. He yearns for a full life, which at first he understands in terms of unrestricted sensual pleasure. But his ideas soon take a more revolutionary turn when, at a 'club for the preservation of joy', he addresses the members, inciting them to a 'revolution of the young' against their fathers.

The central theme of the play is the irreconcilable enmity between father and son. The father personifies the rational, firmly established order of bourgeois society against which his son rises in revolt. When he coldly rejects the hand of friendship offered to him, the son renounces all filial obligations: 'Let me leave the desert of this house and the daily company of your person. I feel I am setting forth into a happy world. I want to be its prophet.' In the closing act, the son challenges the father with a pistol. But he is spared the extreme act of parricide as the father conveniently dies from heart failure.

Der Sohn was the first drama to reveal fully the revolutionary ferment of Expressionism. In no other work was the spiritual kinship to *Sturm und Drang*, especially to the early plays of Schiller, more manifest. The parallel is explicitly emphasized by the son:

Remember that our fight against our fathers is equal to the vengeance wrought on the princes a hundred years ago. To-day it is we who are in the right! Then, crowned heads oppressed and enslaved their subjects, robbed them of their money, and imprisoned their spirit. To-day it is we who sing the Marseillaise!

The father-son conflict recurs in a great number of expressionist plays, either as a central or as a secondary theme. The most extreme case was without any doubt *Vatermord* (Parricide) by Arnolt Bronnen (1895-   ) which was written in 1915 but not performed until 1922, when it caused an uproar. With regard to style, this play is realistic, indeed, naturalistic. But the son's rebellion burns with the unmistakable expressionist fire. He sees in his father the chief obstacle to his untrammelled self-realization: 'You have hindered me in everything I have felt. You have destroyed everything I have accomplished. I will love the whole world except you!' The conflict rises to a paroxysm of mutual hatred and culminates in actual parricide. The play closes with the son's rapturous exclamation, 'No one before me, no one beside me, no one above me: my father – dead!'

In all these plays, the struggle between father and son was carried on within the walls of the middle-class home, and the son's revolt had a purely spiritual aim. When war broke out, this aim took on a more concrete form: the son became the herald of a new world of peace and social justice – in short, a revolutionary. The call for the spiritual rebirth of the individual was the primary impulse; only subsequently was it bound up with social and political issues. The son left as it were the nursery sphere of domestic conflict, and stepped out into the world to proclaim his message to mankind. The father, up to then his most powerful opponent, receded into the background; his place was taken by society at large, which the son, transformed into a revolutionary leader, now openly challenged. Consequently, the father-son theme disappeared almost entirely during the later stages of Expressionism, following the revolution of 1918. The scene shifted from the limited sphere of the parental home to the vast field of social conflict where the herald of revolution waged his battles against militarism, capitalism, the State, and all the other demons of the modern world.

III. WAR AND REVOLUTION

The 1914-1918 War had undoubtedly a deeper and more far-reaching effect upon Germany than upon any of the victorious nations. Starting as the powerful self-assertion of the German Empire, it ended with its collapse and the establishment of a new political and social order. The revolution was a direct outcome of military events. During the first half of the war, marked by the successes of the German armies and the general belief that the war had been imposed on Germany against her will, active support of the existing order was almost universal. The year 1916 marked the turning-point: for the first time, a premonition of coming disaster dawned upon the more far-sighted. From then on, opposition to the war gathered in momentum. It gained a vital impulse from the Russian Revolution of 1917 which pointed a way to peace by the overthrow of the ruling powers. The year 1918 presented the last act of the drama, the military collapse and the dissolution of the empire.

This development was faithfully reflected in the dramatic output of those years. During the early part of the war, patriotic plays held the stage. They were mainly of the historical type, evoking heroic figures from the national past. By far the most popular was, for obvious reasons, Frederick the Great: in the first few months of the war, no fewer than three plays about the Prussian king appeared – *Katte* by Hermann Burte, *Friedrich Kronprinz von Preussen* (Frederick, Crown Prince of Prussia) by Emil Ludwig, and *Preussengeist* (Prussian Spirit) by Paul Ernst, all of them centring on the notorious conflict between the young prince and his father, and the former's submission to the call of duty. The series continued with Hermann von Boetticher's *Friedrich der Grosse* (1917) and Joachim von der Goltz' *Vater und Sohn* (Father and Son, 1921). Other historic figures who served as a source of national inspiration were *Bismarck* (by Frank Wedekind, 1916, and by Emil Ludwig, 1922) and *Yorck* (by Paul Ernst, 1917), the Prussian general in the war against Napoleon.

Significantly, all these plays moved on the traditional lines of realistic drama; their retrospective attitude was mirrored in their form. Only those writers who reacted to the war in a revolutionary spirit employed the expressionist technique. The war furnished them with the reality they had anticipated in their vision; it shattered the material world they had denounced, and undermined the middle-class society they had challenged. Politically, the expressionist movement was in violent opposition to the Wilhelmine state. It prepared the way for the overthrow of this state and the establishment of an order diametrically opposed to it.

During the early part of the war, this subversive literature was confined to a few undaunted outsiders some of whom took refuge in neutral Switzerland. From 1916 onwards, the first outspoken anti-war plays were written, often in the front line. In 1917, some of the most prominent were published – Reinhard Goering's *Seeschlacht*, Stefan Zweig's *Jeremias*, Fritz von Unruh's *Ein Geschlecht*. Moreover, a number of pre-war expressionist plays were now performed for the first time, e.g. Sorge's *Der Bettler*, Kornfeld's *Die Verführung*, and the first essential plays of Georg Kaiser, *Die Bürger von Calais, Von morgens bis mitternachts*, and *Die Koralle* – all of them carrying the message of revolution in one way or another. Finally, in 1918, the full flood of revolutionary expressionist drama burst forth, partly before the end of the fighting.

In this way, contemporary German drama reflected clearly the change of spirit working behind the façade of the Reich, and preparing the way for the revolution of 1918.

Any account of the impact the First World War made on German drama must take its starting-point from that remarkable instance of prophetic inspiration, *Krieg* (War) by Carl Hauptmann (1858-1921), which was written in 1913 and published early in 1914. The author cannot be classified as an expressionist; he belonged to the older generation, and his earlier plays alternated between naturalism and symbolism, very much like those of his younger and more famous brother Gerhart Hauptmann. Nevertheless, *Krieg* showed a distinct approach to Expressionism. The whole action, centring on a devastating European war, has, for all its realistic detail, a visionary nature. A note of unreality is struck from the outset: in the old-world setting of a German castle, an international gathering is in progress; but the guests have animal heads, symbolizing the various European nations. The meeting soon degenerates into a heated argument in which each power puts forward its territorial claims. While the dispute continues, an archangel strides down the village street and, through the mouth of a poor miner, announces the coming of war.

The war scenes themselves have a strangely anachronistic touch: the author's vision is still determined by the wars of the past, with their pitched battles and bivouac fires. The demon of war appears, in the mask of Napoleon, standing on a triumphal chariot drawn by frantic crowds. The last act shows the world plunged into utter desolation; the survivors dwell in earth holes, greedily digging for relics of the past and living in constant fear of one another. Yet a faint message of hope rings out at the end. A hermit is seen building a temple; a group of women, bearing their children on their arms, approach it, followed by a procession of cripples. The closing lines are spoken by one of these women as she holds out her new-born child with a fervent prayer:

> The new morrow is here . . . oh Lord, instill from Thy great and gracious heart into this child's blood love for this poor, beautiful earth. . . .

This remarkable play reflects strikingly the tension and foreboding that marked the years immediately preceding 1914. The final message of love and reconciliation sounds a note that was to become the dominant chord of revolutionary drama. Carl Hauptmann not only anticipated in his vision the universal cataclysm of the Great War, but foresaw the faint ray of light which illumed its end.

One of the first published plays to voice a clear protest against the war was *Jeremias* (1917) by Stefan Zweig (1881-1942). A native of Vienna, Zweig followed in the wake of Hofmannsthal and Schnitzler and won international fame through his work as a novelist and historical biographer. His cosmopolitan mind was deeply roused by the folly of war – a feeling which found expression in *Jeremias*, his only important dramatic work. The biblical subject of the play served ·merely as a guise for its real theme. The drama is in nine scenes, starting with the outbreak of war against the Assyrians and ending with the destruction of Jerusalem. The only fully developed character is the prophet himself, who dominates each scene with his eloquent soliloquies and exhortations. All the others – his mother, the king, officials, priests and the people of Jerusalem – are no more than accompanying voices of a chorus. This concentration on one character serving as the author's mouthpiece stamps the work as expressionist. The language, closely modelled on the Scriptures, is couched in a florid, figurative prose, rising in the more emotional passages to irregular metre and rhymed verse. The course of events, while following the biblical account, reflects the contemporary war. In the opening scenes, the Jewish people are roused by the leaders of the war party. Jeremiah raises his voice in emphatic protest:

> But I say unto you, people of Jerusalem, war is a wild and wicked beast, he eats the flesh from the strong and sucks the marrow from the mighty ones, he crushes the cities between his jaws and with his hoofs he tramples the land. He who rouses him cannot put him to sleep, and he who draws the sword might easily fall upon it himself.

The prophet suffers martyrdom for his belief; he is thrown into a dungeon by the king whom he has in vain implored to make peace. Eventually, the city's resistance is broken by famine, and the people turn against the 'warmongers'. Jeremiah, freed from his prison, accuses each and all of a common guilt:

> Those who now cry peace I heard clamouring for war, and those who now abuse the king hailed him joyfully. . . . You have debauched yourselves with war, bear you now its fruit!

Deeply stirred by the plight of the people, Jeremiah changes from a prophet of wrath to a herald of love. He sets out at the head of the Jews on their march into exile. In his last rhapsodic speeches, he preaches the gospel of brotherhood and of redemption through suffering. Defeat, he proclaims, is a blessing bestowed by God to purify the hearts of men.

Because of its outspoken pacifist tendency, the play was first produced in Zürich, in 1917, though it was widely read in Germany and Austria.

It was another Austrian author, Karl Kraus (1874-1936), who wrote what was undoubtedly the most comprehensive denunciation of the war in dramatic form. His *Die letzten Tage der Menschheit* (The Last Days of Mankind, published completely in 1922), is, of course, not a drama in the accepted sense – it has, in fact, never been performed. Its *dramatis personae*, of whom there are many hundreds, are to a large extent real people, including well-known statesmen, generals, writers, actors and journalists of the period; its time of action is from 1914 to 1918; its setting the streets, cafés, offices, theatres of Vienna, army headquarters and the trenches, in short, a cross-section of the world at war. The whole work is largely based on documented fact. As a drama, it lacks any development or climax save that implicit in the subject itself. Yet so powerful is the intrinsic dramatic momentum of events that the play produces the effect of tragedy in the full sense of the word.

For the most part, the drama is realistic in the extreme: the scenes of action are precisely specified; the language reproduces accurately the particular idiom of every social stratum. But there are also unmistakable expressionist elements: the cast includes a large number of mere types, designated by their professions, qualities, or incidental functions, such as Optimist, Patriot, Subscriber, a Regular, or even Old and Young, The Public, etc. Only the epilogue, entitled *The Last Night*, completely transcends the realistic plane. It is throughout in verse and replaces all individual characters by unnamed types – Dying Soldier, Gasmask, a Blinded Man, and supernatural Voices from Above and from Below.

Despite its poignant sense of tragedy, the work is primarily a satire. Karl Kraus, who in his one-man periodical *Die Fackel* (The Torch) had carried on a relentless fight against corruption in public life and, in particular, the Press, saw in the war an outgrowth of a civilization run riot. One of its main causes was the deliberate incitement and deception of the masses by the Press. Many of the characters perpetually re-echo clichés from the daily papers, incapable of experiencing the war otherwise than through the medium of 'printed words':

> The printed words have enabled depraved humanity to commit atrocities they can no longer imagine. . . . Everything that happens happens only for those who describe it and for those who do not experience it.

In the face of unspeakable horrors, life goes on as usual, with material profit and shallow dissipation as its sole objects. An atmosphere of fatalism prevails throughout the drama. No reference is made to any positive factor working for the future: even the end of the war, in the author's view, will not bring about a regeneration of mankind. The only sane voice is that of the author himself who speaks through the mouth of the *Nörgler* (grumbler). This character, a kind of *raisonneur* making his scathing comments, is the only one to see through the fallacy of war. However, he remains a passive onlooker who registers and laments the calamity without offering any constructive idea of how to overcome it. Several times, he invokes God as the supreme authority above the depraved world. But God, too, is merely a passive spectator of the evil which He was powerless to prevent and for which He bears no responsibility. The drama actually ends with the Voice of God speaking words attributed to the Austrian emperor at the outbreak of war: '*Ich habe es nicht gewollt!*' (I didn't want this to happen!).

It is in the epilogue, *Die letzte Nacht*, that realism is superseded by an approach to expressionist form. This epilogue sums up the argument of the drama, symbolizing the cataclysm of the war in a sequence of visions, and ending with the total destruction of the world through an invasion from Mars. In keeping with the playwright's negative attitude, no other solution is conceivable than universal doom – a transcendental day of judgment.

Die letzten Tage der Menschheit stands out as a unique attempt to show up the corrupting effects of the Great War. It contents itself with a resigned fatalism, without pointing a way to a new conception of social and moral values. Such a way is indicated only in those plays that rise above the mere depiction of facts to an appeal for the spiritual regeneration of man – that is, in the expressionist war plays. Of these, Reinhard Goering's *Seeschlacht* is one of the first eminent examples.

Seeschlacht (Naval Battle), published in 1917, was the first play of Reinhard Goering (1887-1936) and remained his only important work. The play is in a single act, set in the gunturret of a battleship before and during the battle of Jutland. The cast consists of seven unnamed sailors who are killed to the last man during the battle. The dialogue is in short, irregular verse, rising from wistful reflection to passionate outburst. The drama opens on the quiet conversation of the sailors, their nostalgic memories of peace, and their vague presentiment of imminent battle. Their attitude is fatalistic; they do not

question the right or wrong of war but resign themselves to
their fate:

> What else is there for us
> but to do our work
> as it falls to us?

The central scene is an argument between the first and the fifth
sailor on the problem of obedience, leading up to a first dim
conception of rebellion. The fifth sailor realizes the tragedy of
war:

> For two years has the merry song been silent.
> For two years we have been drifting on the waters,
> blind and obsessed, killing, dying.
> None remembers anything else,
> none knows of anything
> but killing and dying.

Step by step, he rises to the first clear denunciation of war,
springing from his realization that

> there are things between man and man
> which to achieve
> is a duty more sacred
> than any other fight.

The argument culminates in the fifth sailor's resolution to
disobey battle orders. But at the very moment when he sets
out to stir his comrades to mutiny, enemy ships are sighted, and
the battle is joined. One after another, the sailors are hit.
Finally, an explosion wrecks the gun-turret. The play closes
with a question, raised by the dying fifth sailor:

> I've fired well, what?
> I would also have mutinied well, what?
> But firing was easier, what?
> was obviously easier?

The idea of mutiny is once more lost in the fever of battle.

The war is conceived as a superhuman force, embodied in the battleship to which the sailors are bound as mere automatons, without a chance of resistance or escape. The whole work has the sweep and force of ancient tragedy, with its dominant idea of inexorable fate.

Reinhard Goering tried to recapture the qualities of *Seeschlacht* in a sequel, *Scapa Flow* (1919), but failed. This play glorifies the scuttling of the German fleet after the surrender; it is virtually one long lament for the lost fatherland. The revolutionary urge gives way to nostalgic retrospection. The rest of Goering's production consisted of a play *Die Retter* (The Saviours, 1919), with a distinctly anti-revolutionary bias, and, after a silence of more than ten years, a dramatization of Captain Scott's last expedition, *Die Südpolexpedition des Kapitän Scott* (1930).

The revolutionary impulse is far more outspoken in another play published in 1917, Walter Hasenclever's *Antigone*. Hasenclever had made his name before the war with his play *Der Sohn*, one of the first expressionist dramas.'[1] In 1915, he had produced in *Der Retter* (The Saviour) what must be one of the earliest plays expressing opposition to the war. Here the Poet, roused by an apparition of St. Paul, sets out to preach the gospel of love and human brotherhood in the trenches. The ideas expressed in this play are fully developed in his *Antigone*. It is illuminating to compare Hasenclever's re-creation of the Greek legend with Anouilh's, written during the Second World War in occupied France. While Anouilh concentrates on the personal drama of the heroine who defies tyranny, Hasenclever's attention is focussed on the social aspects of the story. He uses the ancient myth merely as a pretext to proclaim his message of peace and raise the call for revolution. The revolutionary attitude is apparent in the very order of the *dramatis personae*: the People of Thebes head

[1] Cf. pp. 119f.

the list, followed by the king and the other characters. The stage, too, is divided into two levels, the back representing the 'scene of the king', while the foreground is reserved for 'the people'. The play presents a perfect example of the expressionist style: the language, austere and sparing, is shorn of all poetical adornments and occasionally rises to impassioned outbursts, always with the sole intent of conveying the author's message.

When the play opens, a war has ended in victory, and Creon is proclaimed king of Thebes. He is characterized as a ruthless autocrat, and is evidently intended as a portrait of Wilhelm II. Some of his utterances clearly allude to sayings of the Kaiser:

> God has given me majesty
> That I may lead you worthily,
> To Him alone I am accountable!
> Whoever opposes me shall be crushed!

He calls upon the people to prepare for new wars:

> Arm for new deeds!
> We are surrounded by enemies.
> Only the strong will conquer the world.

The great majority of the people are opposed to war. In a vague and as yet undirected spirit of rebellion, their dissatisfaction turns upon the 'rich'. However, the threatened revolt is quelled by brutal force.

The action follows, in outline, the drama of Sophocles. Antigone, defying the king's order, buries her brother and is sentenced to death. Her action, springing from a simple human impulse, becomes a symbol of universal love. Her call 'All men are brethren!' rings out to the masses, stirring them to revolution. In vivid images, she depicts the horrors of war and urges the people to resist any incitement to military glory. She accuses herself of having lived in luxury while others were starving. To the king's face, she announces the end of the reign of power and the dawn of a new world of freedom:

> Your power has passed. Your world is no longer.

The first to be converted by her appeal is the king's son who is betrothed to Antigone and kills himself beside her body. His death has a wider significance:

> The first man of the new earth
> Has been converted at her grave.

Creon himself, shaken by a vision of the war he has unleashed, resigns the throne of his own free will, and sets forth to atone for his crimes:

> The day has come when the barriers fall,
> When the king is one with the people
> Before the throne of Justice.

The masses surge forward to establish the new world of freedom and peace, led by a humble 'man of the people':

> Palaces totter. Power is at an end.
> Those who are great fall into the abyss.
> Those who have owned lose everything.
> The slave in the sweat of his hands
> Is richer than they.
> Follow me! I shall lead you.
> The wind rises from the ruins,
> The new world dawns.

This closing scene of the play, though written at the height of the war, strangely foreshadowed the mood prevailing at its end. At its numerous performances in the immediate post-war years, the drama was acclaimed as a revolutionary manifesto.

Along with *Der Sohn*, *Antigone* remained the most important achievement of Hasenclever. In the following years, he spent his talent in experiments which carried the expressionist manner to the point of absurdity. In *Die Menschen* (Men,

1918) the dialogue is reduced to bare exclamations while the dramatic action is relegated to stage-directions – a device approaching the silent film. Each character utters only two or three words indicating his profession: the gambler – 'the bank', the worker –'strike', the prostitute – 'lilac silk', the prosecutor – 'death sentence', and so on. The action is purely symbolic: a murdered man rises from his grave, intent on expiating the crime committed against him. He is himself accused of the deed and is sentenced to death. When he returns to his grave, the real murderer, converted, exclaims, 'I love!' This staccato technique, which leaves everything to the imagination, is carried on in *Jenseits* (Beyond, 1920), a metaphysical play enacted by two characters. The 'new man' comes to the conclusion that only in death can he rise to the realm of pure thought. In a later play, *Mord* (Murder, 1926), expressionist and realistic elements are strangely mixed. The case of a man wrongly accused of murder serves to denounce the legal system, the state, and society in general.

This was Hasenclever's last attempt at serious drama. Like many of the expressionist playwrights, he turned to conventional comedy, in which he achieved a measure of success: *Ein besserer Herr* (Man of Distinction, 1926), *Ehen werden im Himmel geschlossen* (Marriages are Made in Heaven, 1928), *Napoleon greift ein* (Napoleon Intervenes, 1930). He, too, fell a victim to Nazi persecution. Driven out of Germany in 1933, he committed suicide in a French internment camp in 1940.

The denunciation of war and the call for a new world rising from the ruins were generally inspired by a fervent belief in the fundamental goodness of man. This idea found expression in the very title of Leonhard Frank's famous book, *Der Mensch ist gut* (Man is Good), written in 1916-1917, which came to be regarded as one of the main literary documents of the revolution. The same idea inspired a large number of plays written round about the year 1918; but constant repetition soon debased it to a hackneyed formula, derisively termed 'O *Mensch*' drama. In the best examples, however, the underlying impulse was undoubtedly genuine. This is true in particular of the works of three playwrights who have come to be representative of German expressionist drama – Fritz von Unruh, Ernst Toller, and Georg Kaiser.

IV. FRITZ VON UNRUH

The year 1917 saw the publication of yet another anti-war play of importance, *Ein Geschlecht* by Fritz von Unruh (1885-). This work put its author into the front rank of expressionist playwrights. Following the traditions of his class – he was the scion of an aristocratic Prussian family – Unruh became an officer in a distinguished lancer regiment. Both in his origin and mental make-up, he showed a certain likeness to Heinrich von Kleist, the pre-eminent Prussian dramatist – an affinity of which he himself was clearly aware. But unlike Kleist, he underwent a radical change by breaking away, under the impact of the war, from the traditions in which he had been reared. His first two plays, *Offiziere* (Officers, 1912) and *Louis Ferdinand Prinz von Preussen* (1913), showed him still in harmony with his inherited set of values. The first is a vivid picture of garrison life in peace-time, with the officers thirsting for a chance to go into action. The second has as its central figure the highly gifted nephew of Frederick the Great, Prince Louis Ferdinand, who was killed in action in 1806, on the eve of the battle of Jena. In Unruh's play, it is the prince who persuades the irresolute king to declare war on Napoleon, in order to save the honour of Prussia. The conflict underlying both plays is between duty and insubordination – a typical Kleistean issue. Despite their prevailing realism, their consistently high emotional pitch foreshadows Unruh's subsequent turn to Expressionism.

The vital transformation was wrought by the war in which

Unruh took an active part as a cavalry officer. This transformation evidently took place at a very early date, for the first work reflecting it, a dramatic poem *Vor der Entscheidung* (Before the Decision), was written in October 1914. Though indifferent as a work of art, it reveals the conflict between the author's inbred convictions and his direct experience of war. The hero (an obvious self-portrait), deeply stirred by the horrors he has witnessed, awakens to a new conception of the brotherhood of man. The work is cast in highly emotive verse, and the scenes have a dream-like, visionary quality. In the world of shadows, the hero encounters the symbols of his former life, the tombs of the Prussian kings and the figure of Kleist. Renouncing the spirit of hate, he returns to earth to impart his message of love to the soldiers. Finally, the sun rises over the battlefield, announcing the dawn of a new world.

Unruh's denunciation of war found its full expression in his one-act tragedy, *Ein Geschlecht* (A Race, 1917). In its lofty grandeur and its concentration on a small set of characters, members of one family, the work aspires to the spirit and form of classical drama. The action, set on a hill-top overlooking the battlefield, unfolds within a single night; it is 'tied to no particular period'. The language, cast in rhetorical blank verse, is sustained throughout at a highly emotional level.

The play opens at nightfall outside a graveyard. The Mother, assisted by the Daughter and the Youngest Son, has just buried her favourite son killed in battle. A military detachment brings her two remaining sons in chains, both guilty of insubordination and due to be executed in the morning. They have disobeyed orders for different reasons: one has deserted out of cowardice, while the other has committed an outrage from sheer physical exuberance. This eldest son rises in revolt – but it is a revolt without any definite aim, actuated merely by a self-centred desire to 'live' to the full. He tries to commit incest with his sister, then turns against his mother, and finishes up by jumping to his death from the cemetery wall. By this very action, he brings about the spiritual transformation of the Mother. It is she who becomes the herald of a new age, calling to the mothers of the world to rise against the powers of darkness:

> *Wie können wir den Wahnsinn weiter dulden,*
> *der diesen Bau der Menschheit, den wir schufen,*
> *sinnlos zerschlägt und in die Gräber schleift!*
>
> How can we go on suffering this madness
> Which shatters senselessly and drags to the grave
> The edifice of man that we created!

When the soldiers arrive to take away her son's body, she stands in their way and snatches the staff of office from one of the commanders. Raising it aloft, she pronounces her message of love and hope:

> *O Mutterleib, o Leib, so wild verflucht*
> *und aller Greuel tiefster Anlass erst,*
> *Du sollst das Herz im Bau des Weltalls werden*
> *und ein Geschlecht aus deiner Wonne bilden,*
> *das herrlicher als Ihr den Stab gebraucht! –*
>
> O mother-womb, o womb so wildly cursed,
> and deepest source of all atrocities,
> thou shalt become the core of the universe
> and from thy ecstasy create a race
> that wields the staff more gloriously than they!

The Mother is killed by the commanders. But her message is taken up by the youngest son who rouses the soldiers to rebellion and leads them down into the plain. The last lines are spoken by the two commanders: the one follows the soldiers to maintain discipline and law, while the other casts off his red cloak, the symbol of authority, leaving it to bleach in the sun of the new day.

Ein Geschlecht, for all its immature extravagance, expresses more powerfully than any other work of the period the emotional upheaval and the fervent hope for a new world rising from the war. This hope was not conceived in terms of social or political change but as a purely spiritual rebirth. The play was designed to form the first part of a trilogy; the second was *Platz*, published in 1920.

Platz (Square) dealt with the problems arising from the accomplished revolution; but it lacked the dramatic power and unity of its predecessor and failed to make a similar impact. The action carries on where *Ein Geschlecht* left off; the scene is transferred to a public square flanked by stately buildings – a symbol of the old established order. The central character is the younger son who is now named Dietrich. He appears at the head of the rebellious soldiers, intent on overthrowing the old order and setting up the new world founded on love and human brotherhood. In this purpose he is thwarted by the exponents of the past, represented by three characters with symbolic names: the Overlord stands for the outdated order based on authority; Count Gutundblut (Blood-and-Honour) for the 'nobility of the sword', while Schleich (Sneak) is the opportunist who exploits the revolution for his own ends. Dietrich is diverted from his mission by his love for two women who personify spiritual and sensual love respectively. After a prolonged mental struggle which forms the main part of the play, he decides for Irene, the embodiment of spiritual love. He even renounces his leadership, realizing that the new order cannot achieve perfection unless it is founded on the love of man and woman. From this love there would spring the 'new man' who would attain the ultimate goal, the regeneration of mankind.

The accomplishment of this final task was to be the subject of the concluding part of the trilogy; this part, however, was never written. Most likely Unruh realized the incompatibility of his vision with the hard facts of reality. Moreover, the initial impetus of the revolution had meanwhile subsided, and with it the taste for expressionist drama in its extreme form.

In his post-expressionist works, Unruh maintained his missionary zeal. He belonged to that 'lost generation' which was never able to rid itself of the memories of the Great War. In a festival play *Heinrich von Andernach*, written for the millenary celebrations of the Rhineland in 1925, he evoked the spirit of the Unknown Soldier, admonishing the nations to desist from their unceasing strife. During the last years of the Weimar Republic, Unruh tried his hand at more realistic plays, though with little success. After a historical play, *Bonaparte* (1927), he wrote a comedy, *Phaea* (1930) about an ex-officer who tries to proclaim the message of peace through the medium of the film. His idealism, however, is thwarted by the purely commercial interests of the film producers. Realizing the futility of his efforts, he withdraws in despair – a poignant parallel to Unruh's own position in the post-war world.

In 1933, Unruh left Germany for the United States; after the war, he returned for a short time without, however, succeeding in re-establishing his position as a writer.

Fritz von Unruh was the leading representative of the idealistic and visionary side of Expressionism. He was not concerned with social and political revolution but with the spiritual rebirth of man from within. His fervent pacifism had the militant note of the former Prussian officer; at his best, he had something of the white-hot idealism of the young Schiller or Kleist. But his power of translating his vision into convincing character and action was too weak to produce a work of lasting value. Thus his plays have faded with the hour that inspired them.

V. ERNST TOLLER

Ernst Toller (1893–1939) has come to be more widely known outside Germany than any of the other expressionist playwrights. This is due not so much to his superior stature as to the fact that his works proved more easily translatable and lent themselves to definite political interpretation. In contrast to Unruh, Toller was the chief exponent of the political side of Expressionism. His main theme, too, was the revolt against the old order which brought about the war, and the proclamation of a new age of love and human brotherhood. But he treated it in terms of social and political reorganization; his approach, for all its emotional impulse, was predominantly intellectual. Moreover, he took an active part in the political struggle during the immediate post-war years.

At the outbreak of war, Toller, then twenty-one years old, joined the army as a volunteer. Fighting in the front line, he underwent, like so many others, a profound transformation and was released from active service owing to a physical break-down. In Munich, he joined the extreme Left and was imprisoned for his pacifist views. During this imprisonment, in 1917-1918, he wrote his first play, *Die Wandlung* (Transfiguration, 1919).

Both in its content and form, this play is typically expressionist, unfolding as it does in a sequence of *Stationen* (stages), which denote the spiritual evolution of the hero towards a new conception of life and society. The drama is enacted on two different levels, realistic and symbolic. While the realistic scenes present the hero's actual experiences, the symbolic ones depict the workings of his subconscious mind. The theme of the play is the gradual conversion, under the impact of war, of an ardent patriot into a revolutionary leader. At the beginning Friedrich (as he is called) is seen in his home, in violent conflict with the older generation, his mother and an uncle. When war breaks out, he welcomes it as a release from the drudgery of an aimless life, and enlists as a volunteer. The following 'dream-picture', however, shows a troop train full of dead soldiers in one of whom we recognize Friedrich. Throughout the play the dream-pictures, alternating with the realistic scenes, present the hero one step ahead of his actual experience. For instance, he is shown wounded in hospital, receiving a war medal for his heroic conduct. In the corresponding dream-scene, wounded soldiers are seen in a hospital where Death, in the guise of a surgeon, demonstrates on skeletons. The following scene marks the turning-point: Friedrich is working on a sculpture representing Victory when two war cripples approach him. The sight of them moves him so deeply that he smashes the statue and sets out to rouse humanity from its apathy. A sequence of dream-pictures symbolizes his mental struggle in search of the ideal. Finally, he pronounces his message to a crowd gathered in a public square:

> You are all of you no longer men and women; you are distorted images of your real selves. And yet you could still be men and women, still be human, if only you had faith in yourselves and in humanity, if only you would grant the spirit fulfilment. . . .

His concluding words sound the clarion-call of revolution:

> Go to your rulers and proclaim to them with the organ tone of a million voices that their power is but illusion. Go to the soldiers and tell them to beat their swords into ploughshares. Go to the rich and show them their hearts, their hearts that were buried alive under the rubbish. . . . Now march! March forward in the light of day!

> (Tr. E. Crankshaw)

His appeal stirs the masses who join in a rousing song of revolution.

Die Wandlung, immediately preceding the revolution of 1918, marked the climax of the anti-war movement, the point where it materialized in the actual overthrow of the old régime and the establishment of a new order. The following plays of Toller were milestones on the way this new order took from its initial struggles to its eventual eclipse in disillusionment and failure.

Masse Mensch (1920) and *Die Maschinenstürmer* (1922) were written during Toller's second imprisonment in a Bavarian fortress to which he was sentenced for his part in the Munich communist rising of 1919. Of these two plays, the first was purely expressionist, while the second marked a return to a more realistic form. But their fundamental theme is much the same, namely, the conflict between the inspired leader and the materialistic masses who fail to live up to his lofty vision and, eventually, turn against him.

In *Masse Mensch* (Masses and Man), this theme is presented through an abstract plot enacted by anonymous types, the Woman, the Husband, the Nameless One. The dramatic pattern is almost identical with that of *Die Wandlung*, consisting of alternating realistic and symbolic scenes. The central character is the Woman who, though a member of the middle class, has joined the revolutionary movement. Her husband, a stern exponent of the old order, tries in vain to win her back to her former way of life. In the first part, the war is still raging. The close connection between war and capitalism, as seen from the Marxist viewpoint, finds vivid expression in a dream-scene where stockbrokers buy and sell war bonds and, when the war is lost, perform a macabre dance round the exchange desk. The Woman calls upon the masses to abstain from work in order to stop the war, but is opposed by the Nameless One who incites the people to active revolution. When she objects, he denounces her as a bourgeoise:

> The individual, his feeling and his conscience,
> What do they count?
> The masses count!

The second part deals with the civil war which follows. Violent street battles rage between the revolutionaries and the army. Once again the Woman and the Nameless One stand on opposite sides: the latter, representing the masses, cold-bloodedly orders the fight to continue, irrespective of the loss of life, while the Woman is torn by doubt:

> Did I not cry to heaven against war
> Yesterday – and to-day
> Suffer my brothers to be done to death?
>
> (Tr. Vera Mendel)

The revolution fails, and reaction triumphs. The heroine is arrested. In the last scene, her husband comes to offer her freedom. She rejects him, but she also refuses to be liberated by the Nameless One at the price of killing a prison guard. In this last dialogue, the contrast between her idealism and the materialism of the masses is clearly defined. To the rigid dictum of the Nameless One, 'Our cause comes first!' she retorts. 'Man comes first!' – The Woman is led away to be executed. But her death causes a change of heart in two fellow-creatures: as the volley rings out, two female prisoners, about to grab some of her belongings, drop their spoil and fall on their knees, stammering, 'Sister, why do we do such things?'

A problem only touched upon in *Masse Mensch* forms the main issue of *Die Maschinenstürmer* (The Machine-Wreckers) – man versus machine. The play is based on the revolt of the English Luddites in 1815, the characters have individual, partly historical names: altogether the work approaches a more realistic style.

The protagonist, Jimmy Cobbet, fulfils the role of the Woman in *Masse Mensch*. He, too, has a middle-class background; he, too, is eventually denounced by the masses as an intellectual. The Woman's husband has a parallel in Jimmy's brother, who has worked his way up and now holds an important position in the factory of Ure, the plutocrat. The spokesman of the masses, corresponding to the Nameless One, is John Wible, who incites the workers to violence. At a meeting in Wible's house, the antagonism between him and

Cobbet reaches a climax. The former stirs the assembly with his cry, 'Death ·to the machine! War to the tyrant steam!' whereas Cobbet accepts the machine as an irrevocable stage in man's progress: 'I know that the machine is our inevitable lot – our destiny.' He advocates a new conception of the machine instead of its destruction. His appeal culminates in the cry, 'Man shall rule, not machinery!'

The pivot of the drama is Cobbet's clash with Ure, the exponent of capitalism. Cobbet propounds his idea of a just social order, founded on the brotherhood of mankind. Ure, impressed by his appeal, offers him an influential position. Cobbet declines in order to remain faithful to his mission. Finally, he falls a victim to his idealism: he is killed by the very men he hoped to liberate. The last act is laid in a factory, illustrating, in a scene of lurid realism, the enslavement of the workers by the machine. Rioters enter to wreck the machinery. Incited by their leader, John Wible, they denounce Cobbet as a traitor and kill him. However, in the closing lines, his message finds an echo in the words of an old weaver as he stands over the body: 'We must be good to one another.' As in *Masse Mensch*, the prophet's death kindles a spark in the soul of a fellow-man.

Toller's reversion to a realistic style – in line with the general trend of German drama – was taken a step further in his play *Hinkemann* (1922). This belonged to a type of play much in vogue in the immediate post-war years, the so-called *Heimkehrer* drama, depicting the return of a soldier from the war and his inability to adjust himself to civilian life. It fully reflected the cynicism and moral anarchy into which the revolution had degenerated. A show-man in a suburban fair-ground sums up with brutal cynicism the spirit of the times:

> Peep-show 'the horrors of war' won't earn sixpence. Nowadays Progress is the word. Hundred per cent profit in it. Got to make good nowadays. That's the spirit of the age. Whatever you do make a success of it. . . .

Against this background unfolds the drama of the ex-soldier who has lost his virility through a war injury. Hinkemann sees in this physical defect a symbol of his time:

> I am a mere laughing-stock, and so is everything else in our time – as miserable and ridiculous as I am. The world has lost its soul, and I have lost my sex.

Embittered by his suffering, he reproaches men for their callousness and apathy. In one scene, reality is transcended: in a sequence of nightmarish visions, a cross-section of the contemporary world unfolds before Hinkemann – war cripples singing martial songs, revolutionaries storming barricades, news-vendors crying out sensational headlines, and so on. The play ends in utter despair, with Hinkemann lamenting the futility of war and the apathy of men:

> The war came and took them and they hated their chiefs and obeyed orders and killed each other. And it's all forgotten. They'll be taken again and kill each other. Again and again. That's what people are. They might be different if they wanted to. But they don't want to. They mock at life. They scourge it and spit upon it and crucify life.

> (Tr. Vera Mendel)

In terms of the theatre, *Hinkemann* was probably Toller's most successful work. Here for once he contrived to create live characters instead of mere abstractions. Hinkemann, the clumsy, inarticulate ex-soldier lost in a hostile world, is anything but an inspired prophet, like the heroes of Toller's earlier plays: he is a plain man of the people whose protest springs from real suffering and a dim perception of life's injustice.

The process of disillusionment reached its nadir in *Hoppla, wir leben!* (Such is Life, 1927), the last play in which Ernst Toller tried to present a comprehensive picture of the political scene in post-war Germany. This play was designed for the

5. UNRUH, *Ein Geschlecht*. Berlin, 1918 (design: Ernst Stern)

6. TOLLER, *Die Wandlung*. Berlin, 1919

stage of Erwin Piscator, making full use of such technical devices as film, loudspeaker, simultaneous scenes, etc. Despite an introductory note, 'The action takes place in many countries, eight years after the suppression of a rebellion', the play reflects faithfully the contemporary German scene: the association of the government with plutocratic and reactionary forces, the general materialistic outlook, the growing menace of a nationalist counter-revolution. The central figure is Karl Thomas, a former revolutionary who has spent eight years in the isolation of a mental home. His chief antagonist is Kilman, a former comrade who saved his own life by betraying the revolution and has since risen to the position of a minister of state. The confrontation of these two men, the idealist and the opportunist, reveals the gulf dividing the lofty idealism of 1918 from the cynical realism of 1927. Broken by his experiences, Thomas comes to the conclusion that he is out of place in the present world: 'I sometimes think I belong to a generation that has vanished.' To shatter the general apathy by a striking action, he plans to kill the minister who, he feels, has betrayed the revolution. In this intention he is, however, anticipated by a nationalist fanatic who manages to escape, while Thomas is arrested as the assassin. In prison he commits suicide, despairing of mankind.

Hoppla, wir leben! presents a vivid picture of the political and moral state of Germany in the late twenties. It also reveals the limitations of Toller's range: like most of the expressionist writers, he was unable to outgrow the vital experiences of his life – the war and the revolution of 1918. Accordingly, he passed judgment upon a world which was moving further and further away from these events. Nothing could illustrate his case better than the story of a man who has spent the intervening years in enforced isolation and awakes to find himself in a changed world.

This retrospective attitude was also borne out by a later play,

Feuer aus den Kesseln (Draw the Fires!, 1930), which deals with the abortive naval mutiny of 1917. Toller called it 'a historical play'. The change he had undergone is clearly indicated by a comparison between this play and those written under the direct impact of war and revolution. There is no trace left of expressionist passion, no lofty vision of a future world founded on love. Instead, the theme is presented in a realistic and matter-of-fact style, the characters appear under their real names, among them such historical personages as Admiral von Scheer, Scheidemann and Liebknecht. The action begins with the battle of Jutland in the summer of 1916 and ends with the execution, in 1917, of the two ringleaders of a mutiny among German sailors. But their message is taken up a few months later when, in November 1918, the sailors at Kiel refuse to obey orders and thus give the signal for the revolution.

Feuer aus den Kesseln was the last work of Ernst Toller reflecting the political history of Germany during and after the First World War. A play *Die blinde Göttin* (The Blind Goddess, 1932), based on a notorious court case of the time, challenged the soulless mechanism of the judicial system. The plot centres on a pair of lovers convicted on false evidence of having killed the man's wife. After five years of prison, the verdict is revoked, and both are released. But their sufferings have broken their spirit and killed their love. (An English version of this play, written in collaboration with the Irish playwright Denis Johnston, appeared under the title *Blind Man's Buff*, 1938).

Ernst Toller was the foremost exponent of what may be called the Left wing of the expressionist movement, i.e. that group of writers who conceived the spiritual upheaval in terms of social revolution. It is mainly owing to this direct political appeal that his plays have become better known outside Germany than those of any other expressionist. These plays – in particular the five ranging from *Die Wandlung*, in

1918, to *Hoppla, wir leben!*, in 1927, present a broad picture of the political history of Germany during that decade, as seen from the communist viewpoint. Their protagonists – from the youthful hero, Friedrich, in *Die Wandlung*, who is roused by the war to a new conception of social responsibility, to Thomas in *Hoppla, wir leben!* who ends his own life in despair – reflect the mental development of their author through these crucial years. Toller's own suicide in a New York hotel room, on the eve of the Second World War, sealed the tragedy of his life.

VI. GEORG KAISER

Georg Kaiser (1878-1945) was undoubtedly the leading playwright of German Expressionism. He alone contrived to mould its chaotic elements into a balanced and consistent form, re-uniting, as it were, its diffuse components in a new organic whole. Except in a few plays, he ignored the usual loose pattern of expressionist drama, adopting a solid construction in three or five acts, built with mathematical precision. The explosive force of expressionist fervour was counterpoised by his sense of proportion, akin to the spirit of modern architecture.

This mastery of dramatic form was partly due to the fact that Kaiser, unlike most of the expressionist writers, had reached full maturity when he came into prominence. He was in his fortieth year when the performance of *Die Bürger von Calais*, in 1917, carried him to fame overnight. At that time, he had already published a number of plays, although they attracted little attention. The peak of his career coincided with the full tide of the expressionist movement, that is, the years 1917-1923, when his plays were produced in rapid succession on all the major stages of Germany. After that, his amazing productivity continued, with varying success, until his exile in 1938, and further on, to his death in 1945. During all these years, he refused to yield to the change of literary fashion but sustained the moral passion of Expressionism, long after the movement had run its course.

Kaiser's dramatic output, amounting to more than fifty plays, includes every variety of style and subject-matter – social drama, comedy, farce, romance, legend and history. This bewildering diversity caused him to be regarded, by some of his critics, as merely a skilful concoctor of effective stage plays. However, on closer examination, this variety reduces itself to two or three basic themes which recur with an almost obsessive insistence. Kaiser himself claimed one single idea or 'vision' to underly all his works; he called it *die Erneuerung des Menschen* (the regeneration of man). With this dominant creative impulse, he proved himself a true exponent of Expressionism.

Like all expressionist drama, Kaiser's plays are plays of ideas. But unlike Ibsen or Shaw, he does not attempt to create a semblance of reality and psychologically convincing characters. His *dramatis personae* are types: shorn of any individual subtleties, they are embodiments of ideas pure and simple. Frequently he points to Plato's dialogue as the supreme model of drama. 'Plato', he writes, 'formulates his ideas in the shape of dialogues; characters enter and speak.' And again, 'To write a drama is to follow a thought to its conclusion.' He scorns the conventional stage play with its petty sex conflicts which he dismisses as '*Anlässe für erbärmliche Spannungen*' (incidents for contemptible thrills).

Kaiser's peculiar diction is fully adapted to his purpose. While free from the excesses of other expressionists, it is far removed from colloquial language. It sets its own rules of grammar and syntax, contracting to terse dialogue, or rising to flamboyant oratory in moments of high emotion.

Kaiser's early plays, written before 1914, still bore the stamp of Wedekind's and Sternheim's social satires. They were for the most part satirical comedies and must be valued as attempts

to evolve a personal style.[1] They are set among the lower
middle class, and filled with a throng of clerks, shopkeepers,
dried-up schoolmasters, elderly spinsters, with their petty
cares and stuffy living-rooms. But Kaiser did not, like Wedekind, set this social stratum against an underworld of adventurers
and social outcasts; nor did he see salvation in a life of sexual
emancipation. His central idea points in a different direction.
It may be defined as a quest for a fuller and more intense
awareness of 'life'. Man, roused by some trivial experience,
breaks away from his accustomed life of stale conventions and
attains to a higher plane of existence. This idea, containing the
very essence of Kaiser's mature plays, is clearly foreshadowed
in some of the earlier comedies.

Frequently, the external cause of a man's transformation is a
large sum of money that suddenly falls to a humble *petit
bourgeois*, be it the first prize won in a sweepstake or an unexpected legacy. This event flings him out of his daily routine;
it unbalances him to the point of casting him into a mental
vacuum. Often this sudden wealth is connected with a fraud
of some kind. The principal characters involved are in one
way or another engaged in the circulation of money. One is an
employee at a savings-bank, another an agent of a life-insurance
company, a third a post-office clerk. Money passes through
their hands as an abstract quantity, unrelated to their personal
lives. The suddenly acquired fortune, however, offers them
the chance of a new and fuller existence. In these comedies,
the hero ultimately resists the lure of wealth and finds his way
back, recognizing the superior value of security within his
circumscribed world. In *Der mutige Seefahrer* (The Daring
Seafarer, 1925) the hero is expected to sail to America to
obtain a large legacy; at the last moment, he shrinks from

[1] Some of these early works were later re-edited by the author in a slightly different
version, often under another title – a habit which makes the chronology of Kaiser's
plays difficult to ascertain.

the journey, sells his ticket, and thus inadvertently saves his life as the ship is wrecked on the voyage. In *Zwei Krawatten* (Two Ties, 1930), a waiter wins a trip to America on a sweepstake ticket; but he renounces a promising career and returns to his former life. In the last of this series, *Das Los des Ossian Balvesen* (The Lot of Ossian Balvesen, 1936), a post-office clerk who has won the first prize in a lottery has his eyes opened by a philosophical puppet-maker to the value of inner contentment; he tears up the lottery ticket and resumes his place at the counter where he finds satisfaction in the fulfilment of his humble duties.

The deeper implications of the theme, however, are explored in those plays which carry it to a tragic conclusion. This is the case in some of Kaiser's most significant works, written at the peak of his expressionist phase. In these plays, the sudden uprooting of a man from his habitual way of life is seen in a tragic light. In every instance, an ordinary man, stirred by some experience, trifling in itself, 'sets out' on his way to an unknown destination. To his fellow-men, he is a lost soul, a man possessed. But he himself has entered a sphere where the former standards no longer apply. Often this departure is accompanied by some legal offence, a fraud, or even murder, which makes him an outlaw. In these tragic versions of the theme, the rupture is irremediable. When the hero realizes the incompatibility of his quest with reality, suicide offers itself as the only solution. Again, the central characters are, in their normal lives, engaged in some purely mechanical job: in *Von Morgens bis Mitternachts* it is a bank cashier; in *Kanzlist Krehler* an office clerk; in *Nebeneinander* a pawnbroker. The characters no longer bear individual names but are merely types – Cashier, Wife, Daughter, Lady, etc. – the sure stamp of expressionist technique.

The first of this group, *Von Morgens bis Mitternachts* (From Morn till Midnight, 1916) is probably Kaiser's most famous play and, incidentally, the one that made his name known outside Germany. It is a *Stationen* drama, depicting a man's evolution in a succession of stages. A bank cashier, acting on a sudden impulse, abandons his job and his family, absconds with a large sum of money and strives, within the space of a single day, to make up for a lifetime of frustration. This is how he describes his home, surveying it for the last time:

Within four walls – a family life. Comfortable, cosy, contented. The magic of familiar things . . . the household spell. Let it work. Parlour with table and lamp. Window with geraniums. Piano on the right, fireplace. Kitchen, daily bread. Coffee in the morning, chops for dinner. Bedroom, four-poster . . .

In the course of twelve hours, he hurries through various stages, in a frantic quest for a new and intense experience of life. He stakes a huge sum at a bicycle race, merely to relish the frenzy of the crowd; but he leaves disillusioned when the same crowd bows in respectful silence before royalty entering the box. In another scene, he turns in disgust from a public dance-hall where he hoped to buy love with his money. Eventually, he ends up in an assembly hall of the Salvation Army and realizes the vanity of all material values:

You can buy nothing worth having, even with all the money from all the banks in the world. You get less than you pay, every time. The more you spend, the less the goods are worth. Money corrupts them; money veils what is genuine – money is the sorriest fraud of all!

Mounting the platform, he scatters his money to the crowd who instantly start to fight for it. Thoroughly disillusioned, he shoots himself. 'His groaning rattles like an *Ecce* – his breathing hums like *Homo*', runs the last stage direction.

Kanzlist Krehler (Krehler the Clerk, 1922) is a variation on the same theme. But here the hero – a humble clerk –

experiences his transformation within the narrow limits of his home. He is thrown out of his stride by the mere fact that he is sent home from the office for his daughter's wedding. The unaccustomed sight of the streets on a week-day completely unbalances him. He, too, grows estranged from his family and his everyday life: 'Total rupture of time-worn relations. Transformation in a single day.' Without ever leaving the scene of his normal domestic life, he escapes, by a purely mental process, from the confines of his habitual world and attains a more intense awareness of existence. However, he realizes that he is too old to live up to his newly gained insight. He ends by throwing himself from the balcony, in complete mental derangement.

In these two plays, the hero's quest is utterly self-centred. The issue assumes a new aspect in *Nebeneinander* (Side by Side, 1923), one of Kaiser's most arresting plays. Here a man's metamorphosis involves his awakening to a sense of responsibility towards his fellow-men. The action is set against the background of the German inflation, with its harsh contrasts of wealth and poverty. By an ingenious device, three plots run 'side by side', internally connected, but never meeting. In the main plot, the owner of a small pawnshop comes by accident across a letter left in a pawned dinner-jacket: he infers from it that a young girl is about to take her own life. He 'sets out' to save the girl whom he has never seen, but his urgent appeal is dismissed with cynical indifference. At a police station, he seeks help from the law which, he fervently believes, should apply all means at its disposal to save a human life. For him the case has universal significance: 'No letter on earth has ever been as important as this one is! This incident involves each and all! Everyone is now under an obligation!' But his cry falls on deaf ears. Realizing the futility of his search, he returns to his shop and gasses himself. His despair is lit by a ray of hope; he visualizes a future in which his experience will be shared by all:

Might not what has now befallen a wretched pawnbroker be repeated – multiplied a thousand times? To-day it costs my life to ensure what I have gained. It was too early to spend oneself, the others trample upon the seed!

The two other plots centre on the girl who succeeds in finding new happiness, and the callous seducer who has caused her misfortune – both of them completely unaware of the tragedy they have set in motion. In this drama, the self-centred pursuit of a fuller life develops into an ethical challenge, affecting society at large. *Nebeneinander* thus stands on the border-line between the plays which trace the transformation of a solitary individual, and those postulating a regeneration of society. It is in this latter group, containing some of the principal works of Georg Kaiser, that the spiritual impact of the 1918 revolution is most apparent.

This group of social dramas was opened by *Die Bürger von Calais* (The Burghers of Calais, 1914), the first performance of which, in 1917, established Kaiser as the leading playwright of Expressionism. It is, on the surface, a historical play, based on the medieval story of the six burghers of Calais recorded by Froissart. However, the historical incident serves merely as a parable to convey the author's message. In this work, Kaiser's dramatic art reached heights he perhaps never surpassed. The language is fully expressionist, of rich and glowing eloquence. The very grouping and gestures of the characters, as shown in the stage-directions, have a statuesque quality reminiscent of Gothic sculpture. Only the bare outlines of the story are given. The military commander of the beleaguered city has ordered resistance to the last man. Against this order, one of the citizens, Eustache de Saint-Pierre, extols the superior value of constructive work, symbolized by the newly built port. He persuades the citizens to accept the humiliating terms of the enemy and offers himself as the first of six hostages who are to go to the English camp, offering surrender. Others volunteer to join him – but instead of five, six more come forth. A contest ensues as to who should withdraw. The drawing of lots is thwarted by a ruse of Eustache. Finally, to overcome the impasse, he kills himself, thus setting a shining example of self-sacrifice for the common good. Over his body, laid out in the open square, his aged and blind father, in an ecstatic speech, pronounces the universal significance of the deed: 'Go you out into the light, from this night. The great day has dawned – darkness is dispelled.' Here, for the first time in his work, Kaiser's proclamation of the 'new man' rings out with full force: 'I have seen the New Man; in this night he was brought to birth!' – *Die Bürger von Calais* was received, at the height of the war, as an open challenge to the ruling powers, and as an appeal for peace and moral renewal. It was the first outstanding expressionist play to herald the coming revolution.

The full impact of the revolutionary upheaval is reflected in those plays Kaiser published just before and after 1918, above all, in the so-called *Gas* trilogy, comprising *Die Koralle* and the two parts of *Gas*. In these plays, Kaiser's fundamental theme, the regeneration of man, is no longer veiled in a historical guise but presented in terms of contemporary social conflicts. The characters have no individuality whatever but are types designated by their social functions – Billionaire, Engineer, Secretary, Worker, etc. – or by some external attribute – Gentleman in Grey, Lady in Black, Blue and Yellow Figures. The scenes of action are not localized but stand for any of their kind: the industrial plant in *Gas*, for instance, symbolizes industrialism at large; its explosion signifies the destruction of the mechanized world. The principles of typification and generalization, essential features of expressionist drama, are carried to the extreme.

The three plays form a sequence ranging over three generations, very much like Carl Sternheim's trilogy of the Maske

family. But Kaiser's scope reaches far beyond that of Sternheim. Instead of a strictly defined stratum of German pre-war
society, his cycle encompasses the entire evolution of capitalism, presented in an abstract scheme. He begins where Sternheim, in *1913*, left off. The central figure in *Die Koralle* (The
Coral, 1917) is the Billionaire, an industrial leader who has
climbed the social ladder from the very bottom. To assuage
his conscience, he offers material assistance to anybody seeking
aid in his office. His wealth serves him as a means of escaping
the haunting memories of an unhappy childhood. His foremost
aim in life is to spare his son the hardships he himself experienced; the son, however, renounces wealth and enlists as a
common stoker on a cargo-boat. The Billionaire, in his
frantic quest for mental peace, now seeks to exchange his
life for another man's. 'In whom can I submerge and lose
this dread and raging tumult? Who has a life, smooth and good,
to give for mine?' With this aim in mind, he shoots his
secretary (who is also his double, engaged to replace him at
public functions) in order to efface his own identity and thus,
by a mental *tour de force*, to acquire the memories of a carefree
childhood. For this crime, he pays the death penalty. But he
has gained a deeper happiness than he has ever known: 'I
forced my entry into paradise through an act of violence!'
As he is led to his death, he clutches a bit of coral (the
secretary's mark of identity), in which he sees a symbol of
peace and oblivion:

> We are all driven from our paradise of tranquillity – pieces
> broken from the glimmering coral tree, bearing a wound from
> our first day. It never closes, it burns us, and the terrible pain
> drives us along our path!

The main theme of *Die Koralle* – the exchange of a man's
identity to gain a new lease of life – is a motif recurring in
several of Kaiser's plays. Here spiritual renewal is still attained

by a single individual who breaks away from his former self and finds peace in escape. In the sequel, *Gas*, however, the idea of regeneration encompasses society at large. This play (which was first performed in November 1918, a few days after the Armistice) ranks as one of the central works of Kaiser, and of Expressionism in general. The story continues where *Die Koralle* left off. The Billionaire's son has taken over the industrial plant; but he has introduced a system of collective ownership by which the workers share in the profit. Capitalism has reached a new phase. 'Gas', the product of the plant, is the motive power of industry, the very life-blood of the machine age. Contrary to all calculations, an explosion wrecks the plant, and the industrial process comes to a standstill. The Billionaire's son, profoundly shaken by this event, refuses to rebuild the works and to deliver man once more to the tyranny of machines. His warning rings out at a workers' meeting. This fourth act of *Gas*, with its calculated symmetry of speeches, its alternation of individual oration and choral repetitions, its contraposition of ideas, represents the zenith of Kaiser's dramatic art and stands as a model of the expressionist style. The Billionaire's son, in a passionate appeal, points to the fundamental cause of the workers' plight, their enslavement by the machine. He offers instead to provide them with land on the former site of the factory. Man, a settler once more, must regain his balance from the soil:

> To-morrow you shall be free human beings – in all their fullness and unity! Pastures broad and green shall be your new domains. . . . You are dismissed from bondage and from profit-making. You are settlers – with only simple needs and with the highest rewards – you are men – Men!

However, he is opposed by the Engineer, the exponent of industrialism, who persuades the workers to rebuild the plant and resume the work which gives them mastery over nature –

even at the price of new explosions. The prophet has failed.
Fatally wounded by a stone thrown in a workers' riot, he sets
his hope on a distant future when his vision will come true:

> Can Man be extinguished – must he not return again – now that
> one man has seen him? Must he not arrive – to-morrow or the
> day after to-morrow – every day – every hour? Am I not a
> witness for him – and for his origin and advent? Do I not know
> him – his brave face? Can I doubt any longer?

The last line, spoken by his daughter, contains a promise:
'I shall give him birth!'

The second part of *Gas*, written two years later (1920),
carries the theme to its logical conclusion. Industrial mechanization has reached its final phase. The works are now controlled
by the state, and 'gas' is used exclusively for war production.
Men are reduced to mere automatons tending the machines.
This complete mechanization is illustrated by the very setting
of the scene:

> Concrete hall. Fluorescent light from arc-lamps. From the high
> and misty dome wires lead vertically to the iron platform where
> they diverge to small iron tables – three right, three left. At each
> table a blue figure, sitting rigidly in uniform, staring at a glass
> disk in the table . . .

A war is in progress. The two sides, designated merely as Blue
and Yellow Figures, are without any individual distinctions;
their speech is reduced to mechanical formulas: 'Report from
third battle section: accumulation of enemy growing.' The
war itself is void of any emotional impulse, an impersonal
process involving units of efficiency and output.

However, from this non-plus-ultra of dehumanization there
springs a longing for human values. Owing to a decline in the
output of gas, the war is lost, and the workers assume control
of the plant. The second act, depicting a mass meeting, closely
resembles the fourth act of *Gas I*. The place of the Billionaire's

son is now taken by the Billionaire-Worker: he has completed the cycle of generations and is once more a worker among workers, giving voice to their soaring hopes:

> Once more it is day around you – a whole day with morn and noon and evening. . . . You are once more yourselves, emerged from enslaving compulsion into supreme obligation!

He exhorts the workers to appeal to the enemy, to renounce the production of gas, and to unite with all mankind in a rapturous sense of universal brotherhood. But the enemy disregards the call, invades the country, and seizes control. The bondage of machines is re-established and the workers are made to produce gas for the enemy. The Great Engineer incites them to annihilate the enemy with a poison-gas bomb he has invented. The Billionaire-Worker objects: not through violence, but by tacit submission must true freedom be gained. His call re-echoes the words from the Scriptures, 'The Kingdom is not of this world!' Once again, the choice marks a cross-roads in man's history: 'Be silent and listen how heaven and earth hold their breath at your decision which will seal the world's fate!' The workers decide for poison-gas, that is, for brute force. Thereupon the Billionaire-Worker offers to throw the bomb himself. The end is a lurid tableau of total annihilation – a prophetic anticipation of the atom bomb.

As in most of Kaiser's plays, the call for regeneration falls on deaf ears, and the prophet is doomed to pay with his life. In one instance only does his appeal succeed in transforming society – in *Hölle Weg Erde* (Hell Road Earth, 1919). Both in form and in content, this play can be said to present the quintessence of Expressionism. The three words of the title correspond to its three parts, each representing a stage in social and moral evolution. 'Hell' stands for the present state of society, with its rigid laws based on exploitation and selfishness; 'Road' depicts the awakening to a sense of moral responsibility,

while 'Earth' denotes the ultimate goal – the ful'
of the ideal. This general evolution is set in motio.
individual case. An artist, named Spazierer, receives woru
from a friend that only prompt financial aid can save him.
In order to raise the required sum, he approaches a wealthy
woman with the request to buy some of his pictures. She
refuses and spends the money instead on some jewellery.
Spazierer, on learning of his friend's death, assaults the jeweller
whom he holds responsible for the failure of his mission, and is
imprisoned for attempted murder. He appeals to a lawyer, the
soulless functionary of law, to take up his case. By and by, his
persistent appeal changes the hearts of men. From an isolated
case, the plot develops into a matter concerning each and all.
The collective guilt of society is established, and everybody
confesses to his share in it. The prison gates are thrown open,
and convicts and guards alike pour out in an ever growing
procession. In the end, the ecstatic call of the prophet echoes
across the sun-lit plain: 'The earth resounds! Your blood
surges – for you are the earth!'

This drama reveals more clearly than any other the close
affinity existing between the expressionist idea of spiritual
rebirth and Christian concepts. It is, in essence, a morality play,
restated in terms of a modern and highly intellectual mind.
How deeply Kaiser himself was conscious of this affinity is
evident from the explicit allusions to Christian symbols in
many of his plays, e.g., the 'ecce homo' with which the
cashier expires in *Von Morgens bis Mitternachts*, the picture of
the resurrection at the close of *Die Bürger von Calais*, or the
Billionaire-Worker's cry, 'The Kingdom is not of this world!',
in *Gas II*. In one play, *Noli me tangere* (1922), one of the inmates
of a prison cell is revealed as Christ Himself whose hands, at
the climax of the drama, show the stigmata of the Cross. These
references to Christian symbols do not spring from any
orthodox belief (which was entirely foreign to Kaiser) but

from an implicit analogy between expressionist concepts and Christian ideas.

Kaiser resumed the theme of social regeneration in a play *Gats* (1925), in which he tried, rather unsuccessfully, to repeat the pattern of *Gas*. But the time for this sort of revolutionary Utopia had passed; it was his last expressionist play in the full sense. In keeping with the general trend of German drama, Kaiser moved, in his later development, towards a more realistic style. But this change did not imply, as it did with most other expressionist writers, a reversion to conventional forms. He was the only outstanding author to maintain, down to the very end, the high emotional pitch and ethical challenge of Expressionism, though in a purified form. Abandoning the excesses of expressionist diction, he approximated his language to normal speech; instead of an abstract plot enacted by nameless types, he embodied his message in a concrete story, derived from history or legend.

A perfect example of this type of play is *Lederköpfe* (Leather Hoods, 1928), an impassioned denunciation of militarism. The plot is based on a story from Herodotus, according to which the Persian king, to carry out a military action, made his troops wear leather hoods concealing their heads and faces. In Kaiser's hands, this device becomes a symbol of the soulless uniformity of militarism which completely effaces the individual. The captain of the troop, roused by the king's daughter to a new conception of human values, tears off his hood and incites the soldiers to kill the king. He himself falls, but the king's daughter leads the soldiers 'into the desert, to rebuild what lies destroyed'.

Another instance of Kaiser's skill in turning a given story or event to his own purpose is *Mississippi* (1930). This play shows clearly how close was his idea of moral rebirth to the Christian spirit. The plot was suggested to him by the Mississippi floods of 1928. A group of American farmers have founded a

7. KAISER, *Gas*. Amsterdam, 1928

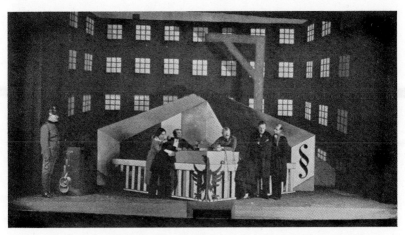

8. KAISER, *Nebeneinander*. Berlin, 1923 (design: George Gross)

religious brotherhood, inspired by the teachings of Christ, and directed against the city of New Orleans, which they see as a citadel of vice. The rising of the river appears to them as a sign from heaven, the 'flowing arm of God' reaching out to punish the city. When they learn that the dykes are to be blown up and their land flooded in order to save New Orleans, they decide to sabotage the scheme by reinforcing the dykes. For them, the issue becomes one of religious faith against the power of Mammon. But their plan is betrayed; the dykes are mined, and the city is saved. The leader of the farmers, Kehoe, dies in the swirling waters. But he is not alone: his wife, the very person who had betrayed the plan to the authorities, joins him in death. 'You alone' (these are his final words) 'have turned your back on the hordes who will not be persuaded. Can more be gained?'

This ending – two lovers uniting in the face of an evil world – points to another prominent theme in Kaiser's work. Side by side with his social dramas, there runs a sequence of plays centring on the union of two lovers and their purification through love. At the very height of his expressionist phase, in 1918, the first two plays of this type appeared, *Das Frauenopfer* (A Woman's Sacrifice) and *Der Brand im Opernhaus* (Fire in the Opera House). Both in form and content, these two set the pattern for the whole series; in fact, the title of the first might well apply to almost any of these plays. Each of them treats of a man's awakening, through a woman's selfless love, to a fuller awareness of life. Fundamentally, this central idea is closely related to that of the social plays; but here a man's regeneration is effected by his experience of an exalted passion. It is worth noting that these plays are, almost without exception, set in France and derive their plots from episodes of French history or literature. In every instance, the story serves merely as a means to illustrate Kaiser's essential idea. *Das Frauenopfer*, for instance, is based on the story of General

Lavalette, a follower of Napoleon, who was freed from prison by his wife taking his place and suffering the most abject humiliation. In *Der Brand im Opernhaus*, the heroine, Sylvette, throws herself into the flames of the burning opera house to preserve her husband's belief in her integrity. Two more plays of this type appeared in 1923 – *Die Flucht nach Venedig* (Flight to Venice), treating of the romance between George Sand and Musset, and *Gilles und Jeanne*, in which the notorious Blue-beard, Gilles de Rais, desperately in love with Joan of Arc, finds redemption through the Maid's death. The most success-ful of these romantic plays was *Oktobertag* (A Day in October, 1928, translated under the title *The Phantom Lover*). Here a girl who is found to be pregnant refuses to disclose the name of her seducer. The suspicion falls on a young officer who, unaware that he has ever crossed her path, denies any acquaint-ance with the girl. Gradually, however, he is drawn to her through her unshakable conviction that he was her lover. Without a moment's hesitation, he kills the butcher boy who is the real father of the child. 'If there are actions which in their frightfulness sunder us from our environment – this is one of them!' he exclaims, and embraces the girl with his final words, 'Now we can live!' Here the issue is stated with full force: the regeneration comes about through the absolute union of two lovers, insulated from the outside world. In order to preserve the purity of their love, they transgress the laws that bind society, even to the point of committing a crime, destroying any intruder who dares to break into their magic circle.

During the latter part of Kaiser's career, this type of play occupied a prominent place in his dramatic production. It was as though the expressionist outburst, spending itself in vain against the hard facts of reality, withdrew to the innermost core of the human heart. After 1933, when his plays were banished from the German stage, he wrote a whole series of intimate plays, such as *Adrienne Ambrossat* (based on a story by Maupassant), *Der Gärtner von Toulouse* (The Gardener of Toulouse, 1938), *Alain und Elise* and *Rosamunde Floris* (both 1940). All these plays centre on the intense emotional experience of two lovers who, through suffering and sacrifice, attain to a higher level of existence. By a curious coincidence, the three last plays mentioned open in a hot-house – a symbol of the charmed isolation of the lovers in a chill and alien world.

In 1938, Kaiser left Germany for Switzerland where he spent the rest of his life in exile. Even then, his stupendous productivity continued unabated. The Second World War roused him to turn once more to wider moral issues. In two satirical comedies, *Der englische Sender* (The English Radio) and *Klawitter*, written in 1940, he poured his scorn on the Nazi régime. *Napoleon in New Orleans*, revolving around an imposter posing as Napoleon escaped from St. Helena, satirizes false hero-worship. The most important works of his exile, however, are two serious plays denouncing the inhumanity of militarism and war. The first, *Der Soldat Tanaka* (The Soldier Tanaka, 1940), is set in Japan. A plain Japanese soldier has his eyes opened to the evil of militarism when he meets his own sister in an army brothel. He kills his sister and one of his superiors, and is sentenced to death by court martial. When he is advised to beg the emperor for mercy, he declares defiantly that it is the emperor who should ask his pardon: for it is only by exploiting the poor that he can maintain his army!

Kaiser's denunciation of war found its final and most poignant expression in a drama *Das Floss der Medusa* (The Raft of the Medusa, 1943), enacted by children only. The scene is set in a life-boat adrift in the Atlantic, manned by English children from a torpedoed liner. When they become aware that there are thirteen of them in the boat, they decide, in a superstitious panic, to throw the youngest and most helpless one overboard. This plan is hotly resisted by Allan, a boy of twelve, who challenges them with the commandment, 'Thou shalt not kill!' Through a heartless ruse the child is drowned behind his back. Deeply shocked, he refuses to board the plane that comes to their rescue, preferring death to life in a world depraved by murder. The plane leaves without him, an enemy plane approaches, and the play closes with the boy lying mortally wounded by machine-gun bullets in the sinking boat, 'as if crucified' – the last of Kaiser's long line of martyrs for an ideal.

In the last year of his life, Kaiser made a new and unexpected departure: he wrote a cycle of three plays based on Greek mythology, *Zweimal Amphitryon*, *Pygmalion*, and *Bellerophon* (published posthumously in 1948). It was his final and supreme attempt to escape from a reality which had become increasingly unbearable to him. For the first time in his career, he adopted verse to convey his message. The three plays are interrelated by a common theme: in each, a deity – Zeus, Athene, and Apollo respectively – singles out a human being, raising him or her above the rest. For the first and only time in Kaiser's work, divine powers intervene in human conflict. But in essence the issue is the same as before. Amphitryon, the general, forfeits his wife by placing war above love; in the end he is condemned by Zeus to walk the earth, atoning for his selfish ambition. *Pygmalion* is the tragedy of the artist who finds himself alone with his vision in the face of a spiteful world, while *Bellerophon* has as its central figure a saintlike youth, caught in the snares of the world, until he is saved by Apollo who turns him into a star. Shortly after the completion of this play, Kaiser died in Ascona, in June 1945, at the age of sixty-seven.

Georg Kaiser is the only one of the expressionist dramatists whose plays have been revived on the German stage since the end of the last war. No doubt a large part of his work is now merely of historical interest, including some of his major plays which made his name at the time, but which are too closely bound up with a bygone period to find a permanent place in the theatre. The diversity of Kaiser's subjects and styles was a constant puzzle to critics and public alike. The question has often been asked, what was the real face behind so many masks, and was there, indeed, a real face at all? A closer inspection reveals that Kaiser pursued one or two central ideas with a persistence bordering on mania. It is in these central ideas, or 'visions', that his true self must be sought – if often hidden behind the mask of the satirist, or distorted by the grimace of a tormented mind. However, it is perhaps for a deeper reason that he falls short of true greatness. His work, for all its dramatic power and far-flung vision, lacks an incalculable element of all great art – the appeal to the human heart. His passion springs from the white-heat of a highly-strung intellect, his vision of the 'regeneration of man' is essentially a rational concept. His entire work is based on contradictions: while extolling the untrammelled freedom of the individual, he presents it in terms of impersonal types; while yearning for the peace and tranquillity of the pure heart, he depicts a world ravished by violence, deceit, and mental torment; while pointing to the abstract thought-process of Plato's dialogues as the supreme model for his plays, he uses every device of modern stagecraft to drive home his message.

For all these unresolved contradictions, Georg Kaiser stands as one of the boldest and most fascinating of modern dramatists, whose impact on the contemporary theatre, both inside and outside Germany, has been considerable.

VII. REVOLUTION IN THE THEATRE

The years following the revolution of 1918 represented the high-water mark of the expressionist movement. The sudden opening of the sluices released a flood of new publications, pent up by censorship during the war years. Expressionism, which had until then been as it were relegated to an illicit existence, now became the dominant literary style. Not only did the political upheaval bring about a flood of new plays reflecting the social revolution, but all those works which had been suppressed during the war for their subversive tendencies were now released for theatrical production.

For a brief moment, it seemed as though the hopes and aspirations of the expressionist writers had come true: the fabric of imperial Germany had disintegrated under the shock of defeat, the war had ended, and the foundations were laid of a new social structure, inspired by the ideas of peace and human brotherhood. The exponents of the younger generation were united in the belief that a new stage in the history of man had been reached.

These messianic hopes found expression in countless publications, theoretical, lyrical, and dramatic, which followed the end of the war.[1] They were all inspired by the firm belief that a turning-point in the evolution of mankind was near at hand. As a typical example, the preface by Alfred Wolfenstein to the year book *Die Erhebung* may be cited. He sets out by denouncing the war as the last manifestation of the 'old powers', and sees in the new era the realization of 'the eternal', which is carried by the masses, as opposed to the merely 'temporal' viewpoint of bourgeois society. Literature is charged with a new mission: 'In the place of the artist's romantic self-indulgence, its purpose is to elevate man to a citizen of the world.' The supreme object of writing must be the rousing of 'man's love for his fellow-man'.[2]

These ideas had often a distinctly communist tinge. The impact of the Russian revolution, which had preceded the

[1] The very names of some of the prominent almanachs and anthologies indicate their spirit: *Kameraden der Menschheit* (Comrades of Mankind, 1919); *Die Erhebung* (The Uprising, 1919/20); *Die Gemeinschaft* (The Community, 1920); *Menschheitsdämmerung* (Twilight of Man, 1920); *Verkündigung* (Annunciation, 1921).

[2] Cf. *Die Erhebung*, Vol. I, Berlin, 1919, pp. 1ff.

German by one year, was of considerable importance. From the outset, there existed a powerful mutual influence between the revolutionary theatres of Russia and Germany. In Germany, however, owing to its different political development, this influence soon waned, or rather, it confined itself to the radical left-wing theatre, whereas the main-stream of drama took a very different course.

The unity of the revolutionary impulse, in Germany, was from the very start thwarted by the conflict existing between a radical and a moderate trend. This conflict came to a head in the civil war of 1919 and 1920; it ended in the defeat of the extremists and the establishment of a democratic parliamentary government. However, the moderate faction achieved its victory only with the aid of the reactionary powers which it was never again able to shake off. Thus the germ which eventually destroyed the Republic from within was latent at its very birth.

It is against this historical background that the development of German drama in the first years after the war must be seen. The actual revolutionary drama, mirroring the political upheaval, centred around the years 1918-1919. It was accompanied by a complete transformation of the theatre, both in its economic structure and in the style of stage-production. Considering that the country had just suffered total defeat, this revolution in the theatre was of truly impressive force and range. It formed an indispensable complement to the development of the drama.

In the first place, the numerous court theatres (*Hoftheater*) which, up to 1918, had been endowed and controlled by the various German princes, were now turned into public playhouses subsidized by the State, the *Land*, or the town (*Staats-*, *Landes-*, and *Stadttheater*). An outstanding example was the Berlin Staatliches Schauspielhaus which, as a royal theatre, had been devoted to a somewhat stagnant repertory of patriotic or, at the best, classical drama. Under the directorship of Leopold Jessner, it now came to be one of the pre-eminent platforms for modern drama. His style of production, dispensing with realistic décor and using as its salient feature a flight of steps (the famous 'Jessner Treppe'), was also applied to classical plays (e.g. the memorable performances of Shakespeare's *Richard III*, Schiller's *Wilhelm Tell*, and Grabbe's *Napoleon*).

At the same time, a large number of new theatrical enterprises sprang up all over the country, directed by new men and imbued with a new spirit. One of the most influential of these was the *Volksbühne*, the 'people's stage'. Its origins reached back to the 1890s when it promoted the cause of naturalistic drama. Up to 1918 it was mainly confined to Berlin; now it spread all over Germany in a vast organization comprising nearly three hundred local centres. Its Berlin playhouse, inaugurated in 1915 as one of the largest and most up-to-date theatres, was re-opened in 1918, under the management of the actor-producer Friedrich Kayssler. The type of play presented during its initial phase reflected the new spirit pervading the German theatre. It included revivals of Strindberg's *Road to Damascus* and *Luther* as well as outstanding specimens of expressionist drama such as Georg Kaiser's *Die Bürger von Calais* and *Gas*, and Ernst Toller's *Masse Mensch*. At a later stage, Erwin Piscator, one of the pioneers of revolutionary drama, became the leading producer at the *Volksbühne*. His style of production, strongly influenced by the Russian theatre of Meyerhold and Tairov, transformed the stage into a maze of geometrical shapes and platforms, supported by the use of film and loudspeaker – a device he applied both to classical drama (e.g. Schiller's *Die Räuber*) and contemporary plays such as Alfons Paquet's *Sturmflut* (1926), Toller's *Hoppla, wir leben!* (1927), or Walter Mehring's vast spectacle of post-war Berlin, *Der Kaufmann von Berlin* (1929).

Even Max Reinhardt, though rooted in the pre-war world, responded to the call of the new era. During the war, he had produced the first fully expressionist drama, *Der Bettler* by Reinhard Sorge. But his main contribution was the opening, in 1920, of the Grosses Schauspielhaus in Berlin, a former circus with a seating capacity of over three thousand, whose vast arena suited the demands of mass drama. The repertory presented on this stage during the first few years reflected the theatrical tendencies of the period: it comprised ancient Greek drama such as the *Oresteia* of Aeschylus (with which the theatre was inaugurated), Sophocles' *Oedipus*, and Aristophanes' *Lysistrata*; a great variety of outstanding plays of past and present suited to mass display, such as Shakespeare's *Julius Caesar*, Goethe's *Götz von Berlichingen* and *Egmont*, Hauptmann's *Die Weber*, *Florian Geyer* and *Der weisse Heiland*, and Romain Rolland's *Danton*; finally, a number of representative works of the expressionist type, such as Hasenclever's *Antigone*, Toller's *Maschinenstürmer*, and Georg Kaiser's 'dance-play' *Europa*. The gradual decline of this theatre, its eventual conversion to the production of operettas and spectacular revues, reflected better than anything the lowering of standards once the impetus of the revolution had subsided.

The theatrical revolution was, of course, not confined to the capital. It swept all the major provincial centres, such as Frankfurt, Darmstadt, Hamburg, Leipzig, Munich, some of which even outstripped Berlin in their bold experiments. In short, the German theatre, under the impact of the political revolution, experienced a vital transformation. Not only was the contemporary drama promoted with all available means, but the works of all times and nations were re-interpreted in the spirit of Expressionism.

The period immediately following the revolution of 1918 presented, in spite of all its variety, a comparatively homogeneous picture of theatrical life. However, along with the political development, this unity of purpose soon disintegrated into various conflicting trends. The actual revolutionary drama expired as soon as the Utopian hopes roused by the end of the war were quenched in civil strife and the economic chaos caused by inflation. By and by, the initial optimism gave way to an ever deepening pessimism and disillusionment. This change of mood found expression in a change of literary style. Expressionism was superseded by a form of writing which reverted to the crude realities of life and renounced all spiritual forces. With this change, there opened a new chapter in the history of modern German drama.

The expressionist movement, seen as a whole, was the symptom of a crisis which affected the whole of Europe, but which impressed itself most deeply on the German mind, owing to Germany's defeat and the revolution following it. This crisis can be summed up as the decline of the middle class, the *Bürgertum*, from the leading position it had occupied for over a century, and the disintegration of the values on which it was based. Expressionism was in its origin and purpose a revolutionary movement and, like every revolution, more clearly aware of what it opposed than of what it aimed at. The only positive ideal it established was the dignity of man – man, naked and absolute, shorn of all historical, social and personal differentiations. It was a purely abstract concept and, therefore, without constructive force.

Unfortunately, the emotional impetus of the movement was greater than the individuals who carried it – at any rate, in the field of literature. Of the actual works, little has survived the passage of time. Yet its total effect was tremendous. It widened the scope of drama, filled it with a new sense of poetry and vision, and revolutionized the methods of stage representation. These achievements have not been lost to this day.

Chapter Five

NEW REALISM

I. DISILLUSIONMENT

The year 1923 may be considered the end of the expressionist movement in Germany. This confirms once again the dependence of literary trends on political developments. The same year marked a turning-point in the history of post-war Germany: it saw both the climax and the end of the social anarchy caused by monetary inflation. Moreover, the various attempts of the extreme Left and Right to overthrow the political structure as it had emerged from the revolution were, at any rate for the time being, thwarted, and a comparatively stable order was established on a democratic basis. The actual period of revolution came to a close. The following six years may be viewed as a time of consolidation and recovery. This, in its turn, was brought to an end by the economic slump of 1929 which resulted in the growth of the nationalist opposition and the eventual downfall of the Weimar Republic in 1933. The entire era between the two revolutions, 1918-1933, can thus be divided into three distinct phases: the period immediately following the revolution; the period of stabilization; and the final relapse into social and political anarchy.

These phases are faithfully reflected in the drama of the time. The immediate repercussions of the revolution were registered in dramatic literature up to 1923, which was still largely under the sway of Expressionism. The following period was marked by the abandonment of social and political themes and, as regards form, by a reversion to realism. During the last phase, about 1930, there was a conspicuous increase in social and political plays, both from the Right and from the Left, foreshadowing the imminent disintegration of the Weimar Republic.

It is much more difficult to sum up, under a single heading, the drama of the twenties and early thirties than that of the preceding period. It lacked the unity of purpose that distinguished the expressionist movement. Generally it can be said that the German theatre, both in the type of plays and in stage production, returned to more conventional forms, that is, to realism. The new style soon came to be known, with the German fondness for labels, by the name of *Neue Sachlichkeit*.[1] Its principles were, at first sight, diametrically opposed to those of Expressionism: for the abstract plot, enacted by types, it substituted concrete action, carried by individual and life-like characters; for the unspecified and timeless scene, a well-defined setting; for the explosive diction, everyday speech.

However, this return to reality was no mere reversion to the Naturalism of the 1890s. In many ways, the new realistic drama still bore traces of the expressionist eruption. It continued to propound ideas and ethical postulations, though they were now presented in a concrete and realistic form. Frequently, the sequence of loosely connected scenes, characteristic of expressionist technique, was maintained. The very language, though in prose throughout, had a terseness and intensity which still bore traces of expressionist fervour.

However, the differences between both kinds of realism were more than formal. The last decade of the nineteenth century, for all its social conflict and criticism, was a time of hope and promise: the dawn of a new age seemed to be just below the horizon. The 1920s knew of no such hopes. Their main tenor was disillusionment and pessimism. New Realism

---

[1] Literally 'New Matter-of-factness', or 'New Objectivism'. In this chapter, the more convenient term 'New Realism' has been used throughout, with reference to the style of writing as well as to the mental attitude.

was the expression of this mood. The ardent hopes roused by the revolution of 1918 had been shattered by the social and moral anarchy following it. The term *Neue Sachlichkeit* indicated an attitude of mind which recognized, with level-headed sobriety, the supremacy of material facts. Literature consciously turned its back upon wider social topics and resigned itself to individual and 'purely human' subjects. The quintessence of this change is vividly defined in the words of Paul Kornfeld, dated 1924:

> No more about war, revolution and the salvation of the world! Let us be modest and turn our attention to other and smaller things. Let us ponder on a human being, on a soul, or a fool. Let us play a little, look round a little and, if we can, laugh or smile a little!

The renunciation of ideological issues was accompanied by some positive factors: the renewed emphasis laid on artistic form which had all but disappeared in the turmoil of Expressionism; the return to a concrete plot and characters of flesh and blood as basic constituents of drama; the assessment of new constructive values both for the individual and for society.

The new realistic style was developed partly by a new generation of writers who had been too young to take an active part in the war. But even those authors who had made their names as the very champions of expressionist drama adopted, in one way or another, the new style. The change from Expressionism to New Realism did not, of course, happen suddenly. At the peak of the expressionist movement more or less realistic plays were produced. On the other hand, the repercussions of Expressionism were felt long after 1923. But generally speaking that year may be regarded as the turning-point. It marked the end of the inflation – one of the crucial factors dominating the immediate post-war years. Its most far-reaching effects in the social sphere were the expropriation of the middle classes and the ever widening gulf separating the impoverished masses from a small minority of *nouveaux riches*. The chaos of inflation, following closely on the revolution as it did, gave the lie to the Utopian visions of 1918.

It was largely because of the inflation and its repercussions in the social sphere that the soaring optimism of the early revolutionary drama ended so soon in utter disillusionment. By way of reaction, this disillusionment led to universal despair of mankind and civilization as a whole. A significant feature of this mood was the escape, in imagination, to distant exotic regions, untarnished by Western civilization. One might almost speak of a *Südsee-Literatur* – with the South Sea providing a kind of paradise, a refuge from war-weary Europe. This mood pervaded, for instance, the two poetic dramas of Gerhart Hauptmann written during those years, *Der weisse Heiland* and *Indipohdi*, the latter a variation on the theme of Shakespeare's *The Tempest*.[1] At the peak of the inflation, no less than three plays centring on a flight from Europe made their appearance on the German stage – *Die Fahrt nach Orplid* (Journey to Orplid, 1922) by A. W. Schmidtbonn, *Südsee* (South Sea, 1923) by Wilhelm Speyer, and *Fahrt nach der Südsee* (Journey to the South Sea, 1924) by Bernhard Blume. In *Südsee*, for instance, a Scotsman is leading a secluded life on a South Sea island to which he has retired from the European scene. 'After the World War, I closed my account with the white race', he declares to the British governor who wants to take him back to civilization and a life of action. These words strike the keynote of all the plays concerned.

The social and moral anarchy of the post-war years formed the background of a large number of plays written in the early twenties. Formally, these plays were realistic, depicting a

[1] Cf. p. 46.

well-defined milieu. But spiritually they were still under the spell of Expressionism; their characters were still types, and their aim was to convey a message. However, there were no more revolutionary meetings, no more impassioned exhortations by an inspired prophet. The moral challenge was now confined to a single individual who sought, not to convert mankind, but to save his own soul. One of the foremost examples of this type of drama was Georg Kaiser's *Nebeneinander*, ironically subtitled '*Volksstück 1923*'. The anarchy of the time, the unsoundness of business enterprise, the harsh contrast between dire poverty and the extravagance of racketeers and crooks, form the sordid background of this play; its ultimate message is frustration.[1]

The same mood prevails in a play by Hans José Rehfisch (1891-), *Wer weint um Juckenack?* (Who weeps for Juckenack?, 1924), which was clearly prompted by Georg Kaiser. This was probably the best play of Rehfisch, a prolific writer who showed a remarkable talent for presenting vital topics of the day in a somewhat conventional form. *Heimkehr* (Home-Coming, 1918) was probably the earliest of the many plays dealing with a soldier's return from the war; *Chauffeur Martin* (1920) treated the central idea of Expressionism, a man's spiritual rebirth, in a realistic style. In *Wer weint um Juckenack?* a minor clerk at the law-courts gains a new understanding of life through a dream in which he experiences death. He believes himself to be rejected by God because he has nobody to weep for him. Moved to a new feeling of love for his fellow-men, he singles out two individuals, a girl to whom he gives all his savings, and a young man whom he saves from prosecution by destroying the legal records. However, he fails to win the genuine affection of these two people who merely offer to pay him back what they owe him. Realizing the futility of his quest, he dies in a state of mental derangement.

[1] Cf. pp. 152f.

The story is presented, quite realistically, in a well-defined Berlin setting. The atmosphere of post-war Germany is caught in a number of vividly drawn types, an ex-officer employed by an insurance company, a self-styled 'poet' who embarks on some fraudulent business enterprise, and so on. The central character, Juckenack, roused by his dream experience of death, severs all ties with his former life. By committing a grave offence against the Law, he places himself outside the established order. He, too, is stigmatized by his time: an ex-soldier from the war, he likes to recall his days as a sergeant and dies with a military phrase on his lips: 'Sergeant Juckenack – reporting back to base!'

The oppressive gloom pervading most plays of the early twenties was occasionally relieved by comedy. Throughout the whole range of expressionist drama, we do not find a single genuine comedy. Expressionism was by its very nature averse to a comic interpretation of life. Whenever comic elements were introduced it was for the sole purpose of satire. It is only with the return to a more realistic drama that we meet the first attempts at comedy – some by the very writers who had been the champions of Expressionism. Paul Kornfeld, for instance, in a comedy *Der grosse Traum* (The Great Dream, 1923), set out to ridicule the Utopian aspirations of the revolutionary era. This he did simply by inverting its main ideas, thus carrying them to the point of absurdity. In a public meeting, various speakers announce their revolutionary programmes; one of them advocates the introduction of polygamy. The play then depicts a future society where polygamy is an accomplished fact and any reversion to monogamy is punished for being anti-social. Now individual love becomes the battle-cry of the 'progressive' minds who acclaim it as the antidote to war and social strife.

One of the most successful comedies of those years, however, was the work of a new author, Max Mohr (1891-1944) –

9. TOLLER, *Die Maschinenstürmer*. Berlin, 1922

10. PAQUET, *Sturmflut*. Berlin, 1926 (Piscator)

Improvisationen im Juni (Improvisations in June, 1922). In this play, expressionist and realistic elements are skilfully mixed. The comedy is tinged with bitter satire; an apocalyptic sense of imminent doom prevails. Yet the final message is one of hope and promise. This ambiguity is succinctly expressed in the introductory motto, 'Europe is dead! Long live the European!'

The scene is set in an old German castle, a refuge of aristocratic tradition and culture, which is about to be sold to an American millionaire. On the eve of the transaction the owner, an elderly princess, conscious that her world has come to an end, chooses voluntary death: she dies with perfect composure, surrounded by her faithful servants. The new proprietor is depicted as the very embodiment of capitalistic power, with a cynical disregard for tradition and sentiment – a typical portrait of the American plutocrat which recurs frequently on the German stage of the twenties. His only worry is his son who suffers from melancholia since he has come to realize the venality of everyone and everything. To distract him, the father engages a travelling comedian who earns his living by impersonating any given character. In one of these 'improvisations', he appears as the Last Man, conjuring up a lurid vision of the end of the world. The only person who proves immune to the temptations of money is an ex-officer of the Czarist army who has found refuge in the castle as a manservant. He rejects a large sum offered him by the American and light-heartedly takes his leave, accompanied by the comedian's daughter who has fallen in love with him. The millionaire's son, cured of his cynicism, regains his faith in 'freedom above the chaos, and the fresh breezes of the heart'.

It is refreshing to come across a play of this period that does not end in despair. Faced with the moral dissolution of the post-war scene, Mohr saw salvation in personal integrity. *Improvisationen im Juni* remained the only noteworthy play of the author who died in exile in Shanghai, in 1944. It was too much bound up with its particular period to be of lasting value; but at the time it was widely acclaimed as a first sign of recovery, both from the excesses of Expressionism and from the spiritual frustration of the post-war years.

II. THE 'ZEITSTÜCK'

The most significant type of play evolved in the twenties and early thirties was the so-called *Zeitstück*. This term was applied to plays dealing with contemporary issues, generally from a critical viewpoint. Most of these plays were too closely bound up with the particular problems of the time to survive the moment for which they were written. But seen in retro-spect, they faithfully reflect the social and spiritual currents of that crucial period in German history. The topics treated include the problems of the returning soldier, the demorali-zation of German post-war youth, the rigours of the Law, the growing violence of political conflict, and so on. The large number of *Zeitstücke* can best be classified according to these various themes.

Frequently the German post-war world was seen through the eyes of a returning soldier who felt unable to adjust himself to civilian life. This theme of the *Heimkehrer* recurred in a long succession of plays extending from the end of the First World War right down to the rise of National Socialism. The general pattern remained unchanged throughout: the returning soldier contrasted the suffering and sacrifice of the war with the demoralization surrounding him at home. By and by, however, the emphasis shifted from violent criticism of the present to romantic idealization of the *Front-Erlebnis*, the emotional experience of the front line, with its nostalgic associations of comradeship and heroic death. This develop-ment led straight to the national socialist glorification of war as an end in itself.

The first play to treat the theme of the returning soldier was *Heimkehr* (Homecoming) by Hans José Rehfisch, which was actually written before the end of the war, and published in 1918. The hero, returning from the trenches to his middle-class home, is deeply moved by a letter left by his brother who has been killed in battle. He leaves home and wife to join the revolutionary movement, only to find that his idealism clashes with the materialism of his fellows. Disillusioned, he returns home and finally commits suicide, overwhelmed by a sense of frustration and hopelessness.

This play established the pattern for most of its kind. The two outstanding instances of *Heimkehrer* drama were undoubtedly Ernst Toller's *Hinkemann*[1] and Bertolt Brecht's *Trommeln in der Nacht*,[2] both published in 1922. Another significant play of this type, though far inferior in quality, was *Die katalaunische Schlacht* by Arnolt Bronnen (1895-   ). Bronnen, who was born in Vienna, made his career as a playwright in Germany. For a short time he was acclaimed, along with Brecht, as an exponent of a new generation which turned its back on Expressionism and reverted to a more realistic manner. Yet for all his stark realism, the explosive diction, the overstrained emotion and the crudity of dramatic effect showed him still under the influence of the expressionist style. In his first play, *Vatermord*,[3] of 1920, Bronnen had carried the theme of the father-son conflict to its uttermost limits. After a comedy *Die Exzesse* (Excesses, 1922), which rises to a sexual paroxysm of almost unbelievable crudity, and a play *Anarchie in Sillian* (Anarchy in Sillian, 1924), dealing in a sensational manner with industrial strife, he wrote his only play about the war and its after-effects, *Katalaunische Schlacht* (Catalaunian Battle, 1924). The title alludes to the legendary battle of Attila where, it is said, the spirits of the slain fought side by side with the living. The play opens in a dug-out

[1] Cf. pp. 143f. [2] Cf. pp. 201f. [3] Cf. pp. 120f.

on the Western Front where a group of soldiers is gathered, among them the wife of one of the officers who has followed him into the trenches, disguised as his batman. When her husband is fatally wounded, she escapes with a few survivors. The same group of people is then seen after the war, first in Paris, then on board a liner bound for America. The action revolves around the frantic desire of the surviving men to possess the woman they met under such strange circumstances. But the spectre of the dead man proves to be stronger than the living. In the end, by a somewhat sensational contrivance, she hears the voice of her dying husband from a gramophone, and commits suicide. The underlying idea of this rather distasteful play is no doubt the continuance of the war, and the ghostly presence of the dead, in the minds of the survivors. But this theme is here confined to the erotic relations of a small group of characters, and it is treated in a crudely sensational manner. Arnolt Bronnen never fulfilled the expectations he had roused in some of his early supporters. After a one-man play, *Ostpolzug* (Journey to the East Pole, 1926), a dramatic *tour de force*, and a patriotic play, *Rheinische Rebellen* (Rebels on the Rhine, 1925), inspired by the French occupation of the Ruhr, he threw in his lot with the rising Nazi movement; curiously enough, he ceased writing altogether after 1933.

One of the most distinguished of the *Heimkehrer* plays was *Karl und Anna* (1929) by Leonhard Frank (1882-   ). The author had made his name with a collection of anti-war stories *Der Mensch ist gut*, which had the effect of a revolutionary manifesto in 1918. *Karl und Anna*, adapted from a novel, concentrates on the human aspects of the theme, without reference to general social issues. The action is carried by three characters only, a woman and two men who are prisoners of war in Siberia. During their long captivity together, one of them paints a glowing picture of his married life, thus kindling in his friend a passionate love for his wife Anna. The unmarried man manages to escape and goes straight to his fellow-prisoner's home, presenting himself to Anna as her husband. By recalling details of her married life, he succeeds in convincing her. When, after the war, her real husband returns, she decides for the man who has taken his place and whom she has come to love more deeply. Although the play confines itself to this rather out-of-the-way case, the story is presented as one of many domestic tragedies caused by the war.

Karl und Anna was one of the first plays to herald the revival of the war theme on the German stage – a notable feature of the years preceding 1933. It was followed in quick succession by some more *Heimkehrer* plays, such as *Toboggan* by Gerhart Menzel, *Douaumont* by E. W. Möller, and *Wunder um Verdun* by Hans Chlumberg (all between 1928 and 1931). Of these three, *Wunder um Verdun* (Miracle at Verdun, 1931) was by far the most arresting. The opening scene is laid in a war cemetery near Verdun. The events of the play form the dream of a German sightseer who has fought on the very spot twenty-five years before. (By a curious coincidence, the time of action is August 1939.) A celestial messenger rouses the dead, calling upon them to return to their homes to dispel the spirit of mutual distrust and hatred which is about to plunge the world into another war. In an apocalyptic scene, the dead, both German and French, are seen rising from their graves and marching off in military formation. The news of their resurrection spreads general dismay. A conference is summoned to discuss measures against the menace of the risen soldiers. When they present their demands, the assembled statesmen point to the economic and moral chaos their return would create throughout the world, and entreat them to go back to their mass-grave.

This haunting play remained the only work of the author who was accidentally killed at the dress rehearsal. It was the last play to express an emphatic anti-war attitude before the rise of Nazism. In the other two *Heimkehrer* plays, memories of the war hold a strange fascination for the returning soldier. Both authors, Gerhard Menzel and E. W. Möller, though vividly portraying the horrors of war and its demoralizing effect on man, shortly afterwards fell in with the Nazi movement. The explanation may be found in the almost pathological intensity with which their heroes are obsessed by their memories, and the nostalgic evocation of the 'comradeship of the front', in contrast to the selfishness and materialism of post-war life. *Toboggan* (1928) opens on the battlefield. The hero, gravely wounded, is left behind by his comrades and drags himself away, in a frantic effort to escape death. In a succession of scenes, we follow his futile attempts to rejoin the living who have written him off as dead. The woman he left behind looks upon him as a ghost whose embrace makes her blood freeze. After this ultimate defeat, he gives up the struggle and goes out into the winter night to be buried by the falling snow.

A similar theme underlies E. W. Möller's *Douaumont oder Die Heimkehr des Soldaten Odysseus* (The Return of the Soldier Odysseus, 1929). Here the hero, one of the few survivors of Fort Douaumont, returns home after an absence of twelve years, only to find his wife courted by two lodgers in her house (the parallel to Homer, emphasized by quotations from the *Odyssey*, seems somewhat contrived). He is still haunted by his war experiences and from time to time falls into a trance in which he confuses the present with the past. Rejected by his wife, and unable to find work, he feels himself to be an outcast in the present-day world: 'There must be a mark on me. Some sign that I was at Douaumont.' When he sees a war film he confuses illusion and reality: jumping on to the stage, he tears down the screen and protests against what he feels to be a profanation of wartime heroism. In the last scene

he contrives, through the sheer power of his imagination, to
hypnotize his two rivals: they believe they are in Fort Douaumont during an artillery bombardment. In mortal terror, they
renounce their claim to the woman and leave the husband in
rightful possession. Finally his reconciliation to his wife frees
him of his obsession: 'We have put it behind us!' runs the last
line of the play.

In a preface, Möller defines the message of the drama and,
beyond it, the general mood of the period preceding the Nazi
revolution: 'The war is still with us. The pain of the recollection can be explained in no other way. . . . The shadow of
Douaumont and its soldiers is still over us all.' These words may
offer a key to the curious fascination the war held for the
German mind more than ten years after it had ended.

A topic frequently treated in the *Zeitstück* of the period
was the moral and spiritual predicament of German adolescents.
The problems of youth and, more especially, the conflict
between two generations, had been a favourite subject of
modern German drama ever since Wedekind wrote *Frühlings
Erwachen*. In expressionist drama, this subject took the particular form of son *versus* father – the son rebelling against the
tyranny of the father and voicing the urge for untrammelled
self-expression. In contrast to this, the plays of the later
twenties reflected the disillusionment of that period. The adolescents depicted were products of the moral anarchy of the
post-war years, disillusioned, cynical, and without any spiritual
aim. Some of these plays were set in a school. However, the
biting criticism of an obsolete school system, which had
formed the main theme of Wedekind's drama of the nineties,
had now lost its sting: the schools shown were mostly of a
'progressive' type; the teachers portrayed had little in common
with Wedekind's narrow-minded despots; rather they surpassed one another in goodwill and understanding towards

the young. The tragedy of adolescence had shifted to a different ground.

The first typical 'school play' of the post-war era was *Anja und Esther* (1925) by Klaus Mann (1906-1949), a son of Thomas Mann. The school portrayed was the Odenwaldschule near Darmstadt, a co-educational school run on progressive lines. The ideas of the children are coloured by the *Jugendbewegung*, the Youth Movement, which exerted such a powerful influence on the younger German generation before and after the First World War. Their attitude towards their elders is not one of rebellion but of contempt and proud self-assurance. Far from wishing to transform the world by revolution, their basic mood is one of resigned withdrawal into their own secluded world. They cultivate an atmosphere of morbid romanticism which finds expression in dancing, singing, and erotic promiscuity (mainly homosexual). This craving for self-expression in eurhythmics and sexual libertinism was an essential feature of post-war adolescence. It was held up to ridicule in Carl Sternheim's comedy *Die Schule von Uznach* (The School of Uznach, 1926) – the only important post-war play of that author whose main work belonged to the pre-1914 era.[1] Its sub-title, *Neue Sachlichkeit*, provided the label for the whole literary movement.

The violent political antagonism which marked the later years of the Republic left its stamp on two more plays dealing with the problems of adolescence. Peter Martin Lampel's (1894-) *Revolte im Erziehungshaus* (Revolt in the Reformatory, 1929) is set in a state reformatory of the Borstal type. The conflicting political currents are embodied in two main characters: a socialist assistant teacher, and a narrow-minded reactionary clergyman who is head of the institute. The former advocates more humane treatment of the juveniles, founded on 'brotherhood' instead of 'contempt'. The action

[1] Cf. pp. 100f.

culminates in a rebellion of the inmates which is brutally suppressed by the police. The juvenile ringleader, as he is led away to prison, stresses the connection between their particular case and wider political issues.

The political antagonism of those years is also reflected in the last of the school plays, Christa Winsloe's *Gestern und Heute* (Yesterday and To-day, 1930) which won world fame under the title *Mädchen in Uniform*. This play depicts an exclusive school for officers' daughters, mainly of the Prussian nobility – a stronghold of the old military traditions where the girls are reared to become 'mothers of soldiers'. Nostalgic memories of the glorious past mingle with the hope of its imminent revival: 'As it was in 1914, so it is in 1930.' Much against her will, the Principal is forced to accept a grant from the detested republican government; but at the same time she cultivates the patronage of a Grand Duchess. The only person opposed to the reactionary spirit of the school is Fräulein von Bernburg, one of the mistresses; but her attitude has no political implications, it springs from a warm human understanding of the pupils. Only in her last impassioned controversy with the Principal, her opposition becomes more outspoken, and the criticism implicit in the play emerges. The Principal discounts her views as 'revolutionary sentiments'. 'In this school', she sternly declares, 'tradition is more sacred than life. The revolution, thank God, has passed us by.' At the height of the argument, news is brought that one of the girls has committed suicide. This human tragedy reveals in a flash the emotional stress to which the children are subjected. Within its limited sphere, the play is a poignant document of the time, reflecting as it does the spirit of Prussian militarism which survived under the very eyes of the republican authorities.

During the later twenties and early thirties, the German theatre saw a remarkable accumulation of plays dealing with various aspects of the Law. In all these plays, the author upheld the cause of the individual caught in the rigid mechanism of legal procedure. In this vindication of the 'humane' point of view, we hear perhaps the last echo of the expressionist cry for the boundless freedom of man. Some of the leading expressionists turned, in their later development, to this type of play – for instance, Hasenclever with *Mord* (1928), or Toller with *Die blinde Göttin* (1932). Others exposed some inhuman or obsolete paragraph of the legal code – e.g. Friedrich Wolf in *Cyankali* (1929), which dealt with the legal aspects of abortion, or Max Alsberg, a prominent Berlin solicitor, in *Voruntersuchung* (Pre-Trial, 1930). The most notable of these court-room plays was undoubtedly *Die Verbrecher* (1928) by Ferdinand Bruckner, which questioned the very foundations of public jurisdiction.

Ferdinand Bruckner (1891–1958) first made his mark with *Krankheit der Jugend* (The Malady of Youth, 1926). This play caused something like a sensation, due partly to the secrecy surrounding the identity of the author. (As it turned out, Bruckner was the pseudonym adopted by Theodor Tagger, who had started as an expressionist poet and had later become the director of a Berlin theatre.) *Krankheit der Jugend* was the sort of play written once in every generation, voicing the frustration and disillusionment of youth in a world hopelessly out of joint. It depicted, with unprecedented candour, the moral corruption and cynicism of a group of medical students. For these young people, youth in itself is a fatal disease. The idea of death by suicide is always present to their minds; they see in it the only alternative to certain disillusionment. 'Either one grows into a philistine, or one commits suicide. There is no other way out,' as one of them puts it. The drama ends with the suicide of one of the girls, and the deliberate provocation of violent death by another. Although confining itself to a specific group of adolescents, the play reflects poignantly the general demoralization of the period.

While *Krankheit der Jugend* was the most striking of the plays dealing with the spiritual plight of German post-war youth, *Die Verbrecher* (The Criminals, 1928), Bruckner's second work, was among the most successful of the court-room plays. It presents a cross-section of contemporary Berlin by showing, in simultaneous scenes, a variety of legal cases all of which end in a miscarriage of justice. The very foundations of the Law are challenged. A counsel's plea before the court culminates in the emphatic question, 'What is Right, unless it be humane? What is the essence of Right?' And in a final soliloquy a writer, acting as the author's mouthpiece, sums up the argument. He has come to realize that the courts of justice constitute 'a world which lies on a plane totally removed from life, a secluded world, petrified for centuries'. Man has established the institutions of Law to evade his own conscience: 'We have set up a retributive authority in order to relieve our conscience, and we numb our souls in fear of ourselves. In this escape from ourselves lies the indestructible power of public jurisdiction.'

Bruckner's next play, *Elisabeth von England* (1930), which carried his name beyond the borders of Germany, was of a very different type. It was one of the large number of historical plays which the new realistic playwrights cultivated side by side with the *Zeitstück*. These historical plays can in fact be considered as *Zeitstücke* in disguise: they were largely stimulated by a vivid interest in political problems, presented in terms of historical personages and conflicts. The realistic type of historical play was of course far removed from classical German drama and its successors in the nineteenth century. It presented the historical characters in terms of modern men, reducing their stature to homely proportions and applying a modern psychological interpretation. The technique employed was usually that of the *Bilderbogen*, the picture book, unfolding the action in a haphazard sequence of short scenes.[1]

Elisabeth von England was easily the most successful of these plays. As in *Die Verbrecher*, Bruckner used his technique of simultaneous action to emphasize dramatic contrasts. At several points, the stage is divided into two sections, showing the English and the Spanish scene side by side. At the climax of the play, for instance, the interiors of St. Paul's Cathedral and of a Spanish church are seen, with Elizabeth and Philip of Spain praying simultaneously to their God. The action, cast in terse, hectic dialogue, concentrates on the treason and execution of Essex, and on the antagonism between Elizabeth and Philip which is interpreted psychologically as a kind of personal 'love-hate'. One of the major characters is Francis Bacon, who stands as the embodiment of the new age of reason, as opposed to the blind fanaticism of the Roman Church. At the close of the play, Elizabeth, all her passion spent, is alone, reading in Petrarch, 'Del dolor' e della ragione'.

Bruckner's last play to be performed before 1933 was *Timon* (1931), based on Shakespeare's drama – the tragedy of the individual who fails to come to terms with the claims of the community. Under the impact of the Nazi revolution, which forced him to leave Germany, Bruckner wrote *Die Rassen* (The Races, 1933), a vivid picture of the conflicts and tragedies caused by racial persecution among German students. Two historical plays about Napoleon, *Napoleon der Erste* (1937) and *Heroische Komödie* (written in 1942), were obviously prompted by the rise of Hitler.

[1] One of the first and most successful of these historical plays was *Neidhardt von Gneisenau* (1925) by Wolfgang Goetz, which had as its central figure the Prussian general famous for his resistance to Napoleon. Other notable plays treating subjects from the national past were *Vater und Sohn* (1922) by Joachim von der Goltz, and *Zwölftausend* (1927) by Bruno Frank. Some of the former expressionists turned to this type of play, e.g. Werfel with *Juarez und Maximilian* (1924) and Unruh with his *Bonaparte* (1927). The line of historical plays continued uninterrupted into the national socialist era when this type of drama attained new significance as a glorification of the German past.

The aggravation of political conflict during the final phase of the Weimar Republic brought about a conspicuous increase of *Zeitstücke*, both from the extreme Left and Right opposition. The gathering strength of the nationalist movement was countered by an accumulation of radical Left-wing drama. This sprang obviously from a desire to recall the spirit of the revolution from which the Republic had been born. Between 1928 and 1932, we find a large number of plays picturing the 1918 revolution and the events leading up to it. Two significant examples were *Feuer aus den Kesseln* by Ernst Toller,[1] and *Die Matrosen von Cattaro* by Friedrich Wolf, both performed in Berlin in 1930. Both plays dealt with a mutiny preceding the revolution, the one in the German, the other in the Austro-Hungarian navy.[2] The two authors may be considered, along with Bertolt Brecht, as the leading exponents of the extreme left-wing, or communist, drama in Germany. But while Toller made his greatest impact during the expressionist period, Friedrich Wolf (1888-1953) became known mainly by his realistic plays. He, too, had started as a full-fledged expressionist with two abstract plays, *Das bist du* (That is You, 1918) and *Der Absolute* (The Absolute Man, 1919). But then he found his true medium in realistic drama, sustained by tense action and by characters of flesh and blood. His revolutionary message was not announced in ardent proclamations but was implicit in the action. The first of this type of play was *Der arme Konrad* (Poor Conrad, 1923), a drama about the German peasant revolt of 1514. *Kolonne Hund* (1926) told the story of a communist-inspired land reclamation scheme in a North German moor, shortly after the war, in which the author himself had taken part. Wolf's greatest success was *Cyankali* (Cyanide, 1929), the drama of a young girl who dies from abortion. This was

---

[1] Cf. p. 146.

[2] A third play, Theodor Plievier's *Des Kaisers Kuli*, treated the same subject as Toller's, and was first performed on the same night.

the latest version of a favourite theme of German drama – the tragedy of the unmarried mother, treated in a long line of plays from H. L. Wagner's *Kindermöderin*, of 1776, to Hauptmann's *Rose Bernd*. In Wolf's hands the subject was turned into a trenchant attack on the law prohibiting abortion.

Die Matrosen von Cattaro (The Sailors of Cattaro, 1930), Wolf's most effective revolutionary play, centres on a mutiny in the Austro-Hungarian navy shortly before the end of the war. The characters are given their actual names, and the action is based throughout on documented fact. The revolt is quelled by the intervention of loyal units, and the four ring-leaders are executed. One of them, as he is led to his death, announces the coming revolution: 'This is not the end, this is only the beginning!' As in all the revolutionary plays of Wolf, temporary defeat is turned into a promise of future victory. The same applies to his last play written in Germany, *Tai Yang erwacht* (Tai Yang Awakens, 1931), which deals with the communist rising in Shanghai of 1927; it was produced by Piscator with all his well-worn devices of film, posters, mime, as a piece of undisguised communist propaganda.

The rise of the Nazis deprived Wolf, like many others, of the main platform for his further work. Under the impact of this event, he wrote one of his most stirring plays, *Professor Mamlock* (1933), the tragedy of a Jewish surgeon who falls a victim to racial persecution. (The play won world fame through its Russian film version.) In his later years of exile, Wolf produced several plays based on topical events, such as *Floridsdorf* (about the uprising of the Vienna workers in 1934) and *Patrioten* (about the French resistance). His last work, *Beaumarchais* (1945), has as its central figure the French play-wright who with his comedies helped to unleash the revolution but felt unable to support it once it had actually broken out. While his Figaro inspires the people, Beaumarchais remains behind, watching from a window the crowds on their way to the Bastille. There can be no doubt that this tragic conflict was intended to portray Wolf's own position. From his return to East Germany, after 1945, to his death in 1953, Wolf did not produce another work. As with his fellow-playwright Brecht, his creative powers faded when he came to live within the social order he had propagated throughout his life. But unlike Brecht, he acknowledged defeat. One of his last public utterances runs: 'I must reproach myself for having abandoned for the first time, after more than thirty years of work on the German stage, the fight against bureaucracy, apathy, and stupidity.' Like Toller, Friedrich Wolf was an idealist who embraced the communist creed on purely emotional grounds. He thus forms a link between Expressionism and the social realism of Brecht.

Another playwright with strong Leftish leanings, though not committed to communism, was Oedön Horvath (1901-1938). Born in Hungary, he rose to brief fame in Berlin and Vienna before his career was cut short by the Nazis. His plays are suffused with a bitter sense of fatalism; though realistic throughout, they have a peculiar lyrical touch which gives them a distinctive quality of their own. His characters are taken from the proletariat and the lower middle class, with their everyday cares, their philistinism, their sad little romances. *Italienische Nacht* (Italian Night, 1930), his first success, satirizes pungently the political antagonism dividing Germany at the time. The scene is set in a beer garden where a party of Republicans drink side by side with a group of Nazis. Horvath ridicules impartially the crude vulgarity of the Nazis as well as the complacency of the Republicans in whom the revolutionary fire has long since died. His subsequent plays – *Geschichten aus dem Wiener Wald* (Tales from the Vienna Woods, 1931), *Kasimir und Karoline* (1932), and *Glaube, Liebe, Hoffnung* (Faith, Love, Hope, 1933) – followed the tradition of the Viennese

Volksstück, mingling tragedy with comedy. Incidentally, one of his last plays, too, was a play on Beaumarchais. When the Nazis seized Austria, Horvath went to Paris. There he met a strange end: he was killed by a tree struck by lightning. –

As this survey shows, hardly any of the authors who emerged in the twenties were given a chance to reach maturity: their careers were cut short by the rise of Hitler. Among the few to survive exile were Carl Zuckmayer and Bertolt Brecht.

These two made their full impact only after the Second World War, when they came to represent the two parts of their divided country. However, their formative years were the 1920s when they had their first signal successes on the German stage. It is therefore justifiable to consider their work as a whole at this point although part of it belongs to a much later period.

III. CARL ZUCKMAYER

The life-story of Carl Zuckmayer is in many ways typical of his generation. Born in 1896, in the neighbourhood of Mainz, in the vinegrowing country of Rhine-Hesse, he was seventeen when war broke out. Like so many others, he welcomed it as a relief from the drudgery of school life and enlisted as a volunteer. For four whole years, he fought in the front line, rising to the rank of captain. In the trenches of Flanders, he wrote his first chaotic verses. He returned a rebel to a country shaken by revolution and the aftermath of defeat. For several years, he drifted from one job to another, making his living as the editor of a revolutionary review, reciting his wild poems in literary cabarets, working in a mine in Norway, and peddling drugs in the streets of Berlin. For a time, he acted as assistant producer at a provincial theatre where he shocked his audiences with his daring experiments. In Berlin, he was caught in the full flood of expressionist writing. His

11. BRUCKNER, *Die Verbrecher*. Berlin, 1928 (Reinhardt)

12. BRUCKNER, *Elisabeth von England*. Berlin, 1930 (Reinhardt)

first play, *Am Kreuzweg* (At the Crossroads, 1920) – the usual compound of ecstatic lyricism and hazy symbolism – was taken off after three performances at the Berlin State Theatre. A second play, *Pankraz erwacht* (Pankraz Awakens, 1925), a savage melodrama set in the Wild West, failed to survive a literary matinée at Reinhardt's Deutsches Theater.

At this point, his literary development took a decisive turn. He recognized that his true powers lay in a very different direction.

> I had grasped a fundamental fact [he records in an autobiographical account] that a house must be built from the basement up, and not from the roof down, that growth does not begin with the blossoms but at the roots. In poems and prose writings I had instinctively pursued this path, portraying the image of a tree, the life of a moth, or relating the story of a pond with all the creatures that live and breathe in it. Now I tried the same in the human realm of drama.

The first fruit of this new insight was the comedy *Der fröhliche Weinberg* (The Merry Vineyard). Its performance in Berlin, in 1925, was a triumph for the new realistic drama. The singular success of this play was symptomatic of a general change of mood, a revulsion from the excesses of Expressionism and a return to sanity. The hilarious laughter it roused from the moment the curtain went up seemed to clear the air from the spectres of war and revolution. On its further course through the provinces, though, the play aroused some fierce protest: the nationalist opposition, already raising its head, was stung by the caricature of a reactionary student which was clearly levelled at it. *Der fröhliche Weinberg*, written throughout in the broad Rhenish dialect of Zuckmayer's native region, is a rustic comedy overflowing with rollicking humour. Its characters are taken straight from life – the carefree and lighthearted life of the vineyards. The action consists of a succession of drinking bouts, riotous tavern brawls and love-making. In contrast to the rough simplicity of the country-folk, the author ridicules the affectations of the townsmen and, especially, the bombast of a nationalist *Corpsstudent* who serves as the general laughing-stock.

With *Der fröhliche Weinberg*, Zuckmayer struck the keynote of his work: although he later expanded its range to include tragedy and history, he was always at his best when portraying characters of flesh and blood. In this elemental quality, he may be regarded as a successor to Gerhart Hauptmann. Like Hauptmann, he drew his finest powers from the soil that had reared him; like Hauptmann, he was at his best when he created his characters, with their unmistakable idiom and temperament, from immediate observation; like Hauptmann, he later extended his range to include Berlin, or to delve into the past, without ever losing contact with his native region. Both dramatists were deeply conscious of this affinity: Hauptmann acclaimed the younger playwright as his 'spiritual heir', and Zuckmayer testified his indebtedness by completing, as late as 1952, a play *Herbert Engelmann*, which Hauptmann had left unfinished.

Zuckmayer's next work, *Schinderhannes* (1927), struck a more serious note. Its hero is a popular figure from the Rhineland at the time of the Napoleonic wars, a kind of Robin Hood who fleeces the rich and protects the poor. Almost unintentionally, he becomes a national hero and martyr when he gets involved in a private war with the French conquerors, is caught, and executed in a public square at Mainz. Once again Zuckmayer draws a crowd of living characters from his native province. The whole play has the simplicity of folksong; it is a *Volksstück* in the best sense of the term, mingling genuine humour with unashamed melodrama. The same is true of *Katharina Knie* (1929), a play set in a travelling circus, depicting the colourful life of jugglers and acrobats which Zuckmayer knew from personal experience. The heroine, a member of a famous circus family, renounces a romance which would force her to settle down, and follows the call of the road. Once again, the play abounds in a multitude of sharply drawn characters, and the language is the broad dialect of the author's homeland.

After a play for children, *Kakadu Kakada* (1930), Zuckmayer wrote what proved one of his greatest successes, the comedy *Der Hauptmann von Köpenick* (The Captain of Köpenick, 1931), ironically sub-titled 'A German Fairy-tale'. For the first time, the scene is Berlin – the Berlin of Wilhelm II in the early years of this century. The notorious incident that set the world laughing at the time forms the nucleus of the plot: an ex-convict, donning the uniform of a Prussian captain, took command of a company to occupy the townhall of a Berlin suburb, arrested the mayor, and robbed the municipal safe without encountering any resistance. This episode served Zuckmayer to ridicule German militarism. Our sympathy goes out to the wretched cobbler, Wilhelm Voigt, who tries desperately to obtain the documents required for finding work, and fights a losing battle against officialdom. When at last he conceives his stratagem of entering the townhall in the guise of a captain, it is with the sole object of obtaining a passport to leave the country. The dramatic core of the play, however, is the uniform which passes from hand to hand until, for a brief moment, it makes history. The arrogance of the military caste and the narrow-mindedness of Prussian bureaucracy are illustrated in sharply profiled types. In Zuckmayer's hands, the story becomes a pungent attack on the revival of the militar-istic spirit which marked the final phase of the Weimar Republic. Despite its satirical purpose, however, the play is aglow with rich humour and humanity. It holds its place, along with Hauptmann's *Der Biberpelz*, as one of the few outstanding comedies in modern German drama.

Der Hauptmann von Köpenick was one of the last attempts, in the realm of drama, to exorcize the evil spirits which were steadily gathering force. A bare eighteen months later, Hitler seized power, and Zuckmayer left Germany. He first went to Austria where he owned an old mill in the neighbourhood of Salzburg. There he was granted five more years of grace. During that time, he produced two plays, *Der Schelm von Bergen* (The Rogue of Bergen, 1934) and *Bellman* (1938). Both were based on historical subjects, perhaps through the author's desire to turn his back on the darkening contemporary scene. The first retold a medieval Rhenish legend (known from a ballad by Heine): the executioner's son becomes the lover of the empress, and is in the end knighted by the emperor for giving him the longed-for heir. In a succession of colourful scenes, the pomp and splendour of medieval Germany unfolds. The language, for a great part in verse, tries to recreate an imaginary medieval diction; yet despite some poetic beauty, it remains strangely lifeless and contrived. The tone rings true only when Zuckmayer falls back on the familiar accents of the Rhineland. This play reveals the limitations of Zuckmayer's creative range: whenever he leaves the realistic plane he is inclined to fall into bathos, and at times comes precariously close to operatic libretto.

This danger is much less evident in the second of his historical plays, *Bellman*, for here Zuckmayer could identify himself fully with his subject. The play has as its central character the eighteenth-century Swedish poet Bellman, a light-hearted minstrel of love and wine. It is evident that the author felt a close affinity to the vagabond-poet, and intended him as a kind of ideal self-portrait. The action is interspersed with Bellman's original lyrics, in Zuckmayer's spirited translation. Some of the characters are in fact drawn from Bellman's own verses – above all Ulla Winblad, the poet's mistress, who becomes the wife of a nobleman, but in the end returns to the dying minstrel whom she has never ceased to love. Court intrigue and the assassination at a masqued ball of Gustavus III, Bellman's royal friend, form a vague background to this fantasy, full of music and song and the cool tang of the Swedish scene.

Under its original title, the play was performed only in Zürich, in 1938. Later it was renamed *Ulla Winblad* (though Bellman still remained the central figure). In this final version, it was revived in 1953, after the author's return to Germany.

Shortly before the outbreak of the Second World War, Zuckmayer went to the United States. After a short stay in Hollywood (where he wrote the scenario for a Rembrandt film), he settled in an isolated farm in the hills of Vermont – a life more in keeping with his natural inclinations. There, at the height of the war, he wrote what was to become his greatest success, *Des Teufels General* (The Devil's General, 1946). It was with this play that he returned to his country after the war and established himself as the leading playwright of West Germany.

It is remarkable that the most authentic play about Germany under Nazi rule was written by an exile in the heart of America. This demonstrates Zuckmayer's intuitive power of creating live characters in their specific setting. The action is laid in Berlin, during the early years of the war, at the height of Nazi power. Harras, a general of the Luftwaffe, is at heart fiercely opposed to the Hitler régime but dulls his conscience with daring witticisms. The aircraft production he is in charge of is found to be sabotaged, and he is called upon to find the culprit. In the end he discovers that the responsibility lies with his chief engineer, Oderbruch, who has all along quietly acted on his convictions. As the Gestapo closes in, Harras takes the air in one of the faulty planes, and crashes to his death. The play, which was performed, after its Zürich première in 1946, all over Germany, gave rise to heated controversy on the moral issues involved; it was criticized for evading a clear-cut decision and for exonerating, in its central character, the

German army. Whatever the political implications, Zuckmayer presents a compelling picture of Nazi power at its zenith, filled with a multitude of vividly drawn characters. There are scenes of genuine dramatic force, as for instance, when Harras tries to convince a young airman, on leave from the Russian front, of the hollowness of Nazi slogans, and opens his eyes to the true values of life.

Zuckmayer never managed to repeat the success of *Des Teufels General*. Another play dealing with the Nazi era, *Der Gesang im Feuerofen* (Song in the Fiery Furnace, 1950), proved less convincing. This play is set in occupied France and centres on a tragic incident of the partisan war: a group of the Maquis, celebrating Christmas in a deserted château, are betrayed to the Germans, who set fire to the building and burn all the inmates to death. In many scenes, and with a vast number of characters, Zuckmayer covers a large canvas depicting France under German occupation. This work reveals more than others the playwright's conspicuous weakness – lack of dramatic concentration and a tendency to lose himself in a profusion of character and incident. What remains in the mind is a number of separate episodes, above all the romance between a German soldier and a French country girl who (a genuine Zuckmayer touch) meet in a byre where a cow is calving. In an attempt to give the events a deeper significance, Zuckmayer sets the action in a symbolic frame, introducing allegorical figures – the wind, the frost, and the mist – who comment on the ultimate issues of human guilt and atonement. These scenes reveal his limitations: whenever he steps outside his proper domain, the realistic portrayal of characters in a definite environment, he comes dangerously close to the banal.

By some immanent law of his creative development, Zuckmayer alternated between topical *Zeitstücke* and legendary or historical plays. Thus *Des Teufels General* was followed by *Barbara Blomberg* (1949) which traces the life-story of a mistress of Charles V, a plain '*Mädchen aus dem Volke*', who fights a losing battle against court intrigue for herself and her illegitimate son, Don Juan d'Austria. After a vigorous opening act, set in the Netherlands, the play rather loses its grip as the scene shifts to Spain where the heroine finds a peaceful haven. Similarly, *Der Gesang im Feuerofen* was succeeded by *Ulla Winblad* (1953), a re-issue of Zuckmayer's earlier play on the Swedish vagabond-poet Bellman.

With *Das kalte Licht* (The Cold Light, 1956) Zuckmayer once more took up a topical theme, in this instance, the nuclear physicist who turns traitor. The time of action ranges from 1939 to 1950; the scene shifts from England to America and back to England. The central figure is Kristof Wolters, a German refugee who finds himself penniless in England at the outbreak of war, is interned in 1940, and shipped to Canada where he is released as a promising scientist. He joins the team of nuclear physicists working on the atom bomb, and gets involved in communist espionage. The final part shows his gradual surrender to a member of the British secret service who, through sympathy and perseverance, eventually obtains his confession. The plot is evidently based on the notorious case of Dr. Fuchs. In fact, the author's method is similar to that employed in *Der Hauptmann von Köpenick* and *Des Teufels General*: in each case, he uses a real character to create a drama in its own right. But compared with his predecessors, the unemployed cobbler Voigt and the Luftwaffe general Harras, Wolters remains curiously lifeless – perhaps because his conflict is by its very nature an intellectual one, not involving the whole personality. The issue is also marred by the introduction of a somewhat conventional romance – a love-affair between Wolters and the wife of his employer – which plays a vital part in his eventual surrender. Once again, the by-play seems dramatically more successful than the central issue – for instance, the scene on board an Atlantic liner crowded with internees, Nazis and anti-Nazis alike: here a whole cross-section of humanity, at a given historical moment, springs to life.

The theme of *Das kalte Licht*, as of *Des Teufels General*, is a man's choice in the main conflict of our age – the choice between freedom and totalitarianism. Like Harras, Wolters sells his soul to the devil; like him, he is prepared to make good when confronted by a man who has retained his moral integrity: 'Throughout my life,' he says to the British agent as he prepares to confess, 'I have stood in the beam of a cold light that came from outside, filling me with an inward frost. But one instant can be like a fire in which everything is transformed.' It is perhaps in this insight that the vital message of the play can be found. Its basic theme is, in the author's words, '*die Denk- und Glaubenskrise der Gegenwart*' (the intellectual and spiritual crisis of our time). In this crisis, Zuckmayer stands unswervingly on the side of human freedom and responsibility. He does so not by an abstract thought-process, but from a natural instinct rooted in his very being. Nothing seems to him more symptomatic of the critical state of our world than its defection from 'nature'. For him, the full and undistorted perception of nature in all its manifestations is the very source of artistic creation. In this belief lie his strength and his limitations: his plays are living organisms, vigorous when drawing their life from the soil, pallid when venturing into the rarefied air of thought.

IV. BERTOLT BRECHT

Bertolt Brecht (or Bert Brecht, as he preferred to call himself in his early years) was twenty-four when his first two plays, *Baal* and *Trommeln in der Nacht*, were published in 1922. He was born in Augsburg in Bavaria, the son of a well-to-do manufacturer. His birthplace seems to have left no imprint on his work save a distinct South-German flavour which characterizes his dramatic diction irrespective of the place of action.

Brecht's attitude towards his origin and social background was from the outset one of violent revolt. He was just old enough to be called up for war service, and joined the medical corps. On his return, he was immediately caught in the revolutionary upheaval of the post-war years. However, his first play, *Baal*, was not in any way related to contemporary events: it is a haphazard sequence of scenes centring on the over-lifesize figure of a poetic tramp and drunkard, a social outcast who spends his life in the reckless pursuit of sensual pleasure, drinking, whoring, and reciting his verses in low taverns. Without any compunction, he seduces and drives to suicide his best friend's girl, and eventually stabs another friend in a pub brawl. His utter nihilism and cynicism are relieved only by an insatiable greed for life, a pagan worship of the open sky, the wind, the plants and beasts of the forest. The quintessence of the drama is contained in the *Choral of the Great God Baal* which precedes it: indeed, the whole play is little more than a scenic ballad, imbued with a haunting lyrical quality. The very headings of the scenes – 'Green fields, blue plumtrees', or 'Plain. Sky. Evening', or 'Highroad. Evening. Wind' – accentuate this poetic quality. Both in form and in language, one feels the influence of the *Sturm und Drang* drama, especially Lenz, of Georg Büchner, and of Frank Wedekind with his predilection for the lower fringes of society and his cynical *épater le bourgeois*.

The same is true of *Trommeln in der Nacht* (Drums in the Night), the first of Brecht's plays to be produced in Berlin, in 1922. This play, however, deals with contemporary events: the scene is laid in Berlin immediately after the war, during the communist rising known as 'Spartakus'. It is a *Heimkehrer* play – the most poignant besides Toller's *Hinkemann*. The homecoming soldier, Andreas Kragler, returns after four years of captivity to find his girl engaged to another man. He has been reported dead, and his unexpected appearance has a weird touch of unreality. He feels himself to be a ghost, an intruder in a world which has switched production from shells to perambulators. From a sense of utter frustration, Kragler joins the rebels who, like himself, feel cheated of their place in life by the war. 'Your sinister associates!' one of the bourgeois types exclaims disdainfully. 'Your comrades who roar in the newspaper quarter and burst into cafés, reeking of murder and arson. Rabble!' Their 'drums in the night' form a constant background to the action, beating a stirring challenge to the peace-loving philistines whose sole aim is to forget the war and settle down to money-making. But there is no hope of a change: 'Injustice!' runs Kragler's cynical comment. 'Make yourselves comfortable on this planet, it is cold here and somewhat dark, and there is no time to remedy injustice, the world is too old for better days to come and brandy is cheaper and heaven is let, my friends.'

This note of resignation is sustained throughout the play. In the end, Kragler turns his back on the revolution and 'goes home' with his girl who has come back to him. 'Is my flesh to rot in the gutter so that your idea may triumph? Are you drunk?' – As with *Baal*, the keynote of the whole drama is struck in an introductory poem, the *Ballad of the Dead Soldier* – perhaps Brecht's best known lyric, satirizing, in the jingling verses of a street ballad, the futile heroism of the common soldier who marches on even when he is dead. The nihilism pervading the play eventually seems to burst the very confines of the theatre. Kragler, in a final savage outburst, hurls his invectives at the audience while beating a drum: 'Don't gaze so romantically! You usurers! You cut-throats! You blood-thirsty cowards!' The subsequent stage-direction runs: 'He hurls the drum at the moon which was a Chinese lantern, and the drum and the moon fall into the river which has no water.' In this calculated debunking of stage illusion, we can see the first hint of Brecht's later 'alienation effect'.

His two subsequent plays, *Im Dickicht der Städte* (1924) and *Mann ist Mann* (1927), may be regarded as a transition from his early to his mature style. Their respective scenes of action, Chicago and British India, point to an important feature of his later works – a preference for non-European settings, especially for the Anglo-Saxon countries. *Im Dickicht der Städte* (In the Jungle of the Cities) is permeated by the same utter nihilism and negation of all moral values as the first two plays. The action hinges on the deadly struggle between two men, Shlink, a Malayan timber-merchant, and Garga, a library clerk, whom he makes his business partner. This struggle has no concrete motive, it is 'metaphysical' – a parable of man's inborn enmity towards his fellow-men. In the course of their fight, the two antagonists deliberately bring one another to ruin. In the end, they meet in a gravel pit on the shore of Lake Michigan; in a moment of weakness, one of them hints that their fight was an attempt to overcome man's utter loneliness:

> The infinite isolation of man makes enmity an unattainable goal. Nor is there any communication possible with animals. . . . Love, the warmth of physical closeness, is our only comfort in the dark! Indeed, so great is the isolation that not even a struggle is possible.

Men, he reflects, have not changed since they tore each other to pieces in the primeval forest; the law of the jungle still rules their lives in the cities.

The comedy *Mann ist Mann* (Man is Man) represents a further step towards Brecht's final dramatic form. It is the first of his plays to introduce 'songs' (Brecht always uses the English term) at the culminating points of the action, voicing general reflections and pointing the moral of the case. These songs are for the most part incorporated in his first collection of poetry, published under the ironical title *Die Hauspostille*

(Book of Family Prayers, 1927), which served as an inexhaustible source of lyrics for his plays.

The play shows, as stated in its sub-title, 'The transformation of the porter Galy Gay in the military barracks at Kilkoa in the year 1925'. The story is told in the manner of a parable: a common porter, on his way to buy a fish in the market, is kidnapped by some soldiers and persuaded to take the place of one of their comrades at roll-call. In the course of his transformation, he loses step by step his individuality, disowns his wife and his very name, and eventually becomes a mere cypher, a 'human fighting-machine'. Towards the end, the army sets out to fight on the northern frontier. The war is cynically represented as serving purely commercial aims: 'If they need cotton it is Tibet, and if they need wool it is Pamir.' When the question is raised as to who is the enemy, a soldier retorts indifferently, 'We have not yet been informed on which country we are about to wage war. But we have been informed that it will be a purely defensive war.' In passages of this kind, Brecht's anti-capitalist attitude is clearly foreshadowed. The basic idea of the play is once again contained in crude verses spoken by one of the characters:

> *Herr Bertolt Brecht behauptet: Mann ist Mann.*
> *Und das ist etwas, was jeder behaupten kann.*
> *Aber Herr Bertolt Brecht beweist auch dann*
> *Dass man mit einem Menschen beliebig viel machen kann.*
> *Hier wird heute Abend ein Mensch wie ein Auto ummontiert*
> *Ohne dass er irgend etwas dabei verliert. . . .*

> Herr Bertolt Brecht declares: man is man.
> That's something anybody may declare.
> But Herr Bertolt Brecht goes on to prove
> That you can do what you like with a man.
> Here to-night a man is remodelled like a car
> Without losing anything in the process. . . .

Despite its exotic setting, *Mann ist Mann* was obviously aimed at the revival of militarism in Germany at the time. (In a note added in 1936, Brecht suggested 'concretizing' the play by transferring the scene of action from India to Germany, turning the British Tommies into Nazi stormtroopers, the porter Galy Gay into a German petty bourgeois, and so forth.) It was the first play to be accepted by the author into his subsequent dogmatic canon. In a later revival, in 1931, he produced it in accordance with his newly developed stage theories, transforming the players, by means of masks, stilts, and artificial hands, into repulsive monsters – with disastrous results.

With *Mann ist Mann* ended what may be called Brecht's early, expressionist phase. His next play, *Die Dreigroschenoper* (The Threepenny Opera, 1928), showed him firmly rooted in Marxist dogma, which from then on formed the solid basis of all his writings. This work proved not only his biggest hit, it was the greatest success achieved by any play during the 1920s. The characters and the plot are taken from John Gay's *Beggar's Opera*, while the traditional English ballads are replaced by translations from François Villon and Kipling, and by Brecht's own verses, with music by Kurt Weill. The time of action is advanced to the beginning of the present century, and the gaoler Lockit is transformed into the chief of the London police, thus sharpening the satirical sting. The beggars, in the English original a picturesque feature of ballad opera, have in Brecht's version a serious social significance. It is in the 'songs' that the revolutionary challenge is most pungently expressed. In conformity with Marxist doctrine, society is ruled by economic factors while all moral and religious concepts are mere ideologies serving the interests of the rich.

> *Erst kommt das Fressen, dann kommt die Moral.*
> *Erst muss es möglich sein auch armen Leuten*
> *Vom grossen Brotlaib sich ihr Teil zu schneiden.*

First comes gobbling, then morality.
First the poor, too, must be allowed
To cut themselves their share from the large loaf.

Die Dreigroschenoper is steeped in the bitter cynicism that permeates all Brecht's writings. His philosophy of life is most concisely formulated in one of the songs, '*Die Welt ist arm, der Mensch ist schlecht*' (The world is poor, man is evil), reversing the basic creed of the expressionists, 'man is good'. For the first time, this cynicism finds vent in a revolutionary challenge, directed at the 'rich' and calling for the overthrow of the social order. The popular success of the play – as of most of Brecht's works – was in fact based on a misconception: while the middle-class audiences relished the antics of Macheath and his gang of cut-throats, Brecht intended these to represent 'bourgeois types', and their exploits to reflect 'bourgeois morality'. In one of his commentaries, he interpreted the action in terms of Marxist doctrine, e.g., 'The robber Macheath must be represented by the actor as a bourgeois character. The partiality of the bourgeoisie for robbers can be explained from the fallacy that a robber is not a bourgeois. This fallacy derives from another fallacy: a bourgeois is not a robber,' and so on.

Die Dreigroschenoper marked a turning-point not only in Brecht's intellectual development but in his dramatic technique and the theories from which it was evolved. These theories – propagated in numerous commentaries which from then on accompanied his creative work – centre around his basic concept of 'epic theatre'. This new epic theatre is opposed to the old 'dramatic' or 'dynamic' theatre; for the traditional form of drama, with its exposition, climax, and dénouement, it substitutes a loose sequence of scenes, each of which is self-contained. The general implications of the action are emphasized by means of posters, projections, and direct apostrophe of the audience. In keeping with these methods of production, a different style of acting is required: the actor must not put himself or the audience 'into a trance'; instead of identifying himself with his part, he must 'demonstrate' it. The spectator, on the other hand, instead of being emotionally involved, must follow the action cool-headedly; he must not 'sympathize' but 'judge', he must take sides and reach a rational conclusion.

These aesthetic theories are subordinated to a single purpose – the 'activation' of the spectator, in other words, the propagation of Marxist doctrine. All the plays of Brecht's maturity are merely parables designed to illustrate this doctrine. The subordination of artistic values to political objects implied the conscious renunciation of those poetic qualities which distinguished his earlier, pre-Marxist writings: from now on, Brecht cultivated an austere, rational, as it were dehydrated style; whenever his innate poetic power broke through it did so almost in spite of himself.

The propagandist purpose is most outspoken in the so-called *Lehrstücke*, or 'didactic pieces', which Brecht produced in the years following the *Dreigroschenoper*. The first was the *Badener Lehrstück* (1929), which was followed by *Der Jasager* (He who says Yes) and its dialectical counterpiece, *Der Neinsager* (He who says No, 1929/30), *Die Massnahme* (The Measure, 1930), *Die Ausnahme und die Regel* (The Exception and the Rule, 1930), and *Die Horatier und die Kuriatier* (The Horatii and the Curiatii, 1934). All these were didactic playlets, designed to illustrate Marxist dogma, usually through a dialectical argument on the right or wrong conduct in a given situation. In these pieces, every vestige of individual characterization is erased; the characters are merely mouthpieces arguing points of the Marxist creed. The very theme of most of the *Lehrstücke* is the ruthless effacement of the individual, his voluntary submission to the will of the Party – even at the price of his life. In *Die Massnahme*, for instance, a communist agent refuses, on humanitarian grounds, to carry out an order of the Party. He tears off his mask, the symbol of his anonymity, and is liquidated by his comrades – with his own consent:

> *Er sagte noch: Im Interesse des Kommunismus*
> *Einverstanden mit dem Vormarsch der proletarischen Massen*
> *Aller Länder*
> *Ja sagend zur Revolutionierung der Welt.*

> He still cried: in the interest of Communism,
> Agreeing to the advance of the proletarian masses
> Of all countries,
> Saying yes to the revolutionizing of the world.

Brecht's conversion to communism was not actuated by any genuine sympathy for the poor or any vision of a better future for mankind, as it had been with many expressionist writers. It was born from a deep-rooted hatred of the bourgeois class from which he himself had sprung; and it was a desperate effort to escape from the total nihilism of his earlier years and accept the absolute values of a rigid, infallible party organization – even at the price of his own poetic substance. It might be compared, in its psychological roots, to the final escape of some of the German Romantics into the Roman Catholic Church.

In the *Lehrstücke*, Brecht's dogmatism took its most rigid form. These were, however, designed not for the theatre proper but for amateur performances, especially at party meetings and in schools. Later on, he receded from their complete rationalism and austerity of style, returning to a more poetical and differentiated dramatic form – without, however, relenting in his strict communist dogmatism.

The first full-length dramatic work to follow *Die Drei-groschenoper* was *Aufstieg und Fall der Stadt Mahagonny* (Rise and Fall of the Town of Mahagonny, 1929), with music by Kurt Weill – Brecht's nearest approach to full-scale opera. Basically, it was a fully developed *Lehrstück*, demonstrating the growth and decline of a capitalist society by tracing the development of an imaginary gold-diggers' town from its foundation to its destruction.

One of the last major works completed before 1933 was *Die heilige Johanna der Schlachthöfe* (Saint Joan of the Stock-yards, 1932). The scene is once again Chicago which evidently represented for Brecht capitalist power at its worst. The main issue of the play is the ruthless struggle raging between capitalists and workers. The economic slump is unmasked as a deliberate machination on the part of the capitalists for the sake of profit. Against this background unfolds the drama of a Salvation Army lass who mixes with the workers to preach the Gospel, inspired by an ardent belief in the supremacy of spiritual over material values. She sees in her mission 'the last attempt to reinstate God in a decaying world, and that through the humblest of men'. Step by step Johanna, under the harrowing impact of unemployment and poverty, comes to realize the supreme importance of economic factors. Torn by doubt, she fails to deliver an important message entrusted to her by the workers' leaders; the general strike fails through her fault. In the end, Johanna lies dying and, in a fervent oration, renounces the Christian faith for the sake of her newly acquired knowledge. In the place of individual goodness, she proclaims the transformation of the world by revolution:

> . . . *Denn nichts werde gezählt als gut . . . als was*
> *Wirklich hilft, und nichts gelte als ehrenhaft mehr, als was*
> *Diese Welt endgültig ändert: sie braucht es . . .*
> *Sorgt doch, dass ihr die Welt verlassend*
> *Nicht nur gut wart, sondern verlasst*
> *Eine gute Welt!*

> . . . For nothing should be counted good . . . but what
> Truly helps, and nothing should be called honourable but what
> Finally changes the world; it needs it . . .
> See to it that when leaving the world
> You have not merely been good, but leave behind
> A good world!

An important stylistic element in this drama is parody: the stockbrokers discuss their business transactions in classical blank verse and, in their closing choruses, adopt the metrical pattern from the last scene of *Faust, Second Part*. And in the final tableau, Johanna is canonized with literal quotations from Schiller's *Jungfrau von Orleans*. These parodies are used for the obvious purpose of exposing the 'bourgeois' character of classical German drama.

For all its intrinsic dramatic power, *Die heilige Johanna der Schlachthöfe* is too closely bound up with the specific conditions of its period – economic crisis and mass unemployment – to be of lasting value. Its publication and performance in Germany were thwarted by the Nazi revolution. Shortly before, in 1932, Brecht completed a play *Die Mutter* (The Mother), after a novel by Gorki. Again a woman is converted, through personal experience, to the Marxist creed: here it is the mother of a worker who dies a communist martyr. The action is set in Russia, starting with the abortive rising in 1905 and ending with the revolution of 1917. The style is deliberately arid and matter-of-fact, enlivened only by some songs of purely didactic character. The rich local colour and emotive appeal of the original are studiously eliminated. In fact, the whole play is little more than an expanded *Lehrstück*, designed to promulgate Marxist doctrine.

In 1933, Brecht left Germany for Denmark where he spent the first few years of his exile. At the outbreak of war, he went to Sweden and Finland, and from there – not to Russia, as might have been expected – but to the United States, where he lived until 1947. Hitler's rise to power gave his writings a new direction. In accordance with the Marxist viewpoint, he identified Fascism with Capitalism and saw in the Nazi tyranny merely another attempt of the bourgeoisie to maintain its hold over the working class. It is in this light that many of his writings in exile must be seen. His first attempt to treat the rise of Nazism dramatically was a parable play, *Die Rundköpfe und die Spitzköpfe* (Round Heads and Peak Heads, 1934[1]), which is set in a fictitious country, Jahoo. Hitler appears as a demagogue, Iberin, who is called in by an impotent viceroy (Hindenburg) to quell a rising of the dispossessed farmers by proclaiming a racial theory based on 'round-heads' (good) and 'peak-heads' (bad). In the end, the wealthy round-heads come to terms with the wealthy peak-heads, thus reasserting the domination of rich over poor – the only distinction valid in Brecht's eyes. Much more effective than this rather tortuous parable was a sequence of realistic scenes, *Furcht und Elend des Dritten Reiches* (Fear and Misery of the Third Reich, 1938, translated under the title *The Private Life of the Master Race*), depicting life in Germany under the Nazi terror. A short play, *Die Gewehre der Frau Carrar* (Señora Carrar's Rifles, 1937), has as its background the Spanish civil war, repeating to a certain extent the theme of *Die Mutter*: a mother is converted through the murder of her son, and joins the revolutionary cause.

During the war, Brecht once more made the rise of Hitler the subject of a play, *Der aufhaltsame Aufstieg des Arturo Ui* (The Resistible Rise of Arturo Ui, 1941), this time in terms of a gangster from the Chicago underworld, a setting much favoured by the playwright as representing an undiluted capitalistic society Here he uses mock blank verse throughout to parody the bogus heroism of the characters involved. This work remained unpublished till after Brecht's death. So did a dramatic sequence *Schweyk im Zweiten Weltkrieg* (Schweyk in the Second World War, written 1941-1944) which revives the hero of Hašek's famous novel, showing him under Nazi domination and as a soldier in Hitler's army fighting before Stalingrad. In Brecht's hands, the character assumes a bitterness

---

[1] This and the following dates quoted refer to the time of writing, since most of Brecht's works written in exile were published much later, some posthumously.

and pungency quite foreign to the original. In the end
Schweyk, the embodiment of the 'common man', leads
Hitler astray in the snowfields of Russia.

Under the impact of the fall of France, Brecht wrote, in
collaboration with the novelist Lion Feuchtwanger (with
whom he had already produced in 1924 an adaptation of
Marlowe's *Edward II*), *Die Gesichte der Simone Machard* (The
Visions of Simone Machard, 1941-1943). Once again, Brecht
uses the story of Joan of Arc as a symbolic parallel. The scene
is set in a French provincial town during the collapse of 1940.
A poor servant girl, still half a child, feels inspired by a book on
Joan of Arc to help her countrymen in their plight. While the
well-to-do citizens try to save their belongings, she distributes
food to the fugitives and finally blows up a petrol-dump to
prevent its falling into the hands of the Germans. Parallel
to this realistic action, there runs a sequence of dream scenes
in which events from the life of Joan are enacted. All the
characters have a double function: Simone is identified with the
Maid, while the others, Germans and their French collabora-
tors, appear in corresponding historical guises. In the end, the
two planes merge: as Joan is burnt at the stake, a swastika flag
dominates the stage. Here, too, the communist viewpoint is
emphasized throughout: the rich associate with the enemy to
save their property, while the poor are the helpless victims.
The object of the play – as Brecht hastens to point out – is not
the glorification of French patriotism but 'an illustration of
the nature of human society'.

Most of these works, related as they were to current events,
are of only secondary importance. At the same time, however,
Brecht wrote, in the enforced isolation of his exile, the series
of plays on which his international fame is mainly founded.
In these works, his genius as a dramatist reached full maturity.
Though still designed to demonstrate the Marxist theory, they
are nevertheless parables of human existence. Perhaps the most

13. BRECHT, *Trommeln in der Nacht*. Munich, 1922

14. BRECHT, *Mutter Courage und ihre Kinder*, Berlin, 1951
(Berliner Ensemble)

compelling is *Mutter Courage und ihre Kinder* (Mother Courage and her Children). Written in 1938, this play is already imbued with the tragedy of war. Its form is that of a chronicle, based on a story by the seventeenth-century German writer Grimmelshausen. The central figure is a camp-follower and sutler-woman who pulls her ramshackle cart through the wreckage and horror of the Thirty Years' War. With her are her children, two sons and a dumb daughter, whom she loses one by one despite her frantic efforts to save them. With her blend of cunning, impudence, common sense, and maternal instinct, Mother Courage is perhaps the most real character Brecht has created. She propagates no doctrines, but by her very nature epitomizes the sufferings of the nameless masses in the cataclysm of war. The dialogue, cast in the crisp and lucid prose peculiar to Brecht, with a touch of the Bavarian dialect, is interspersed with lyrics in the seventeenth-century style. In his customary comment on the play, Brecht insists that it was not his intention to rouse sympathy for the tragedy of a mother. Instead, the drama was designed as an object-lesson demonstrating the effect of war on the masses (represented by Mother Courage) – a striking instance of the discrepancy between the playwright's theoretical reflections and his dramatic intuition. Here, as in so many other instances, his sheer poetic power seems to burst the strait-jacket of his Marxist dogmatism.

The other outstanding play written in the years 1938-1939 was *Leben des Galilei* (Life of Galileo). Of all his later works, this is the one least connected with social theories. In fifteen scenes, it depicts more than thirty years of Galileo's life in a dispassionate, studiously undramatic way, conforming to Brecht's idea of 'epic' drama. The natural climax, Galileo's recantation, takes place off-stage. Brecht carefully refrains from idealizing the central figure: his Galileo is a rationalist, sceptical, dispassionate, for ever compromising with the powers that be. After the recantation – due, as he frankly admits, to fear of physical pain – he turns into a resigned old man, given to material comfort. A pupil of his, however, smuggles a copy of his treatise across the frontier, out of reach of the Inquisition. Even here, Brecht manages to introduce a social slant: street singers chant a ballad, giving the planetary movements a Marxist interpretation; and Galileo himself, in a concluding speech, links the progress of science with ideas of social revolution totally out of keeping with his period. Yet despite these anachronisms and the calculated lack of tension, the play has an irresistible dramatic force of its own. It is perhaps the most personally revealing of all Brecht's works.

During his stay in Finland, in 1940, Brecht wrote *Herr Puntila und sein Knecht Matti* (Master Puntila and his Servant Matti), his nearest approach to downright comedy. This is his happiest, most light-hearted play, full of buoyant humour, and rich with the colours of the Finnish scene. Yet its theme, too, is the class war. The two principal characters, a wealthy country squire and his chauffeur, typify the ruling and the working classes respectively. The main point of the play is that the squire, Master Puntila, is alternately dead-drunk and sober. In his bouts of drunkenness, he is generous and sympathetic towards his subordinates; he makes friends with Matti, his chauffeur, and even offers him his daughter in marriage. In his sober moments, however, he turns into a ruthless businessman: in other words, he reverts to the 'natural' state of a capitalist. In his notes on the staging of the play, Brecht emphasizes that the chauffeur should be clearly the 'intellectually superior', and that the actor of Puntila should be on his guard not to 'carry away the spectators by vitality and charm' in such a way as to 'deprive them of the freedom of criticizing him' – a clear proof that in this play, too, class hatred was his main motive.

In *Puntila* the good and bad are personified in two contrasting characters; this antithesis is contained within a single figure in the Chinese parable of *Der gute Mensch von Sezuan* (The Good Woman of Sezuan, 1938-1940). The heroine is a prostitute whose outstanding quality is unshakable goodness of heart. She is the only person to offer shelter to three deities who have come to earth in search of a 'good man'. With the money they give her she buys a small tobacco shop, but is unable to resist the throng of destitute neighbours who live on her charity. In order to rid herself of their demands, she invents a fictitious male cousin: alternately disguising herself as him and resuming her own identity, she ruthlessly retrieves with one hand what she gives away with the other. She falls in love with a down-and-out aviator for whom she sacrifices all her savings. To provide for her unborn child in a callous world, she runs a tobacco factory in the guise of her cousin, brutally exploiting the workers. At last she finds herself so hopelessly entangled that she reveals her double identity in court. But her heart-rending cry to the gods (who act as judges) remains unanswered. The play is left without a conclusive ending, but by implication Brecht suggests that, since the gods are unable, or unwilling, to protect the good, only a change of the social order can put things right. To avoid any misunderstanding, he states in a prefatory note that the action is set in pre-communist China, when 'men were exploited by men'.

Brecht's last full-length play written during his years in America, *Der kaukasiche Kreidekreis* (The Caucasian Chalk Circle, 1944-1945), is also based on a Chinese fable – a result, no doubt, of his pre-occupation with the Far Eastern theatre. In the original legend, two women, fighting over a child, are asked to pull him out of a circle chalked on the ground: the one who refuses for fear of hurting him is proved to be the true mother. Brecht turns this story upside-down to fit his political purpose. In his version, a 'bad' rich woman, the governor's wife, abandons her child during a rebellion, and a poor servant girl finds it and takes it to the mountains, bringing it up as her own. When after some years the governor's wife reclaims her child, a judge applies the test of the chalk circle: but now it is the poor girl who refuses to use force, and to whom the child is awarded as to the 'true' mother. This story is linked with a second plot centring on the judge who pronounces the verdict. He is a 'man of the people' who has been elected during the rebellion and administers justice by 'common sense', in fact always favouring the poor. The place of action has been transferred from China to the Caucasus, and the play is introduced by a scene enacted among Georgian peasants at the time of the German invasion – evidently to underline the topicality of the story.

For all its obvious propagandist aims, the sheer poetic power of this play, as of its predecessor, is undeniable. Both in *Der kaukasische Kreidekreis* and in *Der gute Mensch von Sezuan*, Brecht employs a deliberately primitive technique: the characters frequently address the audience directly, explaining and commenting on their actions, and pointing the moral. This they do often in a few lines of verse, modelled on the short lyric patterns of Chinese or Japanese poetry. In addition there are the characteristic 'songs', summing up the moral of the story in a concise and trenchant form.

Throughout this sequence of plays, ranging from *Mutter Courage* to *Der kaukasische Kreidekreis*, Brecht is pre-occupied with the problem of 'good' and 'bad'. However, this universal issue he deliberately narrows down to the social plane. Although he does not actually identify good with poor, and bad with rich, he often enough comes close to this simple equation. His rich people are throughout bad by force of their social function as capitalists; but so are many of his poor since they are forced to live in a cold and wicked world. Evidently, the only genuine conviction Brecht held – and had held from the outset – was the conviction that the world is bad, and man is evil. Against this basic belief, his communist doctrines, the hopes he pinned on a social revolution, sound unconvincing – like a frantic effort to overcome the despair of total nihilism. It is this despair, rather than his crude social theories, which has given his work its wide appeal in the years since the Second World War.

When Brecht returned to Germany in 1948 to form his own company in East Berlin, his work was essentially completed. His last comparatively independent play, *Die Tage der Commune* (The Days of the Commune), was written in Switzerland, in 1948-1949. It is no more than a dry account of the rise and fall of the Paris Commune during the Franco-Prussian War, told in long-winded arguments devoid of dramatic interest. It demonstrates once again, with little regard to historical fact, the Marxist view that the bourgeois class prefers to come to terms with the national enemy in order to oppress the working class. – An opera, *Das Verhör des Lukullus* (The Trial of Lucullus, 1951) was in essence a radio play written in 1939: Brecht presented it in two different versions, one for the West, expressing pacifist views, and one for the East, with significant modifications. For the rest, his creative activities were limited to the adaptation of established works of world literature, such as Sophocles' *Antigone*, Shakespeare's *Coriolanus*, Goethe's *Urfaust*, and *Der Hofmeister* by the eighteenth-century dramatist Lenz. In these adaptations, Brecht's method was always to re-arrange what he called the 'social material' of the original play, in other words, to bring it into line with Marxist doctrine.

It is a remarkable fact that Brecht's creative urge subsided at the very moment he came to live under the social system he had glorified in his work. It is no less remarkable that he scored his greatest successes in the Western countries, that is, in the very society he viciously attacked throughout his life.

217

His fame was at its peak when he died in 1956, at the age of fifty-eight.

Like every original writer, Bertolt Brecht defies classification. It may be said that Expressionism and Neo-realism merge in his work. He followed the expressionists in using drama to propagate social ideas, and in abandoning the realistic stage. On the other hand, he reacted violently against their emotional exaltation and cultivated a sober, matter-of-fact style. While the expressionists preached the regeneration of man through a change of spirit, Brecht aimed at the material transformation of the social order on a communist basis; while they put their faith in the untrammelled freedom of the individual, he demanded complete subordination to a collective – the communist party machine. Thus Brecht represented the final phase of a development which had begun before the First World War. Yet, with his bold experiments in new dramatic forms, he pointed the way to the future.

Chapter Six

NATIONAL SOCIALIST DRAMA

I. FORERUNNERS

Hitler's rise to power in 1933 put a sudden end to the cultural life of the republican era, including the drama. Few political events have transformed the intellectual climate of a country so abruptly; for the national socialist revolution was actuated not so much by social and economic factors as by emotional and ideological impulses. The great majority of writers had supported, tacitly or openly, the Weimar Republic, or else held radical Leftist views. All these writers were barred overnight from the theatre and the book market by the rigid Nazi laws; most of them were driven into exile.

The ideas actuating the Nazi movement were diametrically opposed to those of the Weimar Republic and the revolution of 1918. They centred on the Nation as the supreme value. In the eyes of the Nazis, the revolution which ended the First World War had been purely destructive, and the intervening period an era of negation and moral anarchy.

A transformation of such range and violence could not of course happen overnight. In fact, the forces leading up to it were active for a long time before. As in the political field, there was in the realm of drama what may be called a 'nationalist opposition' – a group of writers fiercely opposed to all the republic stood for. Although not all of these writers were necessarily Nazis most of them threw in their lot with the Third Reich once it was established. By cherishing the ideals of German power, of heroism and racial supremacy, which later found their full expression in the Nazi creed, they were justly acclaimed by the national socialists as their spiritual fore-runners.

The nationalist counter-current in drama had its source in the patriotic plays of World War I. During the last phase of that war, and for a short time after, it was temporarily obscured by the flood of expressionist drama. But it never disappeared completely, and after 1922, when the revolutionary impulse had spent itself, it gained new strength, increasing steadily up to 1933.

With regard to style, the nationalist playwrights were little affected by Expressionism. Corresponding to their retrospective and reactionary attitude, they favoured the traditional forms of realistic or blank verse drama. Yet in some instances they too used the expressionist technique.

A striking example of this curious combination was Hermann von Boetticher's *Die Liebe Gottes* (The Love of God, 1919). Its date of publication proves that the germ of nationalist reaction was latent in the republic from the outset. In its form, the play shows the typical pattern of expressionist drama: it pictures the mental anguish of the hero (identical with the author) whose road of suffering through an antagonistic world unrolls in a sequence of loosely connected scenes. The language has the feverish exaltation of expressionist diction; the characters, though bearing individual names, are throughout types and include such supernatural elements as Dead Souls, The Spirit of Decline, The Spirit of Ascension, and so forth. However, the message of the play is in sharp contrast to the spirit of revolutionary drama. The hero is significantly named Achim von Arnim – symbolizing both his pronounced German character and his spiritual affinity to the Romantics. He is described as a writer and mystic, driven by an ardent 'search for God', and yearning for redemption from his mental agonies. The scene is Berlin in 1918. Throughout the play, the sound of rifle and machine-gun fire accompanies the action. The main plot concerns the hero's love for a girl from a wealthy bourgeois home. The demoralization caused by war and revolution is glaringly depicted in her parents and her circle of friends who indulge in a life of superficial pleasures. Achim feels it to be his mission to fight for the girl's 'soul'. His violent criticism of the time is tinged with racial prejudice: he attributes the girl's moral instability to her French and Russian blood and her Jewish environment. It is from these 'contaminating' influences that Achim tries to save her. He sees his ideal in a life of Old-Prussian austerity, which he finds epitomized in the home of a humble artisan in a small provincial town. In this unspoiled haven, he enjoys a temporary respite from his mental torments. Joyfully he acclaims 'the willing militia men who are marching over there in the market square and have found themselves again'.

As can be seen from this outline, Boetticher's play gave the expressionist search for spiritual regeneration an interpretation completely opposed to its original meaning. It contained all the principal tenets of Nazi philosophy: the conception of the 1918 revolution as moral anarchy, the mystical craving for a 'rebirth' of Germany, her 'purification' from foreign, above all Jewish, influence, and the glorification of soldierly virtues.

The embodiment of these ideas in an expressionist play was rather an exception. As already indicated, the reactionary nature of nationalist drama corresponded, as a rule, to traditional forms. The leading exponent of what was termed the 'neo-classical' drama was Paul Ernst (1866-1933), who was later hailed as one of the pioneers of the national socialist theatre. Throughout his lifetime, Paul Ernst was acclaimed only by a limited clique – a fact the Nazis ascribed, as usual, to malicious neglect on the part of dramatic critics and theatre directors. His major works date as far back as the beginning of the century. In a large number of critical essays,

Ernst expounded his aesthetic theories. He was violently opposed both to Naturalism and Neo-romanticism because of their 'passive' and merely 'compassionate' attitudes. By way of contrast, he set forth his ideal of heroic tragedy, centring on the *kämpferischer Mensch* (militant man), who rises to the challenge of fate instead of succumbing to it. He saw the supreme realization of this ideal in Greek tragedy. Drama, for Paul Ernst, had an ethical and religious mission. These theories he tried to realize in some of his own plays which treated subjects from Greek mythology (*Ariadne auf Naxos* (1914), *Kassandra* (1915)), or medieval German legend (*Brunhild* (1911), *Chriemhild* (1924)). But owing to their ponderous and dramatically ineffective character, these works were scarcely noticed by the contemporary theatre.

Under the impact of the war, Ernst resorted to subjects from Prussian history. His plays on Frederick the Great, *Preussengeist* (Prussian Spirit, 1914), and on the Prussian general of the Napoleonic war, *Yorck* (1917), were typical examples of patriotic drama in the First World War. Paul Ernst did not live long enough to reap the fruits of his attempts to revive what he considered the classical and national drama in the grand manner.

Another acknowledged forerunner of national socialist drama was Dietrich Eckhart (a close friend of Hitler), who died as early as 1923. Besides a great number of third-rate comedies, he tried his hand at a series of ambitious historical plays, among them *Heinrich der Hohenstaufe* (1915) and *Lorenzaccio* (performed in 1933) – the latter a wilful interpretation, from a racial and nationalist viewpoint, of Lorenzo de Medici. He also undertook to re-write Ibsen's *Peer Gynt* (1914), transforming the hero into an embodiment of Germanic mysticism.

Two types of plays most favoured by nationalist writers were the historical play and the peasant drama. There was a continuous line of historical plays running through the republican era, linking the patriotic plays of World War I with the national socialist drama. Two early specimens were a play on Frederick the Great by Joachim von der Goltz, *Vater und Sohn* (1922), and Wolfgang Goetz's *Neidhardt von Gneisenau* (1925). The latter proved one of the major successes of the period; it was taken to signalize the recovery of the German theatre from the convulsions of Expressionism, and the revival of a healthy national drama. There followed an uninterrupted chain of historical plays extending beyond the year 1933. The subjects most cherished were Frederick the Great, who stood as the epitome of military virtues and self-effacing submission to the State, and the War of Liberation against Napoleon, which provided a shining example of national resurgence.

Along with the historical play, the nationalist reaction manifested itself in what became known as *Blut und Boden* (blood-and-soil) literature. This type of writing concentrated on a glorification of the soil as the mystical source of the nation's life, in contrast to the corrupting life of the cities. It preached the return to the simple, unchanging values of peasant life as a basis for national regeneration. This line of thought, which found its fullest expression in the novel, left its mark on the drama, too. A typical instance was a play by Hans Franck (1879-), *Klaus Michel* (1925). The author had made his name with a war drama, *Freie Knechte* (Free Bondsmen, 1919), enacted among the North German peasantry. Here a mother's violent denunciation of war, which has robbed her of her sons, is countered by the father who extols the supreme value of self-sacrifice for the fatherland. Franck's nationalist attitude was fully reflected in *Klaus Michel*. The play traces the life-story of a peasant's son who leaves his father's farm to go to the university and thus breaks the continuity of the family tradition. He becomes a famous surgeon, marries, and has a son. When war breaks out, the son enlists as a volunteer while Klaus joins up as a doctor. They meet on the battlefield where the father sacrifices his life to save the son. The tombstone set up on his grave is to bear the epitaph, 'Here rests a German man'. Some years after the war, the son returns to his ancestral farm where his eyes are opened to the permanent values of peasant life which his father betrayed:

> *Wer bin denn ich,*
> *dass ich mich aus dem ewigen Kräftekreis*
> *ablösen könnte? jemals meine Hand*
> *erheben dürfte wider jenes Ur,*
> *durch das ich wurde?*

> Who am I that I should sever myself
> from the eternal cycles of forces?
> that I should ever lift my hand against that mystic source
> from which I have sprung?

He feels himself to be a link in the unending chain of generations, and a part of the collective entity of the *Volk*. Franck's play, for all its immaturity, was one of the more sincere attempts to seek a remedy for the moral instability of the postwar years in a return to the 'soil', the sound basis of the nation.

During the later twenties, and especially after 1933, the 'blood-and-soil' play occupied an ever increasing place in dramatic literature, usually as a vehicle for the propagation of nationalist ideas. One of the few authors of distinction in this field was Richard Billinger (1893-), an Austrian by birth, who made his name in the last years before the Nazi revolution. His plays, set mostly in his native district, the borderland between Austria and Bavaria, present a peculiar mixture of crude realism and poetic mysticism. Their main themes are the conflict between town and country, and the eruption of primeval, pagan instincts under the thin layer of Christian beliefs. His first play, *Das Perchtenspiel* (1928), shows the superstitious belief in demons in conflict with Christianity.

The same conflict underlies his play *Rauhnacht* (Yule Night, 1931): here the.peasants succumb, on Christmas Eve, to an orgy of pagan rites in the course of which a murder is committed. In a terse one-act drama, *Rosse* (Horses, 1931), the antagonism between town and country comes to a head when an old farmhand, passionately devoted to his horses, kills a trader who wants to sell tractors, and then hangs himself in the stable. Perhaps the most accomplished work of Billinger is *Die Hexe von Passau* (The Witch of Passau, 1935), which is set at the time of the peasants' war. A young peasant girl, acting the part of Mary Magdalene in a passion play, so moves an officer by her performance that he saves the convicted rebels from the hangman. Accused of witchcraft, she is thrown into prison and condemned to be burned at the stake. While she dies a martyr's death, the officer sides with the peasants and leads the rebellion to victory. *Der Gigant* (The Giant, 1937), again turns on the conflict between town and country, this time in a Moravian setting. The 'giant' of the title is the city of Prague which lures a peasant-girl into its snares. She returns, broken in body and soul, to her native village. Despised by her father and her friends, she seeks death on the moor. Once again, the mystic powers of the soil prove stronger than the corruption of town-life. 'If you are unfaithful to the plot of land on which you are born as a peasant you will dry up, wither away, and be cut off!' These words express the basic idea of the play – as of all Billinger's works.

Apart from these rare attempts at serious peasant drama, the 'blood-and-soil' plays consisted for the most part of popular farces displaying a crude rustic humour. The foremost example of this type of farce was *Krach um Jolanthe* (Row about Jolanthe, 1931) by August Hinrichs, which had as its central figure – a sow. This play came to be one of the greatest theatrical hits of the Nazi era.

The development of nationalist drama from Expressionism

to the eve of the Nazi revolution is fully reflected in the career of Hanns Johst, who was hailed by the Nazis as one of their principal forerunners in the dramatic field. Hanns Johst (1890-   ) made his first appearance at the beginning of World War I with a one-act war play *Die Stunde der Sterbenden* (The Hour of the Dying, 1914). In *Der junge Mensch* (The Youth, 1916), sub-titled 'An ecstatic scenario', he presented a typical expressionist play of adolescence, portraying a youth who rebels against philistinism and outworn conventions. His next play, *Der Einsame* (The Lonely One, 1917) has as its hero the nineteenth-century dramatist Christian Grabbe who was claimed by the expressionists as one of their precursors. Grabbe, in Johst's play, lives in a permanent state of ecstasy and proclaims the supremacy of *Gefühl* (emotion) over the limitations of reality. The drama opens with this soliloquy of the poet:

> *Oh! Dies Gefühl! Nicht um einen Thron möchte ich es eintauschen! Dieses Gottvatergefühl! Himmel und Erde wird Willkür meiner Gunst! Ich bin der Kosmos! Und ohne mein Wort und ohne die glühende Guirlande meiner Dichtung zerfällt dies alles – Geschichte, Vernunft, Gegenwart und Seele von tausend Gottesäckern – zu wesenlosem Staube.*

> (Oh! This emotion! I wouldn't exchange it for a throne! This divine feeling! Heaven and earth are but a whim of mine! I am the cosmos! Without my words and without the glowing garland of my poetry all this crumbles to insignificant dust – history, reason, the present, and the soul of a thousand of God's fields.

Grabbe's boundless impetuosity brings him into conflict with his fellow-citizens. He transgresses all the moral conventions, seduces his best friend's fiancée, and eventually perishes, mentally and physically exhausted. Evidently this portrait of Grabbe was intended to represent the 'typically German' genius. The author's subsequent development was also foreshadowed in the anti-Semitic outbursts of the hero when discussing his contemporary Heine.

The impact of the 1918 revolution on Johst's work made itself felt in his play *Der König* (The King, 1920). An idealistic young king tries to rule his country on the basis of 'absolute goodness'. He abolishes court etiquette and administers justice from a purely humane viewpoint, in the firm belief that his example will transform the world. However, the king is declared insane by his mother and put under arrest. Broken in spirit, he throws himself from a tower of the palace while the people clamour for his death. The moral of the play is expressed in the words of the king's physician, 'He who believes in the people the people will chastise, but he who chastises the people – in him will they believe.'

Johst's growing obsession with nationalist ideas revealed itself in *Propheten* (1922), a play about Martin Luther. With its passionate 'search for God' and its exalted diction, the play still bore the stamp of Expressionism. Emphasis is laid not so much on Luther's spiritual struggle for the reformation of the Church as on the 'German' character of his mission. In the closing scene, Luther predicts triumphantly the rebirth of Germany; he violently condemns the peasants who acclaim him as their spiritual leader in their fight for freedom. His concluding words, as he meets the soldiers who come to rescue him from the hands of the peasants, run: 'The sword fights, and the sword judges, the name of the sword be praised! Germany takes her heaven by storm!'

In this play, too, Johst's obsession with racial issues is apparent in the portrayal of some Jews as usurers and blasphemers whose brutal murder he openly advocates. *Propheten* clearly marked a turning-point in the author's development towards national socialist ideas.

After a comedy, *Wechsler und Händler* (Money-changers, 1923), in which the heroic German spirit is contrasted, in the familiar way, with the mercantile mind of the Jews, and a play *Die fröhliche Stadt* (The Merry City, 1925), Johst produced what was probably his greatest success, *Thomas Paine* (1927). A Nazi critic later hailed this play as 'the first political drama of the New Germany'. The work is an illuminating example of the deliberate falsification of history for political purposes. Thomas Paine is presented as the main instigator of the American War of Independence, inspiring by his passionate faith the military leaders, Washington and Greene. The American volunteers strongly resemble stormtroopers as they chant in unison Paine's rousing battlesong, with the chorus, 'We, comrades, we!' Washington addresses some merchants, who try to make capital out of the revolution, in unmistakable Nazi jargon, 'A State must be more than mere business. . . . The State – call it God or idol – demands blood!' In the course of the play, Paine crosses to France where he is shocked by the crude materialism of the Jacobins, opposes the execution of the king, and is thrown into prison as a royalist. On his return to America after seventeen years, nobody recognizes him. He ends his life by jumping into the sea, realizing that he has fulfilled his mission since his work, the American nation, is alive.

As is evident from this outline, the historical characters served Johst to proclaim the Nazi philosophy. In his next work, *Schlageter* (1932), he dispensed with the historical guise; this play, though written before the Nazi revolution, was hailed as the supreme dramatic achievement proclaiming the national rebirth. Schlageter, who was executed for sabotage by the French during the occupation of the Ruhr in 1923, is made a national hero, embodying the frantic desire for the 'rebirth' of Germany and her deliverance from the 'fetters of Versailles'. As he is led to his death he bursts into hysterical shouts which, read in retrospect, have an ominous ring of prophecy: *'Deutschland! Ein letztes Wort! Ein Wunsch! Befehl!! Deutschland!!!*

Erwache! Entflamme!! Entbrenne! Brenn ungeheuer!!'
(Germany! A final word! A demand! Command!! Germany!!! Awake! Inflame! Burn immensely!!) This is expressionist ecstasy carried to absurdity. Schlageter represented, as an enthusiastic critic formulated it, 'the last soldier of the Great War and the first soldier of the Third Reich'. The play revealed, like many others of those years, the almost obsessive preoccupation with the First World War, which was one of the most potent impulses of the Nazi movement.

II. DRAMA IN THE THIRD REICH

The national socialist movement which triumphed in 1933 claimed to accomplish the spiritual rebirth of Germany. It looked upon the fourteen years of the Weimar Republic as a period of moral degeneration, every trace of which was to be ruthlessly effaced. It is from this viewpoint that the dramatic production of the Nazi era must be seen. The Nazis vented their wrath on new-realistic and expressionist drama alike. Their criticism even reached back to the neo-romantic and the naturalistic theatre. All these styles of drama were, in their eyes, expressions of a 'liberalistic' and 'individualistic' society which had now come to an end. In that society, the theatre had lost touch with the *Volk*, the people, and had moved in a spiritual vacuum. The foremost mission of national socialist drama was to come once more into contact with the *Volk*. One of the first prerequisites in carrying out this mission was the elimination of all 'foreign', in particular, Jewish influences. The theatre was to become once more, in the words of Schiller, a 'moral institution' – as the Nazis understood it.

These ideas were propounded in countless speeches, proclamations, articles, from the public orations of the 'Minister of Culture and Propaganda', Dr. Goebbels, down to the smallest journalist. They were put into practice by the creation of a *Reichsschrifttumskammer*, from which all unwanted authors were automatically excluded. By this simple device, the entire intellectual life of the nation was brought into line with the tenets of the Nazi creed. The official term, *Gleichschaltung* (rectification), used in this context, likened the nation to an electric current which, at the flick of a switch, could be channelled into one direction.

The first, negative part of this programme was easy enough to realize. By eliminating all the writers who, on racial, political, or any other grounds, were potentially hostile to the new order, complete uniformity was in fact achieved. At the same time, the German theatre was depleted, at a single stroke, of all its major authors. As in every other walk of life, the third- and fourth-rate now came into their own, claiming that they had been studiously ignored under the previous régime. In fact, during the twelve years of Nazi rule, not a single new playwright of importance emerged. And those who were forced upon the public through ceaseless advertisement and lack of competition, vanished without a trace as soon as the Third Reich collapsed.

The intellectual climate of Nazi Germany was, of course, singularly unpropitious to creative art. First, the Third Reich was a totalitarian society moulded into a uniform pattern and directed towards a single aim, namely, the assertion of national power and racial supremacy; any individual efforts not conforming to this pattern were forcibly suppressed. Secondly, the only recognized values were 'heroic' virtues, and the only dramatic conflicts those arising from the struggle of the hero against a hostile and malicious world; all other issues were disdained as pertaining to the 'individualistic' society of the past. Thirdly, Nazi society had sprung, by its very nature, from a revolution of the masses; it scorned every intellectual and artistic activity as potentially dangerous to its interests. Lastly, the self-imposed rupture of all international contacts in the field of art and thought produced a mental isolation which excluded Germany from the intellectual movements of other countries.

Despite these unfavourable conditions, however, the German theatre still maintained a remarkably high standard. To all outward appearances, its highly organized structure remained intact – at any rate, until the middle of the Second World War. The system of large state subsidies, on which it was traditionally based, was fully maintained, and even expanded for propagandist reasons. Nor did the high standard of stage production and acting show any perceptible decline. Moreover, the large proportion of classical drama, so striking a feature of the German theatre, made the absence of any new talent less noticeable. There was, of course, the normal supply of day-to-day theatrical fare – routine comedies and popular farces devoid of literary value. What was conspicuously lacking was any vital development, the emergence of any new talent not artificially inflated by political propaganda. Most surprising of all, even those authors who, during the preceding years, had advocated in their writings the 'national rebirth' (as for instance, Hanns Johst or Arnolt Bronnen) dried up as soon as the event had taken place. As is often the case with revolutionary writers, they were prompted to write only so long as they were in opposition to the existing order, but fell into silence when nothing was left for them to attack.

There was thus a blatant discrepancy between the extravagant claims of spiritual resuscitation, put forth in a flood of cultural propaganda, and the actual achievements in every field of creative art, including the drama. The pattern of national socialist drama followed the trends developed by its forerunners. Emphasis was laid, firstly, on 'blood-and-soil' drama, i.e. plays extolling the regenerating powers of peasant life, and, secondly, on historical plays, glorifying figures and events from the nation's past.

Specially favoured was the war drama, evoking episodes

from the First World War or its immediate aftermath. The revival of the war theme was a striking phenomenon in the years immediately preceding the Nazi revolution – and this not only in Germany but in many other countries. From about 1928 onwards, the theatres of the world were flooded by a spate of plays dealing with the Great War – all the more striking as the war had almost completely faded from literature during the intervening decade.[1] In Germany, this revival was an ominous portent of the Nazi revolution. The glorification of the *Fronterlebnis*, the experience of the trenches, was in fact one of the most powerful impulses of the Nazi movement. It was this emotional experience, exalted to almost mystical heights, which pervaded many (though by no means all) German war plays of those years.

The most successful of this second wave of war plays was *Die endlose Strasse* (The Endless Road, 1930) by Sigmund Graff and E. C. Hintze. The play depicts, in a dispassionate and realistic manner, a single day and night in the life of a company on the Western Front. There is no individual hero: the real hero is the company, or rather the common soldiers of whom it is composed; and their true heroism lies in their unquestioning acceptance of suffering and death in the front line. There is no eloquent outburst nor protest against war, save some grumbling at the officers who enjoy an easy life at base. The attitude of the soldiers is one of unquestioning endurance: 'We've got to go. And this necessity is like one of the commandments. It can't be got round – anyhow.' They feel utterly estranged from their former lives at home; they cannot conceive ever going back: 'Somehow I think we'll

[1] The first play to mark this revival was probably Paul Raynald's *Le Tombeau sous l'Arc de Triomphe* (1926). Its English and Irish counterparts may be seen in R. C. Sheriff's *Journey's End* and Sean O'Casey's *The Silver Tassie* (both 1928) and, in America, *What Price Glory?* by Maxwell Anderson and L. Stalling. All these plays found their way on to the German stage, *What Price Glory?* in an adaptation by Carl Zuckmayer under the title *Rivalen*, produced by Erwin Piscator in 1929.

never get home again – not really home. We've all been caught. And not one of us can ever escape.' One man has even prematurely broken off his leave and returns 'back home to the company'. In the end the company, their promised rest behind the front cut short by a threatened break-through of the enemy, moves up to the line again, to continue on its 'endless road'.

This play presented a true and unbiassed picture of life at the front; by its very objectivity, the effect was profoundly moving. It was all the more remarkable that at any rate one of the authors, Sigmund Graff, soon after wholeheartedly embraced the Nazi creed. His two subsequent plays, *Die vier Musketiere* (The Four Musketeers, 1932) and *Die Heimkehr des Matthias Bruck* (The Return of Matthias Bruck, 1933) treated the familiar theme of the homecoming soldier. The latter play belonged to the 'blood-and-soil' type. A German farmer, returning from Siberia after seventeen years, serves unrecognized as a farm-hand on his own farm. He realizes that life has gone on during his absence, and that he has no right to reclaim his wife who has married again.

Many other war plays, which appeared in quick succession shortly before and after the Nazi revolution, clearly showed the rising of the nationalist tide.[1] They carried a definite message, culminating in the joyful self-sacrifice of the individual for the community. Friedrich Bethge's (1891–   ) *Reims* (1934), for instance, deals with a sergeant who deserts when he learns that his wife is carrying on with a Russian prisoner-of-war. He is caught on his way home and brought before a court martial. When he learns that his regiment has been annihilated during his absence he feels responsible: 'If I had stayed may be they would still be alive!' He is acquitted and volunteers for the

[1] In Austria, a similar nationalist revival showed itself in nostalgia for the bygone glory of the Habsburg Empire. Here the one outstanding war play was Franz Theodor Csokor's *3. November 1918* (1936) which depicted the last days of the Austro-Hungarian army, before it disintegrated into its various national components.

front line in order to atone for his guilt. Eventually he falls at Rheims with the few remaining survivors of his regiment.

The nationalist bias was even more pronounced in a play by Heinrich Zerkaulen (1892-1954), *Jugend von Langemarck* (Youth of Langemarck), first performed in November 1933 in eleven theatres simultaneously. In the early part of the Great War, a German regiment, composed mainly of academic volunteers, was annihilated in an attack in Flanders, with 'Deutschland über Alles' on their lips. This tragic episode is ruthlessly exploited as a shining symbol of heroism and self-sacrifice. The link with the Nazi movement is emphasized in the epilogue: a friend of the fallen hero, realizing that the spirit of front line comradeship must be revived at home, joins the Nazis with the words, 'They died for Langemarck – we live for Langemarck!' In a comment on his play, the author stressed the significance of this conclusion:

> Those of Langemarck marched invisibly with us. They kept on marching with us during the terrible years following the defeat, until the chiming bells of Potsdam rang out. . . . A new youth has unfurled its banners and has taken by storm the first enemy positions in the heart of the fatherland. . . .

The suppression of political opponents inside Germany was thus identified with a battle of the Great War.

The emotional connection between the First World War and the national socialist movement forms the main theme of Richard Euringer's *Deutsche Passion 1933*. Along with Hanns Johst's *Schlageter*, this play was acclaimed as the chief dramatic work celebrating the Nazi revolution. It shows many of the formal features of Expressionism, but also draws on the medieval mystery play. Its central figure is the Unknown Soldier of the Great War, who has risen from his grave and returns, his head adorned with a crown of thorns, as a herald of national resurgence. His call goes out to all classes, exhorting them to unite in the community of the *Volk*. He is opposed by types representing the republican era – intellectuals, war profiteers, Marxist workers, and so forth. His main adversary is the Evil Spirit, who paints a lurid picture of starving children, unemployment, corruption and demoralization, and ridicules the pacifist ideals of the 'charity state'. In the end, overpowered by the rousing call of the Unknown Soldier, the Evil Spirit descends into hell, to the sound of marching troops and celestial choirs, on his lips the incredulous question, 'So there is really such a thing – the Third Reich?'

Euringer's play moved on the borderline between drama and political manifesto. With its lavish use of choral speaking and pageantry, it was specially designed as a *Thingspiel*, that is, for performance on an open-air stage before organized masses. This type of play was particularly cultivated during the Nazi era since it gave expression to 'the monumental and heroic will of the age'. It was usually dedicated to the glorification of the soil and of productive work in the service of the national socialist state. Salient examples are Kurt Heynicke's two *Thingspiele*, *Neurode* (1934) and *Der Weg ins Reich* (The Road to the Reich, 1935), and – one of the more successful – E. W. Möller's *Das Frankenburger Würfelspiel*.

Eberhard Wolfgang Möller (1906-   ) may be regarded as a representative playwright of the Third Reich. He had first made his name with his play *Douaumont oder Die Heimkehr des Soldaten Odysseus* (1929), which combined the familiar theme of the homecoming soldier with a violent protest against the rottenness of the post-war era.[1] This protest grew shriller in his subsequent plays. In all of them, a 'heroic' character is in conflict with a world ruled by ruthless materialism. In *Kalifornische Tragödie* (Californian Tragedy, 1930) the Swiss colonizer, General Suter, wages a hopeless fight against the American authorities who wish to exploit the gold discovered

---

[1] Cf. pp. 182f.

on his Californian estate. *Panama Skandal* (1930) has as its central figure De Lesseps, whose work is brought to ruin by reckless speculators. In *Rothschild siegt bei Waterloo* (Rothschild wins at Waterloo, 1934), the theme has a distinct anti-Semitic slant. The London banker Rothschild, using his advance knowledge of the battle for a ruthless stock exchange manœuvre, emerges as the real victor of Waterloo. In each of these plays, Möller attacked, under cover of a historical theme, the Weimar Republic, which in his eyes was swayed by the corrupt forces of big business.

Das Frankenburger Würfelspiel (The Frankenburg Game of Dice, 1936), Möller's most ambitious work, was also based on a historical subject, the German peasant war. It was, in form and design, a *Thingspiel*, making full use of choral speaking, mass display and allegorical figures. The emperor, Ferdinand II, and a number of German princes are called to account for having betrayed the people by ruthlessly suppressing the peasants in their struggle for freedom. By a ruse, one of the princes gets a number of peasant leaders into his power and wantonly lets them throw dice for their lives. They lose, and are handed over to the hangman. Instead of the hangman, however, a symbolic figure appears and challenges the princes who now in their turn are made to gamble for their lives, and lose. Eventually, both the princes and the emperor are condemned for having forsaken the cause of the *Volk*.

After another historical play, *Der Sturz des Ministers* (The Fall of the Minister, 1937), set in eighteenth-century Denmark, Möller tried his hand at a classical subject. *Der Untergang von Karthago* (The End of Carthage, 1938), written in blank verse, confronts the soldierly virtues of Rome, personified by Scipio, with the corruption of mercantile Carthage, doomed to perish at his hands – perhaps a wishful anticipation of the fate Germany had in store for the Western powers. This was the last major work of Möller whose career ended together with the Third Reich.

The historical play remained by far the most cherished type of drama throughout the Nazi era. Two kinds of subject-matter were particularly favoured – medieval German history and the ascendency of Prussia. These two topics clearly indicate the two main sources from which Hitler's Germany drew its inspiration – the Holy Roman Empire, which constituted the First Reich, on the one hand, and the militant Prussian state, on the other. However, not only the German past but the whole range of world history – ancient and medieval, Spanish, English, and Scandinavian – was eagerly searched for dramatic material, suitable to illustrate some basic tenet of Nazism – the submission of the individual to the state, the hero's fight against a wicked world, or the conflict between legitimate and personal power. The form employed was usually that of the 'picture book' – a loose sequence of scenes leading from one dramatic climax to another. The language, though for the most part in prose, had a terse and dramatically heightened quality, with lavish use of figurative speech and incongruous modernisms. Little regard was paid to historical truth or psychological motivation: the characters were 'demonized', that is, they were over-lifesize and subject to extremes of violent passion and to the uncontrollable power of fate. The 'strong personality' held the centre of the stage, reaching for the ideal or succumbing to the machinations of petty adversaries.

Among the numerous playwrights dedicated to historical drama, Hans Rehberg (1901-) was the most distinguished. From the outset he set himself the task of doing for Germany what Shakespeare had done for England, namely, of depicting the German, and more particularly, the Prussian past in a series of royal portraits, ranging from the Great Elector to Frederick II. This ambitious scheme he carried out between 1934 and 1938 in a cycle of five plays – *Der Grosse Kurfürst* (The Great Elector, 1934), *Friedrich I* (1935), *Friedrich Wilhelm I* (1936), *Kaiser und König* (Emperor and King, 1937), and *Der Siebenjährige Krieg* (The Seven Years' War, 1938). Seen as a whole, these plays unfold a continuous panorama of the history of Prussia, from its beginnings under the Elector of Brandenburg to its emergence as a great power under Frederick II. Rehberg's language, throughout in prose, has a fierce intensity and passion, derived rather from Kleist than from Shakespeare. He has an undeniable talent for contriving dramatic contrasts and building up climaxes. His scenes, austere and harsh like the world they evoke, follow one another with filmlike swiftness. Yet the total effect remains curiously unconvincing. Though he was less concerned with ideas than with individual characters, the ultimate purpose of his plays was that of all historical drama written in the Third Reich – the evocation of the past as an object-lesson for the present.

After completing his cycle of Prussian plays, Rehberg turned to Spanish history in *Isabella von Spanien* (1938), and *Karl V* (1943). Finally he ventured on to Shakespeare's own ground by selecting subjects from English history, *Heinrich und Anna* (1942), *Heinrich VII* and *Elisabeth und Essex* (both in 1949). However, these later works remained ineffective; Rehberg shared the fate of all the writers carried to fame by the Nazis: his spectacular career ended with the fall of the Third Reich, which had provided the background indispensable to his work.

During the last years, from about 1942 onwards, theatrical activities in Germany were increasingly impeded by the growing dislocation of civilian life. Finally, in the autumn of 1944, all theatres were ordered to close down, consistent with the claims of total warfare. Thus an era which had started with the frantic assertion of national resurgence, ended in a welter of destruction.

Chapter Seven

SINCE 1945

The end of the Second World War left Germany in a state of utter physical and mental exhaustion. The destruction of most of the larger theatres deprived the country of the material basis of drama; for several years, theatrical activities were carried on in makeshift halls and backrooms. Moreover, the eclipse of Berlin robbed Germany of the capital which had acted as the focal point for its cultural life, and from which new ideas had spread throughout the country. Political and cultural decentralization led to conditions not unlike those prevailing in earlier centuries: Munich, Düsseldorf, Frankfurt, Hamburg etc. formed independent centres of no more than regional importance. The result was the intellectual provincialism which has marked German life since the end of the war. Above all, the political division of the country brought about a spiritual schism which has grown more pronounced with time. In the theatrical field, as in all other walks of life, there are to-day in fact two Germanys.

More far-reaching than the material destruction caused by the war was the intellectual vacuum which soon became apparent. The downfall of the Third Reich put a sudden end to all the writers artificially inflated by propaganda: of the playwrights who had dominated the Nazi theatre, not a single one survived in the changed climate of the post-war world. In this respect, the year 1945 formed as decisive a turning-point as 1933. On the other hand, the ruthlessness of the Nazi tyranny had crushed any potential opposition. The hidden drawers which, as was hoped, would contain the works of new and unknown authors, were found to be empty. The years following the Second World War thus formed a striking contrast to the early twenties: this time there was no spiritual upsurge comparable to the expressionist movement.

For some time, the absence of any vital new talent was obscured by the tradition, still maintained in the German theatre, of devoting the repertory largely to classical and foreign plays. The long severance from the intellectual life of other nations, enforced by the Nazis, resulted in a passionate desire to catch up with developments abroad. An unprecedented flood of foreign plays swept the German stage; it included the contemporary French and American as well as English and Spanish playwrights. Some of these enjoyed a greater success in Germany than in their own country. Such plays as Thornton Wilder's *By the Skin of Our Teeth* (translated under the title *Wir sind noch einmal davongekommen*) were felt to fit the German situation exactly. The public showed itself particularly responsive to contemporary American plays, with their stark realism and pathos, so closely related to German naturalistic drama.[1]

However, this sudden deluge of foreign plays had its dangers. Germany tried to catch up, within a short space of time, with developments that had taken place in other countries over a period of many years. The result was mental bewilderment.

The vacuum could no longer be filled by the older generation whose work had been cut short by the rise of the Nazis. By a curious coincidence, the downfall of the Third Reich seemed to carry with it some of the leading exiled writers: in 1945, Georg Kaiser died in Switzerland, Franz Werfel in

[1] We are here concerned mainly with developments in West Germany. The situation in East Germany is, in fact, little different; only that here the repertory is of course brought into line with Marxist doctrine, and in the place of plays imported from the Western countries, there is a large proportion of Russian plays.

15. FRISCH, *Als der Krieg zu Ende war*. Zürich, 1949

16. DÜRRENMATT, *Die Ehe des Herrn Mississippi*. Munich, 1952

America. Others had died before – several by their own hands, like Ernst Toller in New York, in 1939, Hasenclever in France, in 1940, and Stefan Zweig in Brazil, in 1942. Of the large number of playwrights who had left Germany for racial or political reasons, only a few lived to return and take up their work where it had been interrupted twelve years before. Of these, Carl Zuckmayer and Bertolt Brecht were the most prominent.

Both these dramatists had started their careers in the early twenties; they had spent their years of exile for the most part in the United States and returned at the end of the war, each to a different side of the Iron Curtain. Zuckmayer brought with him *Des Teufels General* which, after its Zürich première in 1946, started on its triumphal course through Germany and, with more than three thousand performances, scored the greatest success of any German play since 1945. It was followed by *Der Gesang im Feuerofen* (1950) and *Das kalte Licht* (1956), and by the historical plays *Barbara Blomberg* (1949) and *Ulla Winblad* (1953).[1] In all these works, Zuckmayer continued more or less in the realistic style he had developed in his earlier plays, keeping aloof from the new trends in stage technique which had emerged in Western drama since the war. Along with Zuckmayer, Ferdinand Bruckner must be named among the older playwrights who had made their name in pre-Nazi days.[2] Of the numerous plays he had written in exile, *Denn seine Zeit war kurz* (For his Time was Short, 1943) dealt with the Norwegian resistance, while *Die Befreiten* (The Liberated, 1945) depicted the conflict between various political factions in an unspecified European town after the liberation. After his return, Bruckner tried his hand at a revival of ancient tragedy. His first venture in this direction was *Pyrrhus und Andromache* (1951). In two further plays, *Der Tod einer Puppe* (Death of a Doll) and *Der Kampf mit dem Engel* (Fight with the

[1] Cf. pp. 196f.   [2] Cf. pp. 186ff.

Angel), both in 1956, he presented modern characters and problems within the rigid form of classical drama, introducing a chorus and using unobtrusive verse in the manner of T. S. Eliot. Up to his death in 1958, these experiments failed to meet with the success of his earlier plays.

By far the most eminent, and the most challenging, of the older dramatists was Bertolt Brecht. He returned from his exile in America as late as 1949, after spending two years in Switzerland where several of his later plays were performed for the first time in German. In accordance with his political convictions, he followed the invitation of the East German government to settle in East Berlin. After a short interlude at the Deutsches Theater, he took over the Theater am Schiffbauerdamm where, twenty years before, he had scored his first great success with *Die Dreigroschenoper*. Here, lavishly subsidized by the East German authorities, he formed the 'Berliner Ensemble', which carried his name far beyond the German frontiers.

It is scarcely realized, especially by his non-German admirers, that the plays on which his reputation is mainly founded (*Mutter Courage, Leben des Galilei, Der gute Mensch von Sezuan, Der kaukasische Kreidekreis*) were written during his years of exile, in the late thirties and early forties. During the last seven years of his life, his activities (apart from some adaptations and a vast quantity of theoretical writings) were confined to his work as a producer, putting into practice his novel theories of stagecraft. It was this practical side of his work which had the most immediate effect on the Western theatre. The stupendous reputation Brecht won in his last years can only partly be ascribed to the intrinsic quality of his work. It is insolubly linked with political issues, that is, with the pronounced 'Leftist' leanings of large sections of the Western, especially the French, intelligentsia. Moreover, the causes of his success must be sought in the particular situation of the

Western theatre: Brecht's bold experiments in new forms of production coincided with the general tendency to break away from the stale conventions of the realistic stage. His plays broke down the four walls of the middle-class living-room; they seemed to step out into the open air and to encompass humanity at large, on all its social levels. So dazzling was this new vision that some of his admirers went so far as to acclaim him 'Shakespeare reborn'. In fact, however, Brecht studiously narrowed down the range of drama to a single plane – the social. All the larger issues of human existence he subordinated to one purpose only – class warfare. His plays lack any true conflict; they are, in a deeper sense, undramatic since their issue is a foregone conclusion. With all these limitations, the sheer poetic force and originality of Brecht's dramatic work are undeniable. His contribution to modern drama so far over-shadows that of any living German playwright.

The only new name that emerged in the first years after the war was that of Wolfgang Borchert (1921-1947). His short-lived fame was due to his personal tragedy as much as to his only play, *Draussen vor der Tür*. The author was taken prisoner in Russia and returned from Siberia fatally ill, to die at the age of twenty-six, one day before his play had its first performance in Hamburg. *Draussen vor der Tür* (The Man Outside, 1947) is a *Heimkehrer* play, more or less indistinguishable from the numerous plays of that type written after the First World War. There is the same inability of the returning soldier to adjust him-self to civilian life, the same feeling of being left 'outside' in a cold and alien world, the same utter disillusionment and bitterness. The note of despair is if possible shriller. 'I am merely a bad joke the war has made, a ghost from yesterday', cries Beckmann, the ex-prisoner-of-war returning from Siberia – clearly the author himself. The play opens with Beckmann's attempt at suicide: he throws himself into the river but is rescued and forced to face life once more. All his efforts to make contact with his fellow-men end in failure, and he finds himself again and again standing 'outside the door'. For all its realism, the·play has distinct expressionist features. It consists of purely subjective outpourings; the only fully developed figure is the hero, while all the others are mere types or allegories. The river Elbe is personified as an old hag, God appears in the guise of a doddering beggar, powerless to help man in his plight, and Beckmann carries on endless arguments with 'The Other One' – his *alter ego*, who tries in vain to give him courage. In its utter hopelessness and cynicism, this play is a faithful reflection of the general mood prevailing in Germany immediately after the war; its impact waned as soon as this mood passed away.

One of the few noteworthy post-war plays was *Die Illegalen* (1948) by Günther Weisenborn (1902-   ), who is known chiefly as a novelist and poet. It was the first attempt, inside Germany, to treat the anti-Nazi opposition dramatically. The action – evidently suggested by the tragic case of the Munich students – is set among a group of young people some of whom pay with their lives for their subversive activities.

Apart from these isolated instances, the only vital contributions to German post-war drama came from outside Germany, in particular from Switzerland. This is perhaps no mere accident; for it was the only German-speaking country where the continuity of cultural life had not been broken by Nazi rule. Switzerland had never before produced a dramatist of more than local importance. Now, two came into prominence almost simultaneously, Max Frisch and Friedrich Dürrenmatt. To these may be added Fritz Hochwälder who, born in Vienna in 1911, made his home in Switzerland after 1938. It was there that he scored his first, and so far greatest, success with *Das heilige Experiment* (The Holy Experiment, 1943). This play made its full impact only after the war when it was performed in Paris and London (under the respective titles *Sur la terre comme au ciel* and *The Strong are Lonely*). It deals with the fall of the Jesuit state founded in Paraguay in the eighteenth century. The conflict between material and spiritual values comes to a head in the tragic figure of the Father Provincial: in the central scene, when he faces an emissary of the Society of Jesus, he is forced to realize that his bold attempt to set up the Kingdom of God on earth must yield to the superior interests of the Church. He himself must give the order to destroy his work, and is killed in the fight which follows. In this work, Hochwälder proved his remarkable skill in constructing a theatrically compelling action to illustrate a universal moral issue. His second play, *Der Flüchtling* (The Fugitive, 1945) was based on a scenario by Georg Kaiser, written shortly before his death in Switzerland. The drama, set in an unnamed country under German occupation, is enacted by only three characters – a frontier guard, his wife, and a fugitive seeking refuge in their house. In the end, the fugitive escapes with the woman, helped by the guard who is ready to die for a new-found belief in human freedom – a theme more characteristic of Kaiser than of Hochwälder. *Der öffentliche Ankläger* (The Public Prosecutor, 1949) takes its subject from the French Revolution. Fouquier-Tinville, public prosecutor after the death of Robespierre, is induced to conduct a case against an unknown 'enemy of the people' who finally turns out to be himself, and thus unwittingly brings the reign of terror to an end. In *Donadieu* (1953) Hochwälder touches once again on a religious theme. The action, suggested by a ballad of the Swiss poet C. F. Meyer, is set against the background of the French Huguenot wars and centres on an acute moral conflict: a Huguenot nobleman recognizes in a stranger who seeks shelter in his castle the murderer of his wife. After a painful mental struggle, he overcomes his desire for vengeance, and entrusts the punishment to divine justice. The awakening of a man's conscience under the impact of a harrowing experience

– this is again the main theme of *Die Herberge* (The Inn, 1956). The scene is a squalid country inn somewhere in Eastern Europe, and the drama, unfolding in a single night, hinges on the theft of a bag of gold. In the course of the investigation, the past history of the characters is gradually revealed, and a far greater crime brought to light. As always with Hochwälder, the visible action which forms the immediate foreground involves a larger moral issue. *Der Unschuldige* (The Innocent One, 1958) also turns on the subject of hidden guilt, but this time in terms of comedy. A respectable citizen is suspected of murder when a skeleton is dug up in his back garden. Though this is later found to be the remains of a Napoleonic soldier buried on the spot, the event changes the citizen's outlook on life: he realizes that, although in this case he proved innocent, he might well have committed a crime.

In most of his plays written up to date, Hochwälder has turned his back on the present and chosen historical settings. Nevertheless, they are anything but historical plays in the conventional sense. The characters are not revived for their period interest but embody moral forces of timeless relevance; their conflicts are conflicts of ideas. In his dramatic form, Hochwälder eschews all the recent devices of stage technique and adheres to the well-made play on traditional lines, with strict observance of the classical unities.

In contrast to Hochwälder, the two native Swiss playwrights, Max Frisch and Friedrich Dürrenmatt, show themselves to be fully alive to the new trends in drama which have developed since the last war, especially in France and America. Of the two, Max Frisch (1911–) was the first to appear on the scene. He distinguished himself with a play *Nun singen sie wieder* (Now They Sing Again, 1945), sub-titled 'Attempt at a Requiem'. It is a sequence of scenes poignantly evoking the pathos and agony of war – the shooting of hostages, airmen preparing to take off for a raid, the squalor of the air-raid shelter, and so on. As the play proceeds, the realistic plane is gradually transcended; the dead mingle with the living, who are not aware of their presence. Repeatedly the dead hostages are heard singing, giving expression to a fervent hope for peace. In his next work, *Die chinesische Mauer* (The Wall of China, 1946) – a kind of fantastic revue ranging freely over some thousand years of world history – Frisch comments on the fateful impasse man has reached through the invention of the atom bomb. His mouthpiece is *Der Heutige*, the man of to-day, who acts as a kind of compère, stringing together the loosely knit scenes. Stock figures from history and fiction, Napoleon, Columbus, Romeo and Juliet, Cleopatra, etc., make their appearance. In the end, the 'man of to-day' comes to realize that he is powerless to stem the course of history, and that his warning must fall on deaf ears. *Als der Krieg zu Ende war* (When the War Came to an End, 1949) has a more conventional dramatic plot. The scene is Berlin immediately after the capitulation. A German woman is torn between her love for a Russian officer who is billeted in the house, and her husband whom she keeps hidden in the basement. When she discovers that her husband is guilty of war crimes, and that he has quietly connived at her infidelity to save his own skin, she commits suicide. This rather melodramatic story is presented in a form clearly influenced by Brecht: the heroine alternatively enacts her part and steps out of it, commenting 'objectively' on her actions – a technique somehow out of keeping with the conventional content of the play. In *Graf Öderland* (Count Öderland, 1951) Frisch sets out to mirror the chaotic nature of our age: a respected judge, the embodiment of law and order, suddenly breaks with his routine life and turns criminal. He becomes the head of a terrorist movement and, from the sewers beneath the city, challenges the state authorities. At the moment of triumph, however, he cynically reinstates the government, and himself chooses death as the only way of gaining 'absolute freedom'. All along, it is left in doubt whether he is in fact a madman, or acting on a rational plan. With the compelling logic of a nightmare, the play sets out to demonstrate the close proximity of order and chaos in the soul of man, and in society at large.

As if to find release from these apocalyptic visions of our present age, Frisch also produced plays of a purely romantic type. The first, *Santa Cruz* (1946, actually his earliest play in order of writing) centres on three characters – a nobleman, his wife, and a light-hearted rover, named Pelegrin. These three have met long ago in a tropical port where the girl was Pelegrin's mistress. His reappearance in the snowbound manor-house causes the couple to relive the past in their minds – this time, however, with a different outcome: now it is the husband who wants to set out on a life of adventure, and the woman who resists temptation. The attraction of this play lies in its subdued poetry and the skilful interplay of past and present, reality and dream. With *Don Juan oder Die Liebe zur Geometrie* (Don Juan or Love of Geometry, 1953) Frisch once more gave free rein to his romantic mood. In his version of the age-old theme, Don Juan is presented as a woman-hater whose sole interest is the most abstract of intellectual exercises – geometry. By his very detachment, he becomes irresistible to women. In order to free himself from his amorous entanglements, he finally escapes into marriage – the true end to Don Juan's career.

After an interval of six years, devoted mainly to prose fiction, Frisch turned once more to the stage with two short plays, under the common title *Biedermann und Hotz* (1958). By far the weightier of the two is *Biedermann und die Brandstifter* (Biedermann and the Incendiaries), called 'ein Lehrstück ohne Lehre', a morality without a moral. Its central character, Biedermann – a kind of modern Everyman – is an average, good-natured bourgeois. Though disquieted by numerous mysterious fires which have recently broken out in the town, he takes an unknown tramp into his house, and even offers him the attic as a lodging. Presently the tramp is joined by two sinister accomplices and starts piling up barrels filled with petrol. Biedermann, though growing more and more suspicious, fails to take any steps, and goes out of his way to make them comfortable. In the end, he even hands them the matches with which they set fire to his house and, ultimately, blow up the city. All along, a chorus of firemen comment upon the action, voicing, in mock-classical verse, their inability to intervene before it is too late. The wider implications, pointing to the present world situation, are evident. . . . The second play, *Die grosse Wut des Philipp Hotz* (The Fury of Philip Hotz), is no more than a farce: it turns on a matrimonial quarrel, in which the husband, an intellectual, wants to prove himself a man of action by smashing up the furniture and, finally, joining the Foreign Legion – only to be rejected because of his bad eyesight. This slight piece is enlivened by the use of modern stagecraft, with the husband intermittently assuming the role of compère, addressing the audience and commenting upon his actions. In both plays, Frisch shows himself an able disciple of Brecht – without the master's political allegiances.

Friedrich Dürrenmatt (1921-), the other Swiss playwright who has made his mark in the German post-war theatre, first came to the fore with two serious plays, *Es steht geschrieben* (It Is Written, 1946) and *Der Blinde* (The Blind Man, 1948). His first real success was *Romulus der Grosse* (Romulus the Great, 1949), an 'unhistorical historical comedy' about the fall of the Roman Empire and its last emperor. The action is confined to a single day – the Ides of March, A.D. 476 – when the news of final defeat reaches the emperor in his country retreat. More interested in the breeding of chickens than in politics, he stoically accepts the inevitable course of history and hands his crown to the barbarian invader. This play was no

doubt intended as a satirical comment on the present predicament of Western civilization. Another comedy set in ancient
times, *Ein Engel kommt nach Babylon* (An Angel Comes to
Babylon, 1953) is of a purely legendary nature. A girl of
heavenly origin is sent to earth to find the most wretched of
men. The man she chooses turns out to be king Nebuchad-
nezzar who has disguised himself as a beggar for one night.
When she discovers his identity she is forced to reject him, and
is carried off into the desert by a real beggar. The play ends
with the king's resolution to build a tower, pitting his power
against heaven: 'I want to see which is better – my justice or
God's injustice!' This comedy, which the author himself calls
'fragmentary', is as it stands rather obscure. Perhaps a projected
sequel, dealing with the building of the tower, will throw light
on its meaning.

Dürrenmatt's most striking plays to date are set in the present
time. *Die Ehe des Herrn Mississippi* (The Marriage of Mr.
Mississippi, 1952) is a grotesque dance of death: four men
are fighting for possession of one woman, each of them
personifying a specific philosophy of life. The first, a public
prosecutor, with the absurd name of Mississippi, forces the
woman to marry him, for no other reason than to atone for
the murder of their respective marriage partners. He acts from
a rigorous conception of justice, determined to re-establish the
'law of Moses'. His opposite number is Saint-Claude, a social
upstart who works for a communist revolution. These two
claim to be 'the two last great moralists of our time'. The other
two men are a politician who seeks personal power at any
price, and a quixotic count – the only one who loves the
woman for her own sake. In the end all meet with violent
death except the count who survives in his romantic dream-
world. The macabre is mixed with the bizarre: the play starts
at the end, with the mock execution of Saint-Claude by his
communist associates, and proceeds in a series of flashbacks;

the characters frequently step out of their parts, turning to the audience with explanatory comments. By this deliberate debunking of theatrical illusion, Dürrenmatt turns the serious content of the drama into downright comedy. He employs the same method in his most successful work to date, *Der Besuch der alten Dame* (The Old Lady's Visit, 1956, performed in England under the title *Time and Again*). An eccentric old lady of fabulous wealth pays a visit to her birthplace, an impoverished little town off the beaten track. The whole community is bent on extracting a substantial sum from the visitor. However, the lady makes a condition – the death of one of the townsmen who seduced her years ago, and left her with a child. This request starts a violent conflict between righteous indignation and unashamed greed. In the end, the lure of wealth proves stronger, and the man is brutally killed. Again, the macabre theme is presented with a wealth of grotesque detail. The hypocrisy of the townsfolk who protest loudly while yielding step by step to temptation, is depicted with savage irony. The victim, at first a nondescript little man, grows in stature as he gradually comes to accept his fate. In an explanatory note, the playwright insists that the story is not intended as an allegory, nor the old lady as a personification of an abstract idea. Nevertheless, it is evident that the play moves on two levels, and the grotesque plot has wider implications, pointing to the conflict between moral and material values. The citizens, by choosing prosperity at the price of a crime, forgo their integrity.

Though it is obvious that his plays touch upon universal moral issues, Dürrenmatt maintains that his primary object is to tell a story in terms of the theatre. Indeed, what is most striking is his teeming inventiveness as he makes fun of all the time-worn theatrical conventions. In this calculated disillusionment of the stage, he clearly takes his cue from Pirandello, Thornton Wilder, and Brecht. In an essay *Theaterprobleme*

(Problems of the Theatre, 1955), Dürrenmatt argues that the time for writing tragedies has passed. For tragedy, he contends, presupposes a well-ordered world, with established standards of guilt and retribution. Our disintegrating world, however, in which we live 'like Gulliver amongst the giants', powerless to resist the course of events bigger than ourselves, calls for comedy – not a comedy born of despair, but of courage. 'The world, for me, stands as something monstrous, an enigma of calamity that has to be accepted but to which there must be no surrender.' This, if anything, is the message implicit in Dürrenmatt's tragic farces.

Much as Frisch and Dürrenmatt differ from one another in temperament and purpose, they have a peculiar habit in common, that is, to re-write and re-edit their plays – doubtless a sign of the experimental character of many of their works. Of all the younger dramatists writing in German since 1945, they are the only ones to explore the latest developments in dramatic technique. Their plays, though realistic on the surface, transcend reality in many ways. But this surrealism is far removed from the symbolism of neo-romantic drama or the abstractions of Expressionism. It has the oppressive quality of a dream in which every detail stands out with glaring clarity while the whole remains unfathomable and obscure. The characters are frighteningly real, though often distorted into caricature. The fundamental mood is one of profound pessimism, reflecting the fear and insecurity of our present world. But against this background there is a sense of the grotesque, a readiness to laugh, which turns tragedy as if by magic into comedy. It remains to be seen whether this fresh departure is vigorous enough to bring about a new flowering of German drama.

BIBLIOGRAPHY

GENERAL

ARNOLD, R. F.: *Das moderne Drama*. Strasbourg, 1908
   (ed.): *Das deutsche Drama*. Munich, 1925
BAB, JULIUS: *Der Wille zum Drama*. Berlin, 1919
   Die Chronik des deutschen Dramas, vols. 1-5. Berlin, 1922-1926
   Das Theater der Gegenwart. Leipzig, 1928
BITHELL, JETHRO: *Modern German Literature 1880-1950*. London,
   1959
DUKES, ASHLEY: *Modern Dramatists*. London, 1911
ELOESSER, ARTUR: *Die deutsche Literatur*, vol. II: *Von der Romantik
   bis zur Gegenwart*. Berlin, 1931
FECHTER, PAUL: *Deutsche Dichtung der Gegenwart*. Leipzig, 1929
   *Die deutsche Literatur vom Naturalismus bis zur Literatur des
   Unwirklichen*. Leipzig, 1938
   Das europäische Drama. Geist und Kultur im Spiegel des Theaters.
   3 vols. II: *Vom Naturalismus zum Expressionismus*. III: *Das
   Drama im 20. Jahrhundert*. Mannheim, 1956-1958
FEISE, E.: *Fifty Years of German Drama, 1880-1930. A Bibliography*.
   Baltimore, 1941
HOLL, KARL: *Geschichte des deutschen Lustspiels*. Leipzig, 1923
HOLLÄNDER, FELIX: *Lebendiges Theater*. Berlin, 1932
IHERING, H.: *Der Kampf ums Theater*. Dresden, 1922
JACOBSOHN, S.: *Das Jahr der Bühne*. Vols. I-X. Berlin, 1912-1921
KAYSER, RUDOLF: *Das junge deutsche Drama*. Berlin, 1924
KERR, ALFRED: *Die Welt im Drama*. 5 vols. Berlin, 1917
   also: *Die Welt im Drama*, 1 vol. Cologne-Berlin, 1954
LEHMANN, K.: *Deutsche Dramatiker unserer Zeit*. Düsseldorf, 1935
MELCHINGER, SIEGFRIED: *Theater der Gegenwart*. Frankfurt/Main
   and Hamburg, 1956
   Drama zwischen Shaw und Brecht. Bremen, 1957

NAUMANN, HANS: *Die deutsche Dichtung der Gegenwart, 1885-1933.* 6th ed. Stuttgart, 1933

POLGAR, ALFRED: *Ja und Nein.* 3 vols. Berlin, 1926; also: 1 vol. Hamburg, 1956

ROSE, WILLIAM: *Men, Myths and Movements in German Literature.* London, 1931

and ISAACS, J.: *Contemporary Movements in European Literature.* London, 1928

ROSENHEIMER, E.: *Das deutsche soziale Drama von Lessing bis Sternheim.* Constance, 1949

SOERGEL, ALBERT: *Dichtung und Dichter der Zeit.* Leipzig, 1911

STAMMLER, W.: *Deutsche Literatur vom Naturalismus bis zur Gegenwart.* 2nd ed. Breslau, 1927

WALZEL, OSKAR: *Deutsche Dichtung der Gegenwart.* Leipzig, 1925

WIESE, BENNO VON (ed.): *Das deutsche Drama. Vom Barock bis zur Gegenwart. Interpretationen.* II. Düsseldorf, 1958

ZIEGLER, KLAUS: *Das deutsche Drama der Neuzeit.* Berlin-Bielefeld, 1954

SPECIAL PERIODS

Naturalism

BAHR, HERMANN: *Studien zur Kritik der Moderne.* Frankfurt/Main, 1894

BENOIST-HANAPPIER, L.: *Le drame naturaliste en Allemagne.* Paris, 1905

BERG, LEO: *Der Naturalismus. Zur Psychologie der modernen Kunst.* Munich, 1892

BLEIBTREU, P.: *Revolution der Literatur.* Leipzig, 1886

CONRAD, M. G.: *Von Zola bis Hauptmann: Erinnerungen zur Geschichte der Moderne.* Leipzig, 1902

HANSTEIN, H. VON: *Das jüngste Deutschland.* Leipzig, 1900

KERR, ALFRED: *Das neue Drama.* Berlin, 1905

LESSING, O. E.: *Die neue Form. Ein Beitrag zum Verständnis des deutschen Naturalismus.* Dresden, 1910

MARTERSTEIG, MAX: *Das deutsche Theater im 19. Jahrhundert.* Leipzig, 1904

STOCKIUS, A.: *Naturalism in the recent German Drama. With special reference to Hauptmann.* New York, 1903

Neo-Romanticism and Impressionism

BAHR, HERMANN: *Die Überwindung des Naturalismus.* Dresden-Leipzig, 1891
   Renaissance. Neue Studien zur Kritik der Moderne. Berlin, 1897.

HAMANN, R.: *Der Impressionismus in Leben und Kunst.* Cologne, 1907

HILZHEIMER, K.: *Das Drama der Neuromantik.* 1938

PICARD, MAX: *Das Ende des Impressionismus.* 2nd ed. Zürich, 1920

SEILLIÈRE, E. L.: *Néoromanticism en Allemagne.* Paris, 1931

THOMÉSE, J. A.: *Romantik und Neuromantik.* Hague, 1923

THON, L.: *Die Sprache des deutschen Impressionismus.* Munich, 1928

Expressionism

BAHR, HERMANN: *Expressionismus.* Munich, 1916

BRANDENBURG, H.: *Das Theater und das neue Deutschland.* Jena, 1916

CARTER, H.: *The New Spirit in the European Theatre, 1914-1924.* London, 1926

CYSARZ, H.: *Zur Geistesgeschichte des Weltkrieges. Die dichterischen Wandlungen des deutschen Kriegsbilds, 1910-1930.* Halle, 1931

DAHLSTRÖM, C. E.: *Strindberg's Dramatic Expressionism.* University of Michigan, 1930

DIEBOLD, B.: *Anarchie im Drama.* 3rd ed. Frankfurt/Main, 1925

DUWE, W.: *Deutsche Dichtung des zwanzigsten Jahrhunderts: die Geschichte der Ausdruckskunst.* Zürich, 1936

EDSCHMID, KASIMIR: *Über den Expressionismus in der Literatur.* Berlin, 1919

EMMEL, F.: *Das ekstatische Theater.* Prien, 1924

FREYHAN, MAX: *Das Drama der Gegenwart.* Berlin, 1922

FECHTER, PAUL: *Der Expressionismus.* 3rd ed. Munich, 1919

HERFORD, C. H.: *The Post-War Mind of Germany,* Oxford, 1927

IHERING, H.: *Die zwanziger Jahre.* Berlin, 1948

KORNFELD, PAUL: *Der beseelte und der psychologische Mensch. (Das junge Deutschland,* 1918)

LANDSBERGER, F.: *Impressionismus und Expressionismus*. Leipzig, 1919

LEHMANN, KARL: *Junge deutsche Dramatiker*, 1923

MANN, OTTO: *Das Drama des Expressionismus*. In: Friedmann, Hermann, and Otto Mann: *Expressionismus, Gestalten einer literarischen Bewegung*. Heidelberg, 1956

MARTINI, FRITZ: *Was war Expressionismus?* Urach, 1948

PAULSEN, W.: *Expressionismus und Aktivismus*. Berlin-Leipzig, 1935

SAMUEL, R., and THOMAS, R. H.: *Expressionism in German Life, Literature and the Theatre (1910–1924)*. Cambridge, 1939

SCHEFFAUER, H. G.: *The New Vision in German Art*. New York-London, 1924

SCHNEIDER, M.: *Der Expressionismus im Drama*. Stuttgart, 1920

SOERGEL, ALBERT: *Dichtung und Dichter der Zeit. Neue Folge: Im Banne des Expressionismus*. Leipzig, 1925

WIDMANN, W.: *Theater und Revolution*. Berlin, 1920

New Realism (Neue Sachlichkeit)

KINDERMANN, H.: *Das literarische Antlitz der Gegenwart*. Halle, 1930

ROH, F.: *Nachexpressionismus*. Leipzig, 1926

RÜHLE, JÜRGEN: *Das gefesselte Theater*. Cologne-Berlin, 1957.

UTITZ, T.: *Die Überwindung des Expressionismus*. Stuttgart, 1927

WORRINGER, WILHELM: *Nach-Expressionismus*. Leipzig, 1926

National Socialism

BARTELS, ADOLF: *Einführung in das deutsche Schrifttum für deutsche Menschen*. Leipzig, 1933

EMMEL, F.: *Theater aus deutschem Wesen*. 1936

JENSSEN, CHRISTIAN: *Deutsche Dichtung der Gegenwart*. Leipzig, 1936

LANGENBECK, C.: *Wiedergeburt des Dramas aus dem Geist der Zeit*. 1940

LANGENBUCHER, H.: *Nationalsozialistische Dichtung*. Berlin, 1935

MULOT, ARNO: *Die deutsche Dichtung unserer Zeit. I: Das Bauerntum in der deutschen Dichtung unserer Zeit. II: Der Soldat in der deutschen Dichtung unserer Zeit*. Stuttgart, 1937 and 1938

SOERGEL, ALBERT: *Dichter aus deutschem Volkstum*. Leipzig, 1935

WANDERSCHECK, H.: *Deutsche Dramatik der Gegenwart*. Berlin, 1938

INDIVIDUAL PLAYWRIGHTS

Barlach

CARLS, C. D.: *Ernst Barlach*. Berlin, 1931
FECHTER, PAUL: *Ernst Barlach*. Gütersloh, 1957

Beer-Hofmann

LIPTZIN, S.: *Richard Beer-Hofmann*. New York, 1936
WERNER, A.: *Richard Beer-Hofmann, Sinn und Gestalt*. Vienna, 1936

Brecht

HAAS, WILLY: *Bert Brecht*. Berlin, 1958
KLOTZ, V.: *Bertolt Brecht. Versuch über das Werk*. Darmstadt, 1957
LÜTHY, HERBERT: *Vom armen Bert Brecht*. Frankfurt/Main, 1952
SCHUMACHER, ERICH: *Die dramatischen Versuche Bertolt Brechts, 1918-1933*. Berlin, 1955
WILLETT, JOHN: *The Theatre of Bertolt Brecht*. London, 1959
WINTZEN, RENÉ: *Bertolt Brecht, Oeuvres choisies, bibliographie, illustrations*. Paris, 1954

Paul Ernst

LUBINSKA, S.: *Paul Ernst und das neue Drama*. Heidelberg, 1913
MAHRHOLZ, W.: *Paul Ernst*. Munich. 1916

Ernst Hardt

ADLER, F.: *Das Werk Ernst Hardts*. Greifswald, 1921
SCHUMANN, H.: *Ernst Hardt und die Neuromantik*. Lützen, 1913

Carl Hauptmann

GOLDSTEIN, W.: *Carl Hauptmann. Eine Werkdeutung*. Breslau, 1931

Gerhart Hauptmann

BEHL, C. F. W.: *Wege zu Gerhart Hauptmann*. Goslar, 1948
    Zwiesprache mit Gerhart Hauptmann. Munich, 1948
FECHTER, PAUL: *Gerhart Hauptmann*. Dresden, 1922
GARTEN, H. F.: *Gerhart Hauptmann*. Cambridge, 1954
GREGOR, JOSEPH: *Gerhart Hauptmann. Das Werk und unsere Zeit*. Vienna, 1951

MARCUSE, LUDWIG (ed.): *Gerhart Hauptmann und sein Werk*. Berlin-Leipzig, 1922

MULLER, S. H.: *Gerhart Hauptmann and Goethe*. New York, 1949

SCHLENTHER, PAUL: *Gerhart Hauptmann. Leben und Werke* (revised and extended by A. Eloesser). Berlin, 1922

SINDEN, M.: *Gerhart Hauptmann: The Prose Plays*. Toronto-London, 1957

VOIGT, F. A.: *Antike und antikes Lebensgefühl im Werke Gerhart Hauptmanns*. Breslau, 1935

Hauptmann-Studien. Breslau, 1936

and REICHART, W. A.: *Hauptmann und Shakespeare*. Goslar, 1948

ZIEGENFUSS, W.: *Gerhart Hauptmann. Dichtung und Gesellschaftsidee der bürgerlichen Humanität*. Berlin, 1948

Hofmannsthal

ALEWYN, RICHARD: *Über Hugo von Hofmannsthal*. Göttingen, 1958

FIECHTNER, H. A. (ed.): *Hugo von Hofmannsthal. Die Gestalt im Spiegel der Freunde*. Vienna, 1949

HAMMELMANN, H. A.: *Hugo von Hofmannsthal*. London, 1957

JENS, WALTER: *Hofmannsthal und die Griechen*. Tubingen, 1955

NAEF, CARL J.: *Hugo von Hofmannsthals Wesen und Werk* (with bibliography by H. Steiner). Zürich, 1938

SCHAEDER, GRETE: *Hugo von Hofmannsthal. I. Die Gestalten*. Berlin, 1933

Johst

CASPER, S.: *Der Dramatiker Hanns Johst*. Munich, 1938

Kaiser

DIEBOLD, B.: *Der Denkspieler Georg Kaiser*. Frankfurt/Main, 1924

FIVIAN, E. A.: *Georg Kaiser und seine Stellung im Expressionismus*. Munich, 1946

FREYHAN, MAX: *Georg Kaisers Werk*. Berlin. 1926

KENWORTHY, B. J.: *Georg Kaiser*. Oxford, 1957

KOENIGSGARTEN, H. F.: *Georg Kaiser* (with bibliography by A. Loewenberg). Potsdam, 1928

LEWIN, LUDWIG: *Die Jagd nach dem Erlebnis. Ein Buch über Georg Kaiser.* Berlin, 1926
LINICK, L. M.: *Der Subjektivismus im Werke Georg Kaisers.* Strasbourg, 1938

Karl Kraus

RYCHNER, M.: *Karl Kraus.* Vienna, 1924

Schnitzler

KAPP, J.: *Arthur Schnitzler.* Leipzig, 1912
LANDSBERG, H.: *Arthur Schnitzler.* Berlin, 1904
LIPTZIN, S.: *Arthur Schnitzler.* New York, 1932

Schönherr

BETTELHEIM, A.: *Karl Schönherr.* Leipzig, 1928
SEDLMAIER, R.: *Karl Schönherr und das österreichische Volksstück.* Würzburg, 1920

Sternheim

BLEI, F.: *Über Wedekind, Sternheim und das Theater.* Leipzig, 1915
EISENLOHR, F.: *Carl Sternheim.* Munich, 1926

Sudermann

AXELROD, I.: *Sudermann: eine Studie.* Stuttgart, 1907
SCHOEN, H.: *Sudermann, poète dramatique et romancier.* Paris, 1904

Toller

SINGER, P.: *Ernst Toller.* Berlin, 1925

Unruh

KRONACHER, A.: *Fritz von Unruh.* New York, 1946
MEISTER, R.: *Fritz von Unruh.* Berlin, 1925

Wedekind

DEHNOW, F.: *Frank Wedekind.* Leipzig, 1922
FECHTER, P.: *Frank Wedekind. Der Mensch und das Werk.* Leipzig, 1920
KUTSCHER, A.: *Frank Wedekind.* 3 vols. Munich, 1922-1931.

Werfel

BERENDT, H.: *Franz Werfel*. Bonn, 1920
SPECHT, R.: *Franz Werfel*. Vienna, 1926

Stefan Zweig

ARENS, H. (ed.): *Stefan Zweig. Sein Leben und sein Werk*. Esslingen, 1949
 Stefan Zweig. A tribute to his life and work. London, 1951
RIEGER, E.: *Stefan Zweig. Der Mann und das Werk*. Berlin, 1928
ZWEIG, FRIDERIKE M.: *Stefan Zweig*. London, 1947

ENGLISH TRANSLATIONS

BAHR, HERMANN: *The Concert*. Tr. B. Q. Morgan. In: T. H. Dickinson, Chief Contemporary Dramatists, 2. Boston, 1921
BORCHERT, WOLFGANG: *The Man Outside* (Draussen vor der Tür). Tr. D. Porter. Norfolk (Conn.) and London, 1952
BRECHT, BERTOLT: *Round Heads, Peak Heads*. Tr. N. G. Verschoyle. In: International Literature. Moscow, 1937
 Señora Carrar's Rifles. Tr. K. Wallis. In: Theatre Workshop. New York, 1938
 Mother Courage and Her Children. Tr. H. R. Hays. Norfolk (Conn.), 1941
 Dto. Tr. Eric Bentley. In: The Modern Theatre, II. New York, 1955
 The Trial of Lucullus. Tr. H. R. Hays. New York, 1943
 The Private Life of the Master Race (Furcht und Elend des Dritten Reiches). Tr. Eric Bentley. New York, 1944, and London, 1948
 He who says Yes. He who says No. (Der Jasager. Der Neinsager). Tr. G. Nellhaus. In: Accent, VII, 2. Urbana, 1946
 The Horatii and the Curiatii. Tr. H. R. Hays. In: Accent, VIII, 1. Urbana, 1947
 The Measures Taken (Die Massnahme). Tr. Eric Bentley. In: Colorado Review. Fort Collins, 1956/7

BRECHT, BERTOLT: *Parables for the Theatre* (*The Good Woman of Sezuan* and *The Caucasian Chalk Circle*). Tr. Eric and M. Bentley. Minneapolis, 1948, and London, 1956

Galileo. Tr. Brecht and Charles Laughton. In: From the Modern Repertoire, II. Univ. of Denver, 1952

The Exception and the Rule. Tr. Eric Bentley. In: Chrysalis. Boston, 1954, and New Directions 15. New York, 1955

The Threepenny Opera. Tr. Vesey and Bentley. In: The Modern Theatre, I. New York, 1955

St Joan of the Stockyards. Tr. F. Jones. Indiana Univ. Press, 1956

BRUCKNER, FERDINAND: *Elizabeth of England.* Tr. Ashley Dukes. London, 1931

Races. Tr. Ruth Langner. New York, 1934

CHLUMBERG, HANS: *Miracle at Verdun.* Tr. J. Leigh. New York, 1931

Dto. Tr. Edward Crankshaw. London, 1932

ERNST, OTTO: *Master Flachsmann.* Tr. H. M. Beatty. London, 1909 and New York, 1912

FRANK, BRUNO: *Twelve Thousand.* Tr. W. A. Drake. New York and London, 1928

FRANK, LEONARD: *Karl and Anna.* Tr. R. Langner. New York, 1929

Dto. Tr. L. W. Lockhart. London, 1930

GRAFF, SIGMUND, and HINTZE, GERHARD: *The Endless Road.* Tr. Rawson. London, 1930

HALBE, MAX: *Mother Earth.* Tr. P. H. Grummann. New York, 1913-1915

Youth. Tr. S. T. Barrows. New York, 1916

HARDT, ERNST: *Tantris the Fool.* Tr. W. Noble and J. James. St. Louis, 1909

Tristram the Jester. Tr. J. Heard. Boston, 1913

HARTLEBEN, OTTO ERICH: *Love's Carnival* (Rosenmontag). Tr. R. Bleichmann. London, 1904

HAUPTMANN, CARL: *War.* Tr. A. von Ende. In: The Drama, VI. 1916

HAUPTMANN, GERHART: *The Dramatic Works.* 9 vols. (containing all plays published up to and including 1925. Various translators). London and New York, 1913-1929

HAUPTMANN, GERHART: *Hannele*. Tr. William Archer. London, 1894

Dto. Tr. C. H. Meltzer. London and New York, 1908. Also in: International Modern Plays. Everyman's Library No. 989. London, 1950

Lonely Lives. Tr. Mary Morison. London, 1898

The Weavers. Tr. Mary Morison. London, 1899, and New York, 1911

The Sunken Bell. Tr. C. H. Meltzer. London and New York, 1899

The Coming of Peace (Das Friedensfest). Tr. J. Achroch and C. E. Wheeler, London and Chicago, 1900

The Beaver Coat. Tr. anon. In: E. Watson, Contemporary Drama, New York, 1932

The Weavers. Hannele. The Beaver Coat. Tr. H. Frenz and M. Waggoner. New York and Toronto, 1951

HIRSCHFELD, GEORG: *The Mothers*. Tr. L. Lewisohn. New York, 1916

HOCHWÄLDER, FRITZ: *The Strong are Lonely* (Das heilige Experiment). Ad. E. L. Gallienne. New York, 1954

HOFMANNSTHAL, HUGO VON: *Electra*. Tr. A. Kalisch. Berlin, 1908

Dto. Tr. A. Symons. New York, 1908, and in: T. H. Dickinson, Chief Contemporary Dramatists, 3. Boston, 1930

The Rose Bearer. Tr. A. Kalisch. Berlin and Paris, 1912, and London, 1939

Ariadne on Naxos. Tr. A. Kalisch. Berlin and Paris, 1913 and 1924

Death and the Fool. Tr. M. Batt. In: Poet Lore, 1913

Dto. Tr. J. Heard. New York, 1913-1915

Death and the Fool. Tr. E. Walter. Boston, 1914

Dto. *The Fool and Death*. Tr. H. E. Mierow. Colorado Springs, 1930

The Death of Titian. Tr. J. Heard. New York, 1913-1915

Madonna Dianora (Die Frau im Fenster). Tr. H. Boas. Boston, 1916

The Marriage of Sobeide. Tr. B. Q. Morgan. New York, 1913-1915

Venice Preserved. Tr. E. Walter. In: Poet Lore. 1915

Cristina's Journey Home. Tr. R. T. House. Boston, 1916

HOFMANNSTHAL, HUGO VON: *The Play of Everyman.* Tr. G. Sterling and R. Ordynski. San Francisco, 1917

The Salzburg Everyman. Tr. M. E. Tafler. Salzburg, 1933

The Theatre of the World. Tr. T. G. Jones. Llangollen, 1936

Arabella. Tr. John Gutman. New York, 1955

KAISER, GEORG: *From Morn to Midnight.* Tr. Ashley Dukes. London, 1920, and New York, 1922

Gas. Tr. Hermann Scheffauer. London and Boston, 1924

Fire in the Opera House. Tr. W. Katzin. In: Eight European Plays. New York, 1927

The Phantom Lover (Oktobertag). Tr. H. Bernstein and A. E. Mayer. New York, 1928

The Coral. Gas I and II. In: Twenty-Five Modern Plays. New York and London, 1931

MELL, MAX: *Apostle Play.* Tr. M. V. White. London, 1934

MÖLLER, EBERHARD WOLFGANG: *Douaumont, or The Return of the Soldier Odysseus.* Tr. G. and T. Rawson. London, 1930

NEUMANN, ALFRED: *Such Men are Dangerous* (Der Patriot). Ad. Ashley Dukes. New York and London, 1928

SCHNITZLER, ARTHUR: *Anatol.* Tr. Granville Barker. London, 1911 and 1933/4

Free Game. Tr. anon. Boston, 1913

The Green Cockatoo. The Mate. Paracelsus. Tr. H. B. Samuel. London and Edinburgh, 1913

The Reckoning (Liebelei). Tr. G. I. Colbron. New York, 1907

Playing with Love (dto). Tr. P. Morton Shand. London, 1914

Light o' Love (Liebelei). Tr. B. Q. Morgan. In: E. Watson. Contemporary Drama. New York, 1932

Gallant Cassian. Tr. A. L. Gowans. London and Glasgow, 1914

The Lonely Way. Intermezzo. Countess Mizzie. Tr. E. A. Björkman. New York, 1915

Anatol. Living Hours. The Green Cockatoo. Last Masks. Literature. Tr. G. I. Colbron. New York, 1917

(*Living Hours* also in: T. H. Dickinson, Chief Contemporary Dramatists, 2. Boston, 1921)

Professor Bernhardi. Tr. H. Landstone. London, 1927

Dto. Tr. L. Borell and R. Adam. London, 1936

SCHNITZLER, ARTHUR: *Hands Around* (Reigen). Tr. K. Wallis. Newark (N.J.), 1929

Merry-go-round (dto). Tr. F. and J. Marcus. London, 1953

La Ronde (dto). In: The Modern Theatre, II. New York, 1955

SCHÖNHER, KARL: *Faith and Fireside* (Glaube und Heimat). Tr. E. von Mach. New York, 1913-1915

STERNHEIM, CARL: *A Pair of Drawers* (Die Hose). Tr. E. Jolas. In: Transition. Paris, 1927

A Place in the World (Der Snob). Tr. W. Katzin. In: Eight European Plays. New York, 1927

The Mask of Virtue (Die Marquise von Arcis). Ad. Ashley Dukes. London and New York, 1935

SUDERMANN, HERMANN: *Magda* (Heimat). Tr. C. E. A. Winslow. Boston and New York, 1896, and in: E. Watson, Contemporary Drama. New York, 1932

The Joy of Living (Es lebe das Leben). Tr. E. Wharton. London and New York, 1902

A Man and His Picture (Sodoms Ende). Tr. anon. London, 1903

St. John's Fire. Tr. C. and H. T. Porter. Boston, 1904

Dto. Tr. G. E. Polk. *Minneapolis*, 1905

John the Baptist. Tr. B. Marshall. London and New York, 1909

Morituri (3 one-act plays). Tr. A. Alexander. New York, 1910, and London, 1912

Honor. Tr. H. R. Bankhage. New York, 1915

The Vale of Content (Glück im Winkel). Tr. W. E. Leonard. In: H. T. Dickinson, Chief Contemporary Dramatists, I. Boston, 1915

TOLLER, ERNST: *Seven Plays* (containing: *The Machine-Wreckers, Transfiguration, Masses and Man, Hinkemann, Hoppla, Such is Life!, The Blind Goddess, Draw the Fires!*, with *Mary Baker Eddy*, by E. Toller and H. Kesten). London, 1935

Masses and Man. Tr. V. Mendel. London, 1923

Dto. *Man and the Masses*. Tr. L. Untermeyer. New York, 1924

The Machine Wreckers. Tr. Ashley Dukes. New York and London, 1923

Brokenbrow (Hinkemann). Tr. V. Mendel. London, 1926

Hoppla! Tr. Hermon Ould. London, 1928

TOLLER, ERNST: *The Blind Goddess.* Tr. Edward Crankshaw. London, 1934

Draw the Fires! Tr. Edward Crankshaw. London, 1935

No More Peace! Tr. Edward Crankshaw. London, 1937

Blind Man's Buff (Die blinde Göttin). In collaboration with Denis Johnston. London, 1938

Pastor Hall. Tr. Stephen Spender. London, 1939

UNRUH, FRITZ VON: *Bonaparte.* Tr. E. Björkman. New York, 1928

WEDEKIND, FRANK: *The Awakening of Spring.* Tr. F. J. Ziegler. Philadelphia, 1909

Such is Life. Tr. F. J. Ziegler. Philadelphia, 1912, and in: T. H. Dickinson, Chief Contemporary Dramatists, 3. Boston, 1930

Earth Spirit. Tr. S. A. Eliot. New York, 1914

Pandora's Box. Tr. S. A. Eliot. New York, 1918

Tragedies of Sex (containing: *Spring's Awakening, Earth Spirit, Pandora's Box, Damnation*). Tr. S. A. Eliot, New York and London, 1923

Five Tragedies of Sex (containing: *Spring's Awakening, Earth Spirit, Pandora's Box, Death and Devil, Castle Wetterstein*). Tr. F. Fawcett and Stephen Spender. London, 1952

WERFEL, FRANZ: *Goat Song.* Tr. R. Langner. New York, 1926

Juarez and Maximilian. Tr. R. Langner. New York, 1926

Paul among the Jews. Tr. P. Levertoff. London, 1928 and 1943

The Eternal Road (Der Weg der Verheissung). Tr. L. Lewisohn. New York, 1936, and London, 1937

Jacobowsky and the Colonel. Ad. N. S. Behrman. New York, 1944

WINSLOE, CHRISTA: *Children in Uniform* (Heute und Morgen). Tr. B. Burnham. London and New York, 1933

WOLF, FRIEDRICH: *The Sailors of Cattaro.* Tr. K. Wallis, ad. M. Blankfort. New York and London, 1935

ZUCKMAYER, CARL: *The Captain of Köpenick.* Tr. D. Portman. London, 1932

ZWEIG, STEFAN: *Jeremiah.* Tr. E. and C. Paul. New York, 1922, and London, 1929

INDEX

Plays are listed only if described in some detail in the text.

266

INDEX